KILL THE MESSENGERS

KILL
THE MESSENGERS

STEPHEN HARPER'S ASSAULT
ON YOUR RIGHT TO KNOW

MARK BOURRIE

HarperCollins*PublishersLtd*
PATRICK CREAN EDITIONS

Contents

In a city that has no watchdogs, the fox is the overseer.
—SUMERIAN PROVERB

KILL THE MESSENGERS

CHAPTER 1

Democracy, Messengers
and the Harper Revolution

*We campaigned on this new Canadian reality. Not on a dream
or a fantasy or a slogan, but on the reality of this great country rising—
a country founded on great principles—a courageous warrior, a compas-
sionate neighbour, a confident partner—and under a strong, stable, national,
majority, Conservative government—the best country in the world.*
—STEPHEN HARPER, 2011[1]

The King of England stood on a balcony in Westminster, just outside the city of London, and braced himself against the cold. It was a
raw January day in 1649, the crowd was noisy, and only a few people
could hear him. But there was a man near the king who was writing
everything down. Within a few hours, the king's speech was on the
streets in the primitive newspapers of the time.

It was not the sort of rant that Justin Trudeau or even Stephen
Harper would come up with, and it certainly was not the work of a
Barack Obama. King Charles I wasn't running for anything. In fact, his
career was quickly winding down. The words he spoke were his own,
not those of a speechwriter. They're sort of dense and Shakespearean,
but after you read them once or twice, you'll get the drift.

1

"And truly I desire [the people's] liberty and freedom as much as anybody whomsoever, but I must tell you, that their liberty and freedom consists in having of government those laws by which their life and their goods may be most their own. It is not for having a share in government that is pertaining to them," the king said.

"A subject and a sovereign are clean different things, and therefore until you do put the people in that liberty as I say, certainly they will never enjoy themselves." He finished up, turned, knelt down, prayed for a moment, and a chap named Brandon took one swing of an axe and chopped off his head.

Few politicians are as upfront in their contempt of democracy, and fewer still have the opportunity to speak with the honesty that's available to a sentient person who knows he won't have to worry about that evening's dinner because he'll be shorter by a head. But Charles I was a man of his times, and of our times, too: trashing the press, proroguing Parliament, getting very heavy with people who disagreed. Few modern politicians will come out and say the people really have no business being involved in government. A few more will echo the king's assertion that governments exist only to protect people's property and keep taxes down. But not that many are willing to stick their necks that far out to make a point.

Just over two hundred years later, the Americans fought their own Civil War. This one was about crushing secessionist states that had broken up the country because they believed their slave economy was in jeopardy. But this war was, in fact, about something else, about the thing that lies in the heart of Abraham Lincoln's Gettysburg Address, the speech he made at the dedication of the cemetery for the men killed in the decisive battle of the Civil War. Everyone's heard of that short speech—it wasn't much longer than poor Charles's last words— but few people have read it carefully. The address starts with a little history lesson and a very slight side-swipe at the slavery issue. Then it gets down to business: the blood of the Union troops at Gettysburg was spilled so that government of the people, by the people, for the people, should not perish from this earth.

People reading the speech always put the emphasis on the "of, by, for" words. But the real meat of the phrase is in the last six words. In 1863, the United States was the most revolutionary country on Earth. It was the only major power that was anything resembling a real democracy. And it seemed likely to be the last one, an experiment that failed. France had thrice tried to create a democracy between 1789 and 1863 and their revolutions went badly. One ended up bathed in blood. All were undermined by public revulsion and ended with a return to monarchy. Britain was emerging as a democratic state, but few men had the right to vote. Power lay in the hands of aristocrats and industrialists and, among them, "democracy" was a word that was spat out, a euphemism for mob rule. (Nineteenth-century British mobs were quite dangerous things indeed.)

Canada was a little further along, but most politicians gagged at the idea of true democracy. Antidemocratic feeling ran strong among members of Canada's elites, many of them descendants of monarchist refugees from the American Revolution. They feared the political power of French-Canadians and the Irish who were streaming into the country, and many remembered the Rebellions of 1837–1838. Canada had legislatures elected by male property owners, but the country was dominated by colonial officials, railway builders, bankers and lawyers who not only ran the country but also controlled its newspapers.

At the time of the Civil War, the great empires and small countries of Europe were all monarchies. Revolutionaries in Central and South America had overthrown their Spanish colonial masters and had tried to create democracies. All had failed. There were no democracies in Africa. Or Asia. Or, for that matter, in the Confederacy.

Democracy was an anomaly until the end of World War I. Going into it, the great powers consisted of four imperial monarchies (Russia, Germany, Austria-Hungary and Japan), two democracies (France and the United States), a new junta trying to secularize an Islamic state (Turkey), and a parliamentary monarchy that was well on its way to being a democracy but that maintained the power of the landed wealthy (Britain). Most of the rest of the world's countries were military dictatorships, ludicrously small monarchies (the Tsar of Bulgaria comes to mind), colonies or satellite nations of the larger powers. Canada was both a colony and an emerging democracy. By the end of the war, democracy or systems resembling it had been foisted on most of the new European countries created by the Treaty of Versailles and on the enemy Central Powers. The postwar deal of 1919 was a rush forward for democracy in Europe, though many of the people who lived in nations created at Versailles would not get much of a chance to live in a real multi-party, pluralistic state for another seventy years.

After World War II, democracy would get another boost, not just in Europe (outside the Soviet occupation zones) but also in the Third World, where Britain tried, with temporary and minimal success, to create Westminster systems in its old colonies.

No one could have known at the time of the Civil War that democracy would eventually take root in some of the world's great countries. In many ways, Lincoln, when he stood on the platform at Gettysburg, was very much alone as the leader of what he feared was the world's last democracy. Democracy—real involvement by the people in their government, which they, as citizens, rather than subjects, own—is not the default system of government, even in the West. It's something that takes great struggle to create and has to be nurtured, preserved, and, in dire times, fought for. As we've seen in the misfire of the "Arab Spring" of 2010, elections are, in

4

and of themselves, not democracy. Faith in democracy needs to be deep and wide in society. It cannot survive without the rule of law—which, itself, requires honest courts, enforceable agreements, and fair treatment of accused criminals—along with an inquisitive, independent press and a solid, accessible system of public education. State religions undermine democracy because they enforce intellectual and social conformity. So do tribalism and class warfare. People need the freedom to be able to do business together in corporations, but they also need the liberty to work together to form trade unions. Any country that has a huge gap between the wealthy and the poor is so wracked with systemic inequality that the political voice of the impoverished is too weak to be heard.

The fear of being the last, failed steward of democracy drove Lincoln through the Civil War. Like Vladimir Lenin during the years when the Communists were losing the Russian Civil War and the world's first Marxist state was at risk of being smothered at birth, Lincoln became ruthless. Believing freedom could not, on its own, save democracy, he did not back away from censoring the press. At one point, he even considered jailing the chief justice of the United States Supreme Court, who was a diehard pro-slavery, states-rights man. In the end, once the rebellion had been crushed, Lincoln planned to quickly restore state legislatures in Dixie and to bring congressmen from the Confederate states to the newly finished Capitol, but his murder left that work to others. Government of the people, by the people, for the people had been, as much as possible in nineteenth-century America, saved from extinction partly through the use of police-state tactics.

Lincoln ended his life with a bullet in the brain, but the idea of democracy as a practical system of government survived both the war and Lincoln. Public support and the political will for real democracy has ebbed and flowed, but the target was always there.

DEMOCRACY HAS MANY FLAWS, including the obvious fact that it requires an exhausting and frustrating amount of generosity for people to listen to each other and to prevent the strong from dominating the weak. Still, despite the demands it makes on the citizenry, it is the system of government that offers people more freedom than any other. In fact, democracy simply can't work unless people have a deeply ingrained sense of the value of liberty, not only for their own thoughts, speech, and religion, but also for those they disagree with. It's worth it, not just for the happiness that comes with freedom, but also because democracy and freedom pay off economically. Liberty of conscience unleashes all kinds of creativity and inquiry, along with economic opportunity and social mobility. That's one of the reasons why democracies tend to be so wealthy. When things get tough, many people give up on democracy and embrace totalitarianism, believing fascist institutions are somehow more effective and efficient. If they were, we'd all be speaking German.

But our democracy needs work. Canadians have to start feeling as though the government of their country belongs to them. There's a big difference between the constitutions of the United States and Canada. Most obvious, the American Bill of Rights gives unequivocal protection to many rights, while the Canadian Charter of Rights and Freedoms is rigged with escape hatches and loaded with weasel words that allow governments to suspend or subvert the rights of citizens. But more importantly, the American constitution starts with the words "We the People of the United States . . ." while Canada's begins with the less eloquent "Whereas the Provinces of Canada, Nova Scotia, and New Brunswick have expressed their Desire to be federally united into One Dominion under the Crown of the United Kingdom of Great Britain and Ireland, with a Constitution similar in Principle to that of the United Kingdom; And whereas such a Union would conduce to the Welfare of the Provinces and promote the Interests of the British Empire . . ."

Canada's sovereignty rests in the Crown. In the United States, the people are sovereign, and, on all sides of the political divide, Americans have the firm belief that they, as citizens, own their country. Canada, like Britain, is a country of subjects. Perhaps we are less so than we were a few generations ago, but the deference to authority and the class structure of the nineteenth-century colony continues to be a strong part of Canada's political, economic and even media culture. We do have elections, but voter turnout is dismal. Once we install a new regime, usually to punish the last bunch of rogues, most Canadians feel that the country is in the hands of the winners until the next election. Preston Manning's Reform Party did try to float populist American ideas like recall petitions to remove odious politicians, but those policies evaporated when that party became a contender for power.[2]

The ideology of democracy, so taken for granted in places that have benefited from it, is in trouble, not just in Canada, but in most Western countries. The use of corporate communications strategy to hide public information, the development of retail politics, the invention of intrusive technology and the defanging of media and other governmental watchdogs have become normal. Respect for courts and the justice system is being undermined, both from outside and from within. A new kind of controlling, arrogant and often vindictive government has emerged since the 1980s and is getting more emboldened and entrenched. It is not simply a neo-conservative creation. It's loose in Barack Obama's Washington, where "hope" and "change" did not involve the rolling back of the post-9/11 security state and the opening up of government to scrutiny and criticism. The reporters in Obama's White House are treated with the same contempt that Harper holds for the Parliamentary Press Gallery and are subject to the same kinds of controls. The U.S. political system is probably even more dysfunctional than ours.

And if anyone thinks a new regime in Canada, whether a different Conservative prime minister or an NDP or a Liberal government, will roll back this revolution, they're dreaming. If this way of governing becomes entrenched, no prime minister will change it. Harper has built a system that is so favourable to the party in power and so easy to operate that it would take a lot of energy and determination to dismantle it.

Here in Canada, Stephen Harper, like Jean Chrétien before him, relishes the idea of being a "G7 world leader." Because Canada was invited to join the annual summit of world economic powers—in 1975 France got to bring Italy to the table, so U.S. president Gerald Ford insisted his country should bring Canada—Ottawa strangely sees itself as a capital rivaling Paris, London and Tokyo, and the people who run it have developed a swagger that seems somewhat ridiculous. Really, although it's a great place to live, Ottawa's a rather backwater capital of a very decentralized state where power over important issues like education, health care and social services lies with the provinces.

Harper, like Richard Nixon, seems determined to record every moment of his time in power. Nixon said he bugged the White House to create a truthful record for historians. Harper's movements are diligently recorded for propaganda reasons. Fifty years ago, prime ministers simply went about their business with just a handful of aides and political allies. Now Harper's retinue, which moves around the city in a presidential-style motorcade, includes both still and video photographers. Their work is distributed to friendly media and appears on the Internet "program" *24 Seven.* In the fall of 2014, the federal government advertised for a new videographer for the propaganda machine. The job paid about $100,000 a year, but the videographer had to be willing to work every day and night of the year.

The fetish for recording each moment can make things awkward. In 2013, when Prime Minister Harper took his teenage son Ben to the Centre Block's very informal fifth floor cafeteria for a burger, the Harpers were accompanied by at least four skittish, bulky men with wires in their ears and a photographer who snapped almost every second of that magic moment. Much eye-rolling ensued. It must have been strange for the high-schooler who is, by all accounts, a pretty down-to-earth kid. It certainly was for those of us who sat eating our lunches and watching. The situation became comical as the security people filled the tiny cafeteria and eyeballed the journalists, MPs, office workers and political staffers who sat at the rows of tables. There was no reason why the two Harpers could not have quietly walked into the room, without the photographer, and sat down for lunch. But, in true Stephen Harper style, father and son huddled in a secluded corner of the room, protected by prime ministerial staffers, armed heavies and the photographer.

Everything about the prime minister's world is lavish. Alison Redford was forced out of the premier's office in Alberta partly because she spent $45,000 of public money to go, with some of her entourage, to Nelson Mandela's funeral. But Stephen Harper couldn't throw stones. He spent the same amount to go to New York in 2011, where he took in a baseball game and a Broadway show. He also spent $1 million of taxpayers' money to ship a limousine and an SUV to India for a summit in 2012, India somehow being short of luxury vehicles for visiting VIPs. And the cost of the prime minister's security detail had reached $19.6 million in 2014, about double the cost when Harper took power.[3]

If you think the motorcades and the metal detectors are the brainchild of the security staff, and that Harper has no say in how it works, think again. The prime minister is the boss, and if he really thought the head of his RCMP security team was pushing him around, that cop would, within a few weeks, be showing store clerks in Iqaluit how to spot fake toonies. He likes this. He likes this far too much.

Harper and his courtiers spend a lot of time worrying about enemies in the media, universities, bureaucracy, courts, First Nations and even in churches and soup kitchens. And, of course, there are the enemies sitting on the other side of the House of Commons.

Gone were the days of grudging professional respect and sometimes real friendship among Members of Parliament. The House of Commons stumbles toward irrelevance during the Harper regime and the ever more toxic atmosphere and vicious partisanship has worked its way down into the House committees, where most of Parliament's real work gets done.

Whatever people say about former Liberal leader Michael Ignatieff, by the time his political career crashed he understood the danger of separating the people's representatives into "us" and "them," and then trashing the "thems" as unpatriotic, evil, stupid and corrupt. "The opposition performs an adversarial function critical to democracy itself," Ignatieff said in a speech at Stanford University in October 2012. "Governments have no right to question the loyalty of those who oppose them. Adversaries remain citizens of the same state, common subjects of the same sovereign, servants of the same law."[4]

IN HARPER'S WORLD, politics is a game. The informal Calgary School of economists and political scientists headquartered at the University of Calgary (echoing the Chicago School of right-wing academics at the University of Chicago) has a world view built on the market economy economics of Friedrich Hayek and the political modelling concepts of William H. Riker, a games theorist. Riker, who died in 1993, believed politics can be mapped out and manipulated in the same way as any other human activity, including economic behaviour. Riker was one of the crafters of "positive political theory," which he explained in his 1962 book *The Theory of Political Coalitions*. In this world, ideology doesn't matter very much, since the game is one of manipulation. All people are participants in the political game, making rational choices from the options that are placed before them. Riker, a political scientist, thought and wrote like an economist, breaking his theories down to mathematical models and games that change and upset the equilibrium in society and within institutions.

So politics, like all games, can have predictable endings. Politics, Riker's followers believe, is matter of "natural selection" of issues. Most mainstream politicians simply debate within accepted ranges of values and economic options. Political entrepreneurs look for issues and ideas that are, at first sight, marginal. They keep working those issues. Most won't catch on but some will. The idea is to create new cleavages and splits in society and among voters. They can be along regional, social, economic, religious or linguistic lines. If the politician succeeds in developing enough of those "outsider" issues and wins over enough groups, a new, winning coalition can be created. Riker coined the term "heresthetic" (from the Greek word to divide, which also gave rise to the term "heresy") to describe politicians who try to create new political fault lines to develop constituencies, and, eventually, new coalitions with enough financial and political clout to get them into power.

That's why politicians usually debated within what most people saw as "Canadian values" until the early 1990s, when the Reform Party, with Stephen Harper as one of its chief policy architects, came along. Since then, you've heard little about "Canadian values" and a lot about more talk of enemies, domestic and foreign, along with nationalist sloganeering. Riker said majority rule creates, at best, a rare and fragile equilibrium. A politician who upsets and remakes it can win the game. "Disequilibrium, or the potential that the status quo be upset, is the characteristic feature of politics," Riker said in one paper. So, in plainer English, you can win by debating what everyone else is talking about, or you can shake up the whole system and re-make it, generating enough followers to, basically, have a revolution. It helps if you have a much better grasp of information than everyone else.[5]

In the past, politicians could be adversaries in civil debates without being enemies. They could reject each other's arguments without attacking their opponents as people. They could debate facts and lines of logic with vigour and humour, without the vicious, artless mockery and, more and more, outright profanity that's heard in the House of Commons today. They could quibble over their interests without attacking their opponents' patriotism. Canada's Parliament has never been an academy of selfless scholars tirelessly reflecting on the public good. Six years after Confederation, a journalist wrote: "At Ottawa, little enough is done in the way of practical legislation for the country, but the struggle of parties is carried on vigorously, with a shrill accompaniment of organs on both sides."[6] Still, there was a sense of collegiality, perhaps inspired by the fact that Ottawa was a forlorn place and the city was awash in booze.

Now politics is seen as war by other means, with control of patronage and public spending as the prize. It's fought by professional armies of marketers, pollsters, strategists and attack dogs. This makes politics an insider game, one with no place for the public, who have become sick of the noise. In places where politicians look on each other as enemies, "legislatures replace relevance with pure partisanship. Party discipline rules supreme, fraternization is frowned upon, negotiation and compromise are rarely practiced, and debate within the chamber becomes as venomously personal as it is politically meaningless," former Liberal leader Michael Ignatieff told an American audience.

And when political opponents—or any other group—are cast as enemies of the popular interest, it's not much of a leap to label them as enemies of the people and enemies of the state. Ann Coulter, the American right-wing controversialist, has made a good living doing precisely that, peddling books attacking liberals, giving the books titles like *Treason, Demonic, Guilty*, and *High Crimes and Misdemeanors*. "Fascism took the fatal step from a politics of adversaries into a politics of enemies," Ignatieff, still hurting from his own electoral beating, warned. "We are not there yet, but it is worth remembering that the fatal declension occurred in a democracy not so dissimilar to our own, in a society plagued by economic crisis, among a battered population looking for someone to blame."

Democratic politics requires compromise, often a dirty business that can shock and horrify those of us who rarely find the need to hold our noses and make deals with people we don't particularly like, don't agree with, and want to see fail. It's one of the skills that lawyers need, which partly explains why lawyers move so easily into political life. But today's "politics as war" conjures up ingrained concepts of unconditional surrender, scorched earth, take-no-prisoners, and it divides outcomes into victory or defeat. The idea of compromise for the good of the public disappears pretty fast. High-functioning sociopaths flourish in this environment.

War talk, Ignatieff said, should be saved for real enemies. "We should focus martial energies where they are needed: [against]

those adversaries who actively threaten the liberty of other peoples and our own. Towards those within our borders, however heatedly we may disagree, we should work from a simple persuasive, but saving, assumption: In the house of democracy there are no enemies."

Ignatieff said democracy is threatened while money dominates politics. That needs to be curtailed with well-enforced laws. Parties have to loosen their grips on the nomination process so talented people who are unknown to the central leadership can come forward. Elected representatives have to be freed from party whips. Ignatieff had rarely worried about these problems when he held the whip as leader of the Liberal Party, but he was right.[7]

But Ignatieff's visions aren't shared in the Prime Minister's Office (PMO) in the ugly Langevin Block. Even Harper supporters have not been safe from their leader's lust for control: Tom Flanagan, Harper's political and academic mentor, was driven out when he wrote *Harper's Team* in 2007 without approval from the boss. The prime minister had tried to talk Flanagan into killing the book, even though it has very little controversial material and puts Harper in a fairly good light. Flanagan later told author Lawrence Martin that Harper didn't want Flanagan to write *any* book, no matter how supportive it might be.

Flanagan himself, in a 2007 interview, said the goal of Harper and the Tories was to change the very real perception among Canadians that Liberal governments are normal and Conservative administrations are just oddballs and flukes that are elected once in a while and last just long enough to maintain the pretense that Canada is a two-party democracy. "The Liberals had identified themselves as the party of government, people used to talk about the natural governing party and all this bullshit," he told reporter Tim Naumetz of the *Ottawa Citizen*. "[Harper's] got a definite communication strategy to associate the Conservative Party with government and make it seem normal to have a Conservative government after so many years in which the Liberals made it seem that no other party than the Liberals could govern. Conservative parties around the world tend to be successful when they can align themselves with the values of patriotism. That's the norm, that the conservative party is the patriotic party."[8]

And Flanagan has a point. Since the end of World War I, Conservative federal governments in Canada have been rare and relatively short-lived. Almost to the day when Harper was sworn in, conventional wisdom, especially among members of the Parliament Hill media, was that the Liberals, first under Jean Chrétien, then when led by Paul Martin, were mathematically certain to hold power for a very, very long time. Jeffrey Simpson, *The Globe and Mail*'s main Ottawa columnist and the authoritative voice of conventional wisdom for both the bureaucratic and media elites, even published a book, *The Friendly Dictatorship*, about the threat to democracy of the Liberals' seemingly unbreakable lock on power. If he learned anything in the first years of the century, Harper discovered that every political party, including the Liberal Party of Canada—which ranks as one of the world's great political success stories—can be humbled and even broken. There is no "forever" in politics.

THE CREATION OF THE CONSERVATIVE PARTY of Canada took more than a decade, and building it required the co-opting of the Reform Party, a 1980s populist reaction to the sleaze, deficit spending and regional compromises of Brian Mulroney's Progressive Conservatives. The people in Western Canada and rural and small-town Ontario who supported Reform often had legitimate beefs. Starting in the 1970s, Canada has been through a series of recessions that have hit farm country and small towns particularly hard. Cities, riding real estate booms fuelled by immigration, missed much of the pain. In many small communities, the tough recessions of the early 1980s and early 1990s have never ended. Many factories that were shut never reopened. Well-paying jobs in mills, mines, and on railways never came back.

The split from the 1980s onwards between the prosperity of the cities—especially white-collar Toronto, Ottawa, Calgary and Vancouver—and the depopulation and poverty in the countryside and in the near-North opened up enmities and political opportunities that were far more effectively exploited by neo-conservatives. Young people abandoned rural and small-town Canada, causing anguish and bitterness for the parents they left behind. The aging of rural Canada was another factor that helped Reform grow and pick up parliamentary seats. At the same time, Christianity split between dying older denominations and flourishing fundamentalist churches, and Manning, a conservative Christian, was able to pull fellow evangelicals into his political crusade.

Manning's greatest contribution to this country was actually a negative. He could have exploited Western separatist sympathies, but he didn't. Instead, Reform would storm Babylon, muck out the mess in Ottawa, make everyone from every part of Canada equally important in Ottawa, get rid of careerist politicians and those who lied to get elected, and have MPs who really represented their constituents. If they let the people down, voters would be able to "recall" them and throw the bums out. It really was "reform" and much of it was, and still is, badly needed. Reform Party supporters —politically-aware people from small-town Canada who are not thrilled to see fundraising prowess and patronage take over the political system—should be just as horrified as anyone else with what's happening in Ottawa.

16

Politics is run by professional strategists, pollsters and fund-raisers who usually work for lobbying firms and sell their influence to the highest bidder between elections. The professionalization of politics, along with the Conservatives' extreme message control, lack of accountability and almost complete ignoring of the "grass-roots" until the party needs some money or some votes, runs opposite to what the Reform Party stood for in the early 1990s.

Now, former Reformers hold many of the levers of power. The West's biggest economic worries have been taken care of. Alberta's energy sector is safe from high taxation and tough regulations, and the government backs the pipelines that could take Alberta crude to world markets. Farmers don't have to sell their grain to the Canadian Wheat Board. And, probably coincidentally, since not even Stephen Harper can dictate the price of crude, most of the West is booming on $100 oil.

(Harper, though, should reread the books of economist Harold Innis to see where this is going. In a nutshell, Innis, a brilliant University of Toronto economist, warned in 1956 that this country has, too often, relied on just one or two big resource industries and has paid heavily when the world stopped paying us the price we want.)

To win power, the party changed. Readers of George Orwell's *Animal Farm* will be familiar with the storyline. These days, the Conservative Party of Canada bears a striking resemblance to the Mulroney-led party that Preston Manning destroyed. It's hard to believe old Reformers ever expected to see their party defending Mulroney in the House of Commons for taking $300,000 in large bills from German arms dealer–lobbyist Karlheinz Schreiber, with the utterly lame response that the Liberals had skimmed millions through the sponsorship scandal. They never would have said, back when Manning was stumping Prairie villages, that Senate expense account padding wasn't worth much public condemnation because the Ontario Liberals were engaged in a succession of scandals, as though one negates the other in some weird hierarchy of corruption.

So the message has to be controlled. The Harper government has set out to kill many messengers. The media is obviously one of them. And, while Harper's war with journalists has generated some coverage and interest—though perhaps more among journalists than among other people—it's a small and relatively easy part of his re-making of how Ottawa works. The Ottawa media had been withering for years, battered by the collapse of the news business. There are many other watchdogs in Ottawa, and Harper's team went to work defanging them, along with anyone who made much noise about the changes imposed by the Harper government. They set out to make sure only a select few people knew how the country was being run, and to change the way Canadians think about Canada.

First, there was Parliament, an institution, like the media, that has seen better days and has needed serious reform for a long time. Somewhere between Preston Manning's 1980s barn-burners on democracy, made to audiences in rural Alberta and Saskatchewan, and the Harper government's decision to slap time limits on debate of most important bills, someone at the top didn't get the message that MPs are supposed to be more than voting puppets.

The reputations of legislators had already been undercut by neo-cons, who've pretty much erased the concept of "representative" from the public mind and replaced it with "politician." This type of propaganda was expressed in Ontario quite blatantly by the Progressive Conservative government of neo-con darling Mike Harris. His bill to erode local democracy and replace small community councils with less responsive amalgamated city administrations was called the Fewer Municipal Politicians Act, 1999. People might have looked at it differently if it was called the Reduced Representation Act or the Kiss Local Democracy Goodbye Act. (The Harper government has come up with the same triumphal kinds of names for laws, which are discussed in Chapter 11.)

There are federal watchdogs who make sure the government doesn't waste money. There are others who protect people's civil rights. Still more watchdogs advocate on behalf of veterans. Some consult with environmental scientists and engineers to decide whether or not a pipeline can be built safely. Others inspect our food so we don't get poisoned. One group is supposed to make sure the government's spies do not pry into the lives of law-abiding people.

Some of them were never, before Harper's regime went after them, seen as watchdogs at all. For example, very few people ten years ago would have added environmental scientists to any list of people who might be considered dangers to the state. Now, in Harper's Ottawa, they're kept isolated and gagged and, if possible, are turfed from their jobs. Their labs are shut down and their research libraries shuttered. Everyone within the government's grasp is barred from speaking publicly in case they say something that might inconvenience or embarrass the regime. The national institutions paid for by Canadians are to speak with just one voice, and it is linked to the mind of Stephen Harper, an introverted former computer nerd with a master's degree in economics and no real experience in the world of business or professions. He had never managed anything in his life, other than a small and secretive pressure group called the National Citizens Coalition, before winning the leadership of the Conservative Party of Canada, and, within a few years, the premiership of Canada.

A lot of this controlling, targeting and, when need arises, attacking, is done to make life easier at "the Centre"—the Prime Minister's Office, which is the political department run by Stephen

Harper, and the Privy Council Office, the supposedly somewhat objective and brainy group that advises all ministers on policy and finds ways for the public service to carry out the decisions of the cabinet. Both of these agencies are now the personal tools of Stephen Harper, and he uses them with great enthusiasm to enforce his will throughout the government.

Years ago, ministers actually headed government departments. Now they are figureheads, and they can't hire or fire their deputy ministers, who are the real bosses of the bureaucracy, or get rid of the chiefs of staff that run the political side of ministerial offices. The deputies and the chiefs of staff owe their jobs to the prime minister. So government departments aren't really answerable to elected MPs serving as cabinet ministers, and the ministers are no longer answerable to Parliament. The days when ministers would quit, and possibly end their political careers, because of major blunders or corruption in their departments are now far in the past. And it makes sense, in some strange way. Why, the ministers think, would you accept blame for something that really is out of your control, especially when the prime minister gets the credit when things go well?

So WHAT'S THE POINT of the Harper government? Like the men who were the previous two tenants of 24 Sussex, it's difficult to see what great, driving impulse motivates this prime minister. Some prime ministers come into office with goals, like John A. Macdonald's nation-building, Pierre Trudeau's constitution and Brian Mulroney's desire to defuse, or, at least, re-channel Quebec nationalism and forge stronger ties with the United States. Harper's critics used to accuse him of having a hidden political agenda to remake the social fabric of Canada and get rid of abortion rights, non-white immigration and other things that didn't sit well with rural Canada and many Christian fundamentalists. They were wrong.

Harper has refused to go anywhere near the abortion issue. The racial makeup of immigrants to this country has not changed and the number of people coming to Canada has stayed impressively high, even during recession years when the Harper government could easily have argued that reducing immigration would protect Canadian workers from competition. The "hidden agenda," for the most part, has stayed hidden, and, unless Harper radically changes his government priorities, he'll be taking that phantom hidden agenda with him when he leaves.

That's not to say there hasn't been a Harper revolution. It exists, but, except for environmentalists, few people saw where it would break out. First, to a frightening degree, the prime minister has tried to muzzle and delegitimize criticism. That's been done quietly and incrementally, with few people, especially outside Ottawa, noticing. Taken in the bits and pieces that you see in the news, it all seems like insider talk. In fact, it's really the biggest assault on liberty and democracy since Pierre Trudeau imposed the War Measures Act, but, unlike Trudeau's emergency law supposedly aimed at terrorists, these changes are meant to permanently change the way this country is governed and will keep Canadians very far removed from the government that they supposedly own.

Harper is also intent on changing the way Canadians see their own country. He once said Canadians would not recognize the country after he was finished with it, and he's done a lot to make sure that they do see it in a different light: as an energy and resource superpower instead of a country of factories and businesses, as a "warrior nation" instead of a peacekeeper, as an Arctic nation instead of clusters of cities along the American border, as a country of self-reliant entrepreneurs instead of a nation that shares among its people and its regions.

To remake Canada into that kind of country, he had to change the way Canadians think about themselves, their country and the way they are governed. He had to lobotomize a large part of the country's cultural memory by trashing archives and remaking museums. He had to end Canada's "Third Way" diplomacy and pride in peacekeeping and replace it with an almost ridiculous big-stick diplomacy and sabre rattling in places like the Middle East and Ukraine. He had to limit public debate by preventing the people from being able to argue knowledgeably about important issues like the safety of the oilsands and climate change. He had to keep federal experts, who still command the public's respect, from saying anything he doesn't want to hear. He had to delegitimize the political role of his critics by maligning the motives of journalists, opposition politicians and activists of every stripe.

He had to run election campaigns that are just a series of staged events, with media allowed to film him but not to ask questions and ordinary Canadians kept far away. He had to hold cabinet meetings at secret times and in hidden locations, and make sure reporters don't get many chances to question ministers. When ministers are cornered, he demanded they repeat talking points, no matter how incredibly stupid they may sound.

He had to deny that the scrutiny of journalists has any role or value to democracy and to the governance of Canada. And he had to facilitate the creation of arm's-length sycophantic attack media, both mainstream and on the Internet, to handle low-road messaging, float trial balloons and appeal to the most prejudiced and nasty opinions of his base, without much regard for honesty, fairness or civility.

He had to get rid of objective data from the census and from scientists so no one can challenge his narratives on crime, the environmental damage caused by resource exploitation, the extent of climate change or anything else that's complex. He had to follow the Republican Party's blueprint to create bogus think-tanks and pressure groups, some fronted by convicted criminals, to push for "ethical oil," demand tax cuts that cripple governments, and trash his "enemies"—including, in his world, Aboriginal organizations, students, journalists, opposition politicians, pacifists and scientists. When that didn't work, he sent the federal tax department in to threaten the charitable status of the organizations that he doesn't like.

He had to destroy Parliament's ability to scrutinize new laws and the way the government taxes and spends. He had to cloak decision-making in secrecy. He had to spend billions to beef up intelligence agencies and get rid of meaningful oversight, to the point of hiring an alleged criminal and arms lobbyist to be the public's watchdog of the domestic spy agency CSIS (Canadian Security Intelligence Service).

And he always stays on the attack. The election campaign must never stop. People must be diverted by the struggle for power and should not spend time and energy examining how they're actually governed.

The people who create and enforce his will must be utterly loyal and, very often, ruthless. They have to be willing to kill the messengers so that only one message—his—will be heard. In the end, if all goes his way, the government and the country itself will belong to a clique of professional political insiders who serve at Stephen Harper's pleasure, and to their friends in the business world.

If Harper succeeds, he'll have created a new, undemocratic way of ruling Canada. It will be easy for him or his successors to rule, with sham elections maintaining the myth that democracy is the same thing as regular elections. And there won't be much anyone can do about what has happened so far unless people inside and outside of Parliament push back. We're not about to start holding our rulers to the same kind of account that Charles I faced when he tried to trash the rights of Parliament so long ago. That is, unless people demand better from everyone in Ottawa who plays a role in our democracy.

CHAPTER 2

The Perfect Media Storm

Wherever the people are well-informed, they can be trusted
with their own government, that whenever things get so far wrong as to
attract their notice, they may be relied on to set them to rights.
—Thomas Jefferson to Richard Price, January 8, 1789

When I was a kid, I was hired by a newspaper in Midland, Ontario, a small Georgian Bay town. A day or two into the job, I was taken into an office by the editor. In a very low, quiet voice, he told me the newspaper had one sacred cow, one powerful group or thing that was written about positively, if ever mentioned at all. I wondered what it was. The mayor? The town's lawyers? Land developers? Maybe the Rotary Club, which had among its members every business owner and manager in the town, including the newspaper's publisher? Freemasons? Cops? I was about to find out.

I leaned over for the initiation, the sharing of the Great Secret. It was told to me *sotto voce*, so that no one could possibly hear it through the closed door.

"Don't write anything about the grocery stores. Just forget about writing stories about price comparisons or anything like that. They're the one thing that's off-limits. They're our biggest advertisers." So dirty deals at the town hall were fair game? Yes, if we could prove them. So were the dump operators and tank truck contractors who illegally dumped toxic liquid industrial waste in landfills and along hidden trails in the big local forests. I was allowed to write things about the cops, even when the local police force covered up a botched police chase that ended with an innocent sixteen-year-old girl being killed. But I could never compare the price of turnips at IGA and A&P, since both companies bought pages of advertising in our paper every Wednesday. Their ads were the reason we *had* a Wednesday paper, along with an editor, four reporters, four or five ad sales people, a couple of people handling the paper's books and selling classified ads, a printing press, and a building just off the main street.

In 2013, the paper was killed. Its last reporter, who only worked part-time, was fired. The rented office space in an industrial park was cleaned out. The contract with a printing company was cancelled. Nearly everyone who had put out the paper had already been laid off. The community, which had an eighty-year tradition of solid journalism from a newspaper that had once been privately-owned by a former editor of the *Toronto Star Weekly* and had won more than its share of national awards, would now rely on a free, vacuous chain newspaper. The town no longer has a newspaper that sends reporters to every council meeting and court session, that carefully examines the accounts of the local municipalities, argues for public access to local beaches or catches illegal toxic waste dumpers. No one's there to cover amateur sports—high school, junior hockey, recreation leagues. There's no place where people can go to be heard by local journalists who understand the community and who try to do something to help. When the paper died, some of the big Toronto dailies ran short stories on the loss, but they, too, are in trouble.

Probably most readers of *The Globe and Mail* and the *Toronto Star* barely skimmed the story about the demise of my old employer, but it was one more reason for all Canadian reporters to shudder. The news business is dying, root to tree branch. If papers that had been cash cows in the 1980s could die in this century, was anyone's job secure? That kind of worrying hardly encourages controversial reporting and fearless scrutiny—which are both dangerous and expensive—of the powerful.

Canada, like every democracy, needs a vibrant, ideologically diverse press. Our media has always had a hard time being strong enough to do its job. That's partly because we're a big country with a small population, and partly because we haven't really put much value on our own media. It's in the nature of our national inferiority complex to discount our own stories, and to expect the best of our journalists, the Peter Jenningses and the Malcolm Gladwells, to make it big in the States before they can become real celebrities in Canada.

CANADA'S FIRST NEWSPAPER was the Halifax *Gazette*, which hit the cobblestones in March, 1752. Its first story was very Canadian, an apology for coming out late. In 1775, U.S. troops occupied Montreal and brought a printing press with them. They also brought along Fleury Mesplet, a disciple of Benjamin Franklin. He founded the Montreal *Gazette*, which was published in French. The Americans abandoned the city a few months later but Mesplet soldiered on, despite having his republican instincts snuffed out by a stretch in jail. In Upper Canada, (what's now Ontario), the main newspaper in the colony was published by the government. *The Upper Canada Gazette* was not a riveting read. Its editor, Louis Roy, was a francophone from Quebec City, who, according to Elizabeth Gwillim Simcoe, wife of the governor, could not "write good English."[1] After the War of 1812, some local editors began to mimic their "radical" colleagues in Britain who wanted serious reforms of Parliament. When eighty thousand people gathered at St. Peter's Field in Manchester in 1818 to demand real representation, they were attacked by cavalry, who killed eleven of the demonstrators with sabres and muskets. A crackdown on seditious journalists and other troublemakers quickly followed.

William Lyon Mackenzie was one of the Canadians influenced by radical British publishers. He was a friend and follower of William Cobbett, the London publisher and political gadfly who finally succeeded in winning the legal right to publish parliamentary debates. (Until that time, Parliament did not take minutes, and reporting on it was—and still is—technically illegal. Reporters are there, officially, on a "turning a blind eye" basis, and they can be thrown out of the House of Commons and the Senate if a member says, "I see strangers." This happened in the Senate during the 1989 debate on the North America Free Trade deal, although the rule against "strangers" in the chamber probably would not survive a Charter challenge.) After visiting Cobbett, Mackenzie set up several newspapers to fight the governing clique in what's now southern Ontario. The public responded two ways: some supported the cranky little editor-politician, some believed he was leading the province to revolution and republicanism. In a sort of weird imitation of the Boston Tea Party, the sons of some of Mackenzie's rich opponents showed up at night to his printing office on Front Street in Toronto and tossed his press and printers' type into Lake Ontario.

Newspaper work became dangerous everywhere. Mackenzie's printing operation was just one of several that were trashed or wrecked by pro-government mobs. Newspaper offices in Montreal, Brockville, Kingston (where the editor's dog was murdered) and Belleville were ruined in the wake of the Rebellion of 1837. In St. John's, Newfoundland, a mob attacked the office of the *St. John's Ledger* and cut off the editor's ears. Obviously they were not satisfied with the editorial changes that followed, because they returned a short time later and did the same thing to the press room foreman. As late as 1849, the *London Free Press* was sacked.[2] And when Mackenzie came back to Toronto the same year, after spending a dozen years in exile in the United States, the only paper that welcomed him, the Toronto *Examiner*, was menaced by a Tory mob. The surly crowd backed off when they saw that the newspaper's staff was armed and ready to fight. But journalists rarely won these kinds of stand-offs. Over the years, several editors in Upper and Lower Canada were hauled off to jail for seditious and criminal libel.

Technology favoured the wealthy and the savvy, and by the 1840s, Canada had its first daily newspapers, much more slick and authoritative than the dozens of tiny newspapers that came and went in the preceding decades. Almost immediately, they became political party organs, with the *Toronto Globe* the most successful. By then, the bigger papers were sending reporters to the (often brief) sittings of the provincial legislature. The journalists didn't write what we'd recognize today as news stories. Instead, they published transcripts of debates, choosing the topics and speeches that they thought reflected well on their political masters, who often were also the owners or financial backers of their papers.

Confederation probably wouldn't have happened without newspapers, and we'd have no idea how the Fathers of Confederation made our great national bargain if so many of them had not been newspaper publishers or had editors in their pockets. No one took notes at the negotiations where Confederation was crafted, but a steady stream of leaks of the debates was published in the country's papers. Those articles are one of the very few ways of knowing what, exactly, was agreed upon by the politicians who negotiated Confederation.

In the first few years that Canada's federal Parliament met in its new buildings in Ottawa, no one except news reporters took notes of the debates. The Canadian "Hansard" of the post-Confederation years has recently been pieced together by scholars who have culled the newspapers of the 1860s for snippets of debate transcripts. (The first question on the first day of the Canadian House of Commons dealt with whether the Speaker should be bilingual.)

By the end of the 1800s, the financial risks and the overhead of running a newspaper were so high that political parties could no longer afford to dabble in media ownership. After the transition from party press to media run by wealthy investors, papers sent reporters to Ottawa to act as political operatives as much as recorders of debates. That's a tradition that has never changed: many journalists are as much ambassadors of the companies that employ them as they are reporters of facts. And, while parties did not own newspapers anymore, many newspaper owners were up to their necks in politics, as they still are.

The four Toronto dailies that exist today were all founded by people with political axes to grind: the *Toronto Star* was financed by the Liberal Party until Joe Atkinson pried it out of their hands in a sort of reverse takeover. Atkinson went on to write federal Liberal election platforms and helped William Lyon Mackenzie King pick his cabinet after the 1935 election. *The Globe and Mail* was founded by George McCullagh, a rags-to-riches reporter and stockbroker who, at the age of thirty, bought the old Tory *Mail and Empire* and the Liberal *Globe* and merged them into what was Canada's best newspaper, which he used against the country's unions. The *Toronto Sun* emerged from the ashes of the *Telegram* in 1971 underwritten by, and as a voice of, Toronto's Tory community. Its first editor, Peter Worthington, ran as a Conservative in the 1984 federal election and was one of the few Tory candidates to lose in the Mulroney landslide. The *National Post* was founded by Conrad Black in 1998 as his own neo-conservative and libertarian mouthpiece, with the clear goal of healing the rift in Canadian conservatism and uniting the Reform Party and Progressive Conservatives into a single party that could dislodge the Liberals. All Canadian newspapers claim to be objective, at least in their news coverage, but scratch many editors, publishers and political journalists and you'll find a would-be prime minister or political operative just under the skin, playing the game.

At the beginning of World War I, The Canadian Press wire service was formed as a co-operative to share non-partisan stories with papers that couldn't afford to keep a reporter in Ottawa. It changed the way politics was reported in the news pages. Since news stories were shared by all the big papers, much of the partisanship had to be stripped out of them or at least toned down to the point that the stories appeared to be fair and objective. The Canadian Press's coverage of debates left big city reporters free to cultivate sources at the highest levels of the government and become "insiders" gathering news and gossip. The Hill is still full of people who are, or who try to be, insiders. By their very nature, "insiders" aren't really journalists, they're information mongers. The cachet of being an insider comes from having a lot of very interesting secrets that the insider shares with just a very few selected members of the unwashed.

TV reporter Mike Duffy was the textbook illustration of an insider, a man who hoarded secrets about people and policy and used them as currency to get media, social, and, at the end, political power. He used his secrets shamelessly. After prying $30,000 out of *Frank* magazine in 1995 when the magazine claimed Duffy was hiding at a fat farm rather than lecturing at Duke University, Duffy slunk back a few years later and used the magazine to print embarrassing stories about his boss at CTV being in a romantic relationship with Tory cabinet minister Peter MacKay. For years, according to *Frank* publisher-editor Michael Bate, Duffy had dined out on his connections, especially to the Mulroneys. During a pretrial "discovery" hearing on the *Frank* libel suit, Duffy testified that he'd heard through a "back channel" that he hadn't been given the Order of Canada because of *Frank*'s cruel and embarrassing coverage. *Frank*'s lawyer asked who the source was. Duffy's answer: Prime Minister Jean Chrétien.[3]

MEDIA INSIDER CULTURE isn't a Canadian invention and it didn't start with Duffy, who was just part of a string of journalists going back more than a century who played the insider game in Ottawa and ended up in the Senate. Politicians, especially the successful ones, know the game at least as well as reporters.

During William Lyon Mackenzie King's long stretch in power, newspapers printed editorials saying this bizarre man was as silent as a "gagged clam." Yet the memoirs of the now-forgotten journalists of King's time showed he played them well by understanding insider culture and their need for a larder of secrets. King had no "communications" staff, never held press conferences and didn't scrum with reporters, nor would he willingly talk to more than one reporter at a time. When a young Charles Lynch showed up on the Hill and asked for an interview, King's office staff sent him a wad of carbon copies of the prime minister's speeches. All the answers to any questions Lynch might have were in those typewritten pages, the staffers said. King had rightly tagged John Bassett of the *Montreal Gazette* and, later, owner of the *Toronto Telegram* and the CTV television network, as a Tory; he and his ilk would never get into the insider circle. But the Liberals in the press gallery got a different treatment: long chats in King's East Block office or at his house in Sandy Hill, near the University of Ottawa, and lots of attention and help from cabinet ministers and bureaucrats. Most Hill reporters, even some Tories, believed they had a special relationship with King. And, in return for King's candid and often vicious gossip about his own cabinet and mandarins, these reporters learned to keep their mouths shut and to carefully choose what they printed.

Their bosses also played the game. When King picked his cabinet in 1935, the prime minister invited Joseph Atkinson, owner of the *Toronto Star*, and George McCullagh, publisher of *The Globe and Mail*, to Ottawa to give him advice, though neither newspaperman knew the other was in town. Atkinson and King were of fairly like minds, since Atkinson had written the Liberal platform for that year's election, and King often stayed in Atkinson's house when he visited Toronto. King offered Atkinson a Senate seat, which the publisher turned down. McCullagh was new on the block. He supported Mitchell Hepburn and the Ontario Liberals. He had pried the *Globe* out of the hands of the son of the Tory senator who had owned it, merged it with the *Mail and Empire*, and, at thirty-five, stood, it seemed, on the verge of running the country. (Mental illness and, eventually, suicide, stopped that from happening.) It didn't really matter whether the two publishers actually contributed anything to the cabinet-making during the bizarre sitcom moments when the two magnates were in the prime minister's house without each other knowing. King knew it was important to make them each feel important.

Late in his political career, the press gallery made King an honorary member, and a framed picture, autographed with thanks from the seemingly grateful prime minister, still hangs in the press gallery lounge on the third floor of the Centre Block.[4]

It's startling to see the secrets that were kept by Canada's best political reporters. The *Winnipeg Free Press*'s Grant Dexter, once a press lion on the Hill, sat on one tip that has intrigued conspiracy theorists for years: a remark by the prime minister in the first week of November 1941 that Franklin Roosevelt told him the Japanese would make their big military thrust into the Pacific in a month. Four weeks later, as Japanese planes returned to their carriers north of Oahu, Dexter's paper ran the same coverage of Pearl Harbor that was carried in all the other papers.[5]

Dexter's insider tip surfaced years later when his papers were donated to Queen's University. In them were bales of memos, decades of daily notes written by Dexter to his publisher and editors that were full of important inside information that would have been very useful to the public. Instead, this knowledge gave Dexter and his bosses the illusion of being important men. Secrets give people power, they are one of the rewards of access to power. Sometimes, reporters found it difficult to keep their mouths shut: "It frequently disturbed me to be invited to share secrets of the most indiscreet and embarrassing nature, embarrassing, that is, to the cabinet minister or government official if divulged," one senior reporter wrote in his memoirs.[6] Secrets also tend to bind people together. It's just a few baby steps from secret-sharing to conspiracy: during World War II, King and his ministers recruited media friends to be press censors, propagandists and, at least once, secret agents.

Generations of insiders came and went. They survived through the Diefenbaker years, when that rage-fuelled prime minister scorned most of the media but still turned up to be mocked at a press gallery dinner by a reporter wearing an oversized Dief mask. (The mask survives, signed by all but one of the members of the Chief's cabinet. Ellen Fairclough, the country's first woman cabinet minister, couldn't put her name on the relic because women weren't allowed into those off-the-record debauches.) Many journalists knew Lester Pearson from his days as a diplomat, and he was fairly open, if diplomatic, in interviews and media scrums. The world view of Ottawa's Liberal mandarinate, the group of nationalist, centrist, interventionist central Canadian technocrats who had emerged during the King years and held on through the Diefenbaker inter-regnum was in sync with that of the leading members of the press gallery.

Pierre Trudeau cultivated his own insider group, holding pub-lic policy and philosophy seminars for them in a Parliament Hill office and winning important real estate on the editorial and opin-ion pages of *The Globe and Mail* and the *Toronto Star*, among other places. And, while Trudeau did treat most reporters like dirt, he held frequent press conferences and scrums, like the one in 1970 when a radio reporter asked him how far Trudeau would go to limit civil rights to beat the Front de libération du Québec, and the prime minister famously replied: "Just watch me."[7]

Newspaper editors often shuffled their Ottawa bureaus to try to come up with a team that could work with the party in power, and many good careers in the media ended when a government lost an election. Brian Mulroney often had his favourite journalists to dinner at his official residence at 24 Sussex Drive. Two press gal-lery presidents found new work on the Mulroney team—TV repor-ter Luc Lavoie, who stayed with him after he retired, all the way through the Airbus and Karlheinz Schreiber scandals; and Michel Gratton, whom Mulroney fired after a CBC reporter said Gratton sexually harassed her. Gratton enraged Mulroney by writing what passed for a "tell-all" in 1980s Ottawa, and would succumb to his own tough living at a relatively young age.

But, for the most part, conservative journalists on the Hill found themselves sidelined through more than a century of almost unbroken Liberal power. Even in those rare years when the Tories were in office, the top people in the bureaucracy were almost all Liberals, or at least moved in the same social circles as the bureau chiefs and columnists from liberal newspapers like the *Toronto Star*. The Liberals had family and personal roots in Ottawa. The Conservatives always seemed to be just visiting. But even the Chrétien Liberals, who were, especially in their first years in power, treated very gently by Hill journalists, started making it more difficult to get close to politicians.

The 1990s brought a new crop of conservative reporters and pundits who arrived in Ottawa at about the same time as Preston Manning and the Reform Party. They reflected a change in the ownership of most of the country's biggest newspapers. Conrad Black took control of the formerly middle-of-the-road Southam papers, including the *Ottawa Citizen, Montreal Gazette, Calgary Herald* and *Vancouver Sun*, purged them of many of their liberal columnists and editors, and hired conservatives. Then he recruited more neo-conservatives when he founded the *National Post*, a newspaper created to end the split of right-wing voters that kept the Chrétien Liberals in power.

In a lecture at the Canadian Museum of Civilization in 1997, author John Ralston Saul, who had not yet been asked to pick out the drape colours for his spousal study at Rideau Hall, described Ottawa journalists as "courtiers," people jockeying for position, status and influence at the prime ministerial court. It's an apt description: some Hill reporters, especially during the Chrétien years, lapsed fairly easily into using the word "we" to describe what people were doing developing federal policies and actions, especially in the years just after the close-run 1995 Quebec sovereignty referendum. But when Harper was elected in 2006, there was no windfall for the conservative media. All would be manipulated and ignored.

And storms were brewing that would kill the cozy world of Ottawa insider media, no matter who was in charge. Outside of the bubble, the news business had changed, and journalists, who used to be fairly sure that they would always have media work of some kind, were now just one phone call or staff meeting away from losing their careers. The news industry was being re-made, maybe even killed off. Days like February 4, 2014, when Postmedia closed its Parliament Hill bureau, laying off five people and sending its last four Hill reporters to the *Ottawa Citizen*, became common. Don Martin, a CTV news journalist, had walked into that bureau, then called Southam News, as a *Calgary Herald* columnist in 2000, when it had about thirty journalists covering very specialized beats, writing news that focused on issues that were important to the chain's readers in Vancouver, Calgary, Edmonton, Ottawa, southwestern Ontario and Montreal. Now it was over. Mike De Souza, one of the few skilled energy reporters in the country, was let go. It was bad day for more than just the people who had lost their jobs: "After all, a smaller media means a greater chance of bad news staying under wraps," Martin wrote.

"The obligatory coverage of Parliament stretches reporter resources beyond the industry's ability to dig deeper than the press release or scripted news conference. In a drought of warm reporting bodies, investigative journalism becomes a luxury, not a necessity. Add it up and that means victory for a government which has cocooned itself with communications staff programmed to deny, obfuscate or simply not respond to media requests."[8]

IN CANADA IN 1950, the number of daily newspapers sold each day equalled the number of houses in the country. (Of course, some people bought more than one, and some bought none). On average, between 1950 and 2000, circulation dropped by a little more than 1 per cent per year, so that by 2000, just 40 per cent of households bought a daily paper. In 2000–2010, the decade after high-speed

Internet became common and smart phones rolled out, newspaper circulation was at 40 per cent but still gradually falling.

Through the second half of the last century, political conversation in Canada was muted by the gutting of community journalism, as vibrant independent small-town papers were absorbed into national newspaper chains and ruined. Then, in the late 1980s, big city journalism abandoned small-town Canada. *The Globe and Mail* had built itself on regional distribution. It became the dominant political newspaper in Ontario because people in its circulation department memorized railway timetables and made sure every farmer, Main Street business owner and small-town lawyer had the paper first thing in the morning. (The *Globe's* creator, George Brown, made his fortune in the 1850s by getting the paper to the train on time. George McCullagh, founder of *The Globe and Mail*, started in the newspaper business in the 1920s as a kid wandering the back concessions of Ontario, betting farmers that he could plow a straighter furrow than they could, with a *Globe* subscription as the stakes.) *The Globe and Mail*, in a deliberate decision made in 1988, threw away farm and small-town readers and stopped covering most local and provincial issues. The ad industry lusted for the urban, wealthy demographic, even if it's not large enough to support a great newspaper. People in the West and small-town Canada clued in quickly. No one likes to feel unwanted by snobs. Other big papers, especially in southern Ontario, soon closed their small-town bureaus.

Hidden in the stats is a dirty little secret of the newspaper industry: payment for news was dying long before the Internet came along. In the 1980s, big newspaper chains like Metroland, owned by the *Toronto Star*, had begun giving away "community" newspapers in small towns to cut into the incredibly profitable monopoly of the Thomson chain of weeklies and small dailies. These "controlled circulation" papers were toothless local watchdogs. Newsroom staffs were minimal, pages were full of ads, and the give-aways cut prices to scoop up the real estate and grocery ads, which were the guts of the traditional weekly. (That's why the weekly papers were usually printed Wednesday, when grocers published their pages of ads listing specials, which were the ripest fruit of all, and not to be trifled with by young reporters who lusted to write price comparison blockbusters). By the end of the 1980s, most grocers had started printing flyers that were delivered in the freebie "community" newspapers and by Canada Post at a cutthroat rate, using non-union labour.

By the early 1990s, the freebies were in the country's biggest cities, taking the morning rush hour circulation that used to be owned by the big dailies, especially the tabloids. And most of the people picking up the freebies like *Metro* and the short-lived and strangely named *Dose* were the young readers that the paid media so desperately needed.[9] These papers provide just snippets of the news, with no analysis and very little nuance. And none of the freebies have reporters on Parliament Hill. Instead, they chop and rewrite stories sold to them by The Canadian Press wire service and the newspaper chains, some of which own a piece of these "papers."

Still, despite the hemorrhaging of readers, overall ad sales for most "mainstream" media stayed strong until the 2008 recession, when they fell off a cliff. They haven't climbed back. When companies found themselves in a squeeze for profits, it was easy to justify slashing ad budgets, especially since the new conventional wisdom was that the media, as we had known it, was on its last legs anyway.[10]

Smart phones, websites, blogs, iPads, Facebook, Twitter and easily-accessible free wireless didn't kill newspapers. They were already dead from a cancer that infected them some thirty years ago.[11] It's likely no coincidence that newspaper circulation went into freefall in the late 1970s at about the time that *The New York Times* led North American media into a disastrous evolution from being chronicles of current events to arbiters of lifestyle and trends. In fact, if the Internet hadn't come along, most newspapers would have had to do some serious soul-searching to determine why their readers had abandoned them, or, to be more accurate, had never acquired the habit of reading them. The numbers show newspapers throughout the developed world went into a death spiral when Pierre Trudeau was still working on the Constitution and Jimmy Carter was president of the United States.

In 2009, 35.9 per cent of people aged 18–34 read a newspaper regularly. Some 43.3 per cent of Canadians aged 35–49 were regular newspaper readers, while 58.8 per cent of people over 50 still had the habit.[12] People weren't walking away from newspapers. They had never read them in the first place. For example, in the first four years of this century, just 19 per cent of Canadians aged 23–31 read a newspaper every day.[13] In the early 1980s, 59 per cent of people between the ages of 18 and 29 read newspapers. That's 20 per cent more than *all* of the people who read them now.

Maybe TV's to blame. But broadcasting has been around for years. It's always delivered news. Radio networks of the 1930s had correspondents all over the world, the same way the big TV networks do now, and they devoted much more time to serious journalism than any electronic media, even cable news networks, do in modern times. Broadcasts of Hitler's speeches by the big American radio networks scared the hell out of my grandmother and millions of other people, and the blood-chilling eyewitness radio report of the burning of the airship *Hindenburg* in 1937 ranks with the best journalism anywhere. Radio correspondents like Ed Murrow, William L. Shirer, and Matthew Halton were big stars in Canada.

Father Coughlin, the Canadian radio preacher who operated out of Detroit, collected so many coins from his millions of listeners that he created a continent-wide shortage of pocket change and seriously considered cornering the silver market.

Now, viewership for CNN and most other North American news networks—Fox News Network being a notable exception—is declining, although none of them had stellar ratings to start with. In Canada, ratings for flagship national TV newscasts flatlined years ago. None of our major news networks were ever roaring successes. The Sun News Network has laughable ratings, but the CBC's are so bad that they have to fight with Sun and other private news networks to land advertising from peddlers of burial insurance and walk-in bath tubs for geriatrics.

The future of network TV, especially news channels, looks confusing, and not particularly good for the old, big national broadcast networks. A Harris/Decima poll called *Let's Talk TV: Quantitative Research Report*, taken in late 2013, found, of Canadians surveyed:

- 39 per cent watch TV programming through the Internet-on-demand such as Netflix and YouTube
- 47 per cent subscribe to cable
- 19 per cent subscribe to satellite

EVEN SCARIER for legacy broadcasters, just 10 per cent of viewers relied on Netflix and other Internet subscription services in 2011. That number had jumped to 25 per cent by 2013. That year, a bare majority of people under 34 were getting their TV from the Internet, where there are no Canadian content rules, not much serious news, and a lot of crap. A year later, 62 per cent of people in that age group in Canada subscribed to Netflix. The tsunami that's about to hit broadcasting will remake this country's political and regulatory landscape.[14]

Even at election time, young Canadians ignore political coverage, if they come across it at all. (And they certainly won't on Netflix, which doesn't yet carry ads). The supposedly pivotal (though actually stage-managed) leaders' debates during election campaigns have seen a fairly steady decline in viewers. More than 60 per cent of voters under 30 ignored them in 2004, when the Liberal government of Paul Martin came close to being turned out of office. So, since the elderly people actually get out and vote—and also donate money and time to political parties—governments, no matter which party is in power, tailor their policies to the baby boomers and their parents. The Harper Conservatives see this demographic as an important part of their voting and donor base, in contrast to Justin Trudeau's and the Liberals' targeting of young people for both votes and campaign workers.

Why bother with media when it's all about games and spin and manipulation? People know that the "news" is hardly a mirror held up to events, and that coverage of, say, Question Period and the "scrums" that follow is just bad theatre. By 2004, only one in five young Canadians could name the country's minister of finance. The elderly, at 65 per cent, scored much better. And, of seven developed countries surveyed, Canadians, young and old, were the most ignorant about their political leadership. At the same time, and probably not coincidentally, pollsters found people had very little faith in politicians to solve the country's problems. That lack of confidence in politics and the political system was reflected in voter turnout. The 2011 campaign was supposed to be a watershed election that would decide whether the Harper Conservatives would be able to govern unfettered by the compromises of a minority parliament. It was a spring election, so people couldn't be blamed for tuning out politics while they were on vacation. And there were some interesting local races. Yet only about 61 per cent of the voters of all ages felt it worthwhile to go to a polling station and cast a vote. Obviously, in what was called "the Twitter election," tweets had not connected candidates to voters, even if tweeting and reading tweets did make journalists feel important.[15]

Still, according to *Harper's Magazine* publisher Lewis Lapham, while the media has many sins of pride, sloth, incompetence and greed, it's too easy to make journalists scapegoats for the shabby politics that we've been stuck with on both sides of the border for the past couple of generations. Lapham wrote in 2000: "To do so serves no purpose other than to flatter the media's sense of their own self-importance." The idea of a media conspiracy seemed ludicrous to Lapham; at the same time, conformity of thought and ideology among journalists was not only stifling to intelligent political conversation throughout society, but it was also dangerous to the public good.

Not to put too fine a point on it, Lapham said, most of the top journalists in the country were social-climbing poseurs who talked a good fight about liberty, including freedom of the press: "Having attended a good many weekend conferences at which various well-placed figures within the peerage of the fourth estate exchanged decorative platitudes while admiring the view of the mountains or the sea, I long ago learned that nothing so alarms the assembled company as the intrusion of a new idea."[16]

Another problem is that most "news" is not news at all. It's masked advertising, bumph, propaganda, filler and spin that takes up time and space in the media because it's cheap to make, politically safe and seems to have some value to someone. And much of it is eye-splittingly boring. Daniel Boorstin wrote about "pseudo-events" fifty years ago. Back then, pseudo-events were things like newspaper interviews with politicians and celebrities, anniversary commemorations and government announcements. The stories created by coverage of these non-events filled newspaper pages and radio newscasts, but they weren't really written to inform the people. Rather, they were created to help sell ads and fill the space between ads, and they almost always made the subject of the pieces look good. If these stories hadn't been generated by the media itself and by public relations hacks, the "events," this "news," never would have "happened."[17]

Eric Alterman, writing in 1991, just before the Internet hit, realized that journalists had stopped writing for their readers and were trying to make themselves important players in the power game. Rather than expressing readers' issues to the powerful and explaining actions of lawmakers to the people, newspaper executives decided they wanted to make and break politicians. Of course, newspaper executives had always been in that business, but now, as newsrooms thinned out, pages of news stories were dumped and newspapers literally became smaller. Cheap and easy punditry now dominates the media. Newspapers and newscasts are often preachy, disconnected and tedious. "The American body politic is sick and getting sicker as our democratic muscles atrophy from disuse. The very pundits who bemoan the state of American political debate are themselves responsible for its dilapidated condition. For except in the most extreme cases it is the punditocracy, not the general public, to whom our politicians have become answerable," Alterman says.[18]

Award-winning journalist David Halberstam said the rules of objectivity force journalists to write in a "bland, uncritical way" that requires them "to appear to be much dumber and more innocent" than they really are. By trying to keep their news pages looking fair and objective, then by chasing lifestyle trends, news managers had chosen to make them safe and boring, becoming what A.J. Liebling once called "Adolph Ochs' colorless, odorless, and especially taste-less [*New York*] *Times*." Newspapers lost readers in droves. They've tried to become relevant by offering more local news, but that's failed to bring readers back.[19] Not only did newspapers see an impact on circulation and ad lineage, but newspapers' role in the political sys-tem, going back 200 years in the United States and more than 150 years in Canada, started to die.[20]

Blandness was mistaken for objectivity, and the failure of news-papers to explain what was really going on, Halberstam says, "plun-dered the guts out of American politics." And people knew that the "insiders" gave them just snippets of the truth, leading them to believe that whatever was going on in Ottawa or Washington wasn't showing up in their hometown newspapers.

"The resulting abdication from politics," Alterman writes, "coupled with the increasing identification with the culture of celebrity, represents as much as any single development, the foun-dation of the punditocracy's opportunity to hijack our national pol-itical dialogue and direct it toward goals and ambitions that have precious little relevance to most American's lives. Were contempor-ary journalists able once again to recapture the hearts and minds of their readership, the reconstruction of our community conversation might follow."[21]

IN THE EARLY YEARS of this century, the blizzard of puffery and the hours of journalists-interviewing-journalists news coverage was explained away by media experts as "feeding the goat" of the new news channels. Round-the-clock media—whether multiple news-paper editions or hourly radio newscasts—changed the nature of the business more than twenty years before CNN started broadcast-ing in 1980. "The news gap soon became so narrow that in order to have additional 'news' for each new edition or each new broadcast, it was necessary to plan in advance the stages by which any available news would be unveiled," Boorstin wrote in 1961. "With radio on the air continuously during waking hours, the reporters' problem became still more acute . . . it became financially necessary to keep the presses always at work and the TV screen always busy. Pressure toward the making of pseudo-events became even stronger. News gathering turned into news making."[22]

Now it's TV that's the "goat" that needs to be fed, and even though round-the-clock news stations have dismal viewership in Canada, the entire media-political system is being twisted and warped to fit a medium most people ignore. Question Period became the focus of TV coverage because it guaranteed the conflict and images that TV news feeds on. When Question Period ends, the House of Commons empties. Debate on new laws is ignored by the media, so politicians ignore it, too. In fact, Stephen Harper, in his time as a backbench opposition MP, in his brief stretch as leader of the Opposition, and as prime minister, has never debated a bill. In the 1940s, the House of Commons was full on sitting days, and it often met at night, too, with important ministers and opposition leaders sparring over new laws and policies. (During World War II, the House even convened on Saturdays). Now, when a law is debated, usually only a handful of MPs are in the House. Those few people who are watching on television are tricked by MPs who cluster around their colleagues to fill the camera's frame as they speak to an empty house. Democracy in Canada is now what Boorstin called a pseudo-event.

Question Period gives the visuals for the never-ending campaign. "To paraphrase von Clausewitz's famous dictum that war is the continuation of diplomacy by other means, Question Period is the continuation of the election campaign by other means," long-time *Globe and Mail* columnist Jeffrey Simpson wrote during the Chrétien years. "Television, by its visual, kinetic nature, demands conflict. Nuance and subtlety are television's sworn enemies. Question Period provides institutional verbal combat in short, sharp bursts of rhetoric. Better still for television, Question Period offers occasionally genuine but usually rehearsed and packaged emotion. Television treats indifferently the motivation for emotion; it just wants people to show emotion, and the more of it the better. Knowing this, opposition parties place a premium on emotion, anger being for television the most visual and therefore the most appealing emotion." His observation was still valid more than a decade later.[23]

And Question Period, along with the mob-like interviews of politicians in the foyer of the House of Commons right after ("scrums," in Hill lingo), is cheap to cover. In an environment where the greatest volume of words and images at the lowest price is essential to survival, Question Period is vital. Watch TV or go through a few newspapers sometime to see how much coverage, if any, is focused on debates over new laws. You'll likely find none.

Partly, geography is to blame. Toronto, not Ottawa, is the media centre of the country. Toronto media executives, editors and publishers have a Toronto-centric view of national politics. Issues outside Toronto don't catch their interest, and Ottawa, with its arcane culture and strange political rituals, seems very far away and, usually, unimportant, unless there's a lot of easy-to-understand drama.

Lobbyists, media relations strategists, political spinners and others with a large stake in the Ottawa game often appear on cable news-talk shows and on the pundit panels of network news shows. The strategists tend to know Ottawa very well and are eager and, usually, articulate commentators. But they're also on at least two payrolls—the networks, which pay between $200 and $1,000 to these talking heads, and their business or political clients. People watching the shows don't know who the so-called "political strategists" are lobbying for. And even among the journalists themselves, there's some double-dipping. Mike Duffy had a lucrative little guest speaking business before he was appointed to the Senate. Peter Mansbridge, anchor of the flagship CBC nightly newscast, and Rex Murphy, host of CBC radio's national open-line phone-in show and editorialist on Mansbridge's newscast, were both paid hefty fees for speaking to oil producer groups. With many of these people, politics is a game where winners land hefty contracts and get to appear on TV "news" and analysis shows. Credibility is the media's stock in trade, but it's hard to believe, if you're a cable television news junkie, that you're getting a clean product. Knowing that the people giving policy advice and commenting on the political horse race have conflicts of interest and hidden agendas must make people sour about everything on "news" networks.[24]

And much of the media seems thinner, cheaper, more superficial. Media managers have tried to save money and make the media fit together by trying to merge TV, newspapers, the Internet and, in some cases, radio as well. Though embraced by media consultants and journalism professors in the 1990s and early 2000s, "convergence" of media has been a disaster that trashed the media, leaving newsrooms gutted and the surviving reporters overwhelmed. David Olive of the *National Post* wrote that convergence is not a *potential* boondoggle. It is a *proven* one. It failed a century ago when William Randolph Hearst tried to develop a vertically-integrated news company. Rupert Murdoch had not been able to pull it off with newspapers and television. Michael Eisner and Edgar Bronfman Jr. also failed in the modern era. Yes, there are new media, but news managers—a notoriously uncreative bunch on their best day—are nowhere near capable of evolving.[25]

Newspapers finally realized, by about 2010, that they had been fools to give their stories away online. Most of the country's major newspapers have since set up paywalls, giving away a few stories every month, then asking readers to pay for the privilege of reading news online. But it's too late. People don't like to pay for something they used to get free. And, in perhaps the unkindest cut, the CBC has developed the country's most comprehensive news page, with stories and opinion pieces from across the country. That website is free, and it competes directly with all of the country's newspapers. By 2014, the paywall score was being added up and it was grim: just 110,000 people had signed up for Globe Unlimited, *The Globe and Mail*'s paywall service. About half of those subscribers got *The Globe and Mail* delivered to their door and had online access. All of the Postmedia papers—the dailies in Vancouver, the *Calgary Herald*, the *Edmonton Journal, Ottawa Citizen, Montreal Gazette*—are hyping themselves as "digital first" but, in 2014, had only scraped together 137,000 paywall customers, and only 45,000 were digital-only subscribers. The *Toronto Star* said it couldn't give solid numbers because its paywall was new.[26]

SOCIAL MEDIA is the next passing ship for journalists. Twitter is hyped as the great connector between the powerful and the rest of us. The 2011 Canadian federal election was labelled the "Twitter election" by those who embraced the micro-blogging fad. The Canadian Press, probably the brightest collection of journalists in a single Ottawa bureau, hired Ottawa social media consultant Mark Blevis to analyze Twitter's content and blog about its role in the campaign.

Certainly, the volume of election-related "tweets" seems impressive: about 16,000 of them on a typical day, jumping to 25,000 a day in the week of the leaders' debate and levelling at 18,000 in the last week. Twitter fans think those numbers are stellar, but when you consider that 24 million people were actually eligible to vote, they don't look so hot. Blevis counted re-tweets as well as original tweets. The most popular tweeters, like Kady O'Malley, who was paid by the CBC to tweet and blog almost around-the-clock, drew about 35,000 followers, numbers comparable to the viewing statistics of Sun News Network, which everyone in Ottawa's political circles believe had almost no impact on the campaign.[27] Most of the journalist and political insider tweeters had fewer than 1,000 followers.

Academics David Taras and Christopher Waddell, (the latter a former *Globe and Mail* political reporter and CBC Parliament Hill bureau chief), wrote after the election that Twitter had a decidedly negative role in the coverage of the election. In earlier elections, journalistic insiders had communicated with each other by BlackBerry. Twitter had replaced the BlackBerry and had become what Waddell called "the logical next step in the media's turning inwards." Journalists' tweets dealt with what they and the campaign strategists cared about. Energy that might have gone into real coverage and analysis was spent by social- and political-climbing media stars on campaign planes cozying closer to political operatives and distancing themselves even further from voters.

Andrew Coyne from *Maclean's*, David Akin from Sun Media, the CBC's Rosemary Barton and Kady O'Malley, and Susan Delacourt from the *Toronto Star*[28] became the core of a small group of tweeters who tried to dominate the media agenda and frame the campaign's issues. Very little of the material they posted dealt with things affecting the voters. Rather, they focused on the election-as-horse race meme. Twitter stripped away the pretense of objectivity: anyone who cared to examine the opinions of political journalists could pick through their tweets, many of which were remarkably frank about biases. The Hill media rarely followed or talked with outsiders, or even other journalists who worked for unimportant organizations or weren't members of the clique that covered the campaign. Reporters might be able to quickly get comments from candidates (or staffers posing as them on Twitter), but these comments were superficial at best. How could they not be, when even the most thoughtful candidate could reply in just 140 characters or less? Most politicians knew better than to say anything substantial on Twitter. Only two seasoned Conservative Twitter hands, Tony Clement and James Moore—who, not surprisingly, were also two of the handful of ministers allowed to say anything substantial on behalf of the government—made the bulk of the Harper campaign tweets.[29]

Some people point to media scandal-mongering as the culprit for killing political involvement and undermining the watchdog role of the press in Canada. George Bain, a respected *Globe and Mail* writer, made that case in his 1994 book *Gotcha!* But coverage of scandals began long before Confederation. Dozens of newspaper and television news awards grace the walls of newsrooms, home recreation rooms and even some bathrooms for coverage of controversies and wickedness that are long forgotten. And other press critics argue young people might be turned off by regional griping. But Canada's always had that, too, and in fact, those concerned about disenchantment with the federal system should turn public attention to *provincial* politics. Even college and university students, who feel the direct financial hit of increased tuition and residence fees and have the most to fear from today's economy, are very unlikely to engage in politics or rely on the media to follow current events. The notable exception is Quebec, which is unplugged from much of American-dominated media culture. There, in 2012, young people learned by experience that they could throw out a government that they felt was gouging them and that had passed a law to limit their right to protest.[30]

Perhaps, then, people care about their immediate surroundings: roads, bike lanes, policing, urban planning, transit, garbage disposal, parks—all things run by municipalities, with meetings right in the community and representatives who are often easy to call, email or visit at a city hall. But voter turnout at the local level is appalling, even in cities with notoriously inept, even comical, candidates. Yet, where young people actually see the effects of social engagement, you find a very interesting thing: young people volunteer twice as much of their time as their parents did thirty years ago. Some Canadian provinces now require students to volunteer for civic causes, but that simply reinforces a trend among youth that began in the 1990s. (Even taking into account the idea that some students do volunteer work to beef up their résumés for college applications, the doubling of volunteer hours is phenomenal. If anything, universities are easier to get into than they were in the 1970s, and doing free work in, say, a newsroom or a law firm to try to get into a competitive professional program would not count as community volunteer time.) In the United States, young people volunteer more of their time than any demographic segment except people in the 40–49 age group.[31]

Certainly, something is happening to make young people feel like the political system does not want them, and that it's owned and operated by, and on behalf of, other people. Even during the Obama presidency, young people showed very little interest in American politics. While young Americans supposedly swooned over Obama in 2008, wore his buttons and put "Hope" and "Change" posters in their bedrooms, it was black people who actually got off their seats and voted for him.

This is a reversal of the way things used to be. Surveys showed that, between 1948 and 1972, the elderly were less likely to be informed about politics than young people.[32] Back then, young people also found their way to the polling booth. Now, when it comes to democracy and public service taking place in power centres like parliaments, city halls, political parties and voting booths, where there's little obvious impact by each individual, the kids are absent. In places where they see results and maybe get a smile and some praise, more young people are showing up. So we can toss the idea that young people have become too lazy and too pampered to be informed about their government and engaged in democracy. Something else must be keeping them out of the public sphere. Maybe, like most people, they simply don't feel welcome and believe they are lied to.[33]

SO WHAT HAPPENED? Partly, politicians began working hard to delegitimize the role of "mainstream," "lamestream" and "corporate" media. In 1835, the French writer Alexis de Tocqueville had credited the vibrant American press for spurring public participation and the creation of political associations. The death of newspapers— and, it's reasonable to assume, intelligent TV journalism—hurts democracy. Empirical studies confirm that when newspapers scale back coverage or shutter their offices, a rather frightening number of people simply stop caring about the way they are governed. Portland State University professor Lee Shaker took a look at public engagement in Seattle and Denver, two cities that recently lost daily newspapers. The *Seattle Post-Intelligencer* and Denver's *Rocky Mountain News*, which had been bleeding readers and advertisers for years, were crushed by the 2008 recession. In both cities after the papers closed, voter turnout dropped, people made fewer calls and visits to their political representatives, they joined fewer civic organizations and they were less likely to engage in protests such as boycotts.[34]

In the years leading up to the emergence of Stephen Harper, the Canadian media had done a tremendous amount of damage to itself, mainly because of cheese-paring and poor financial and journalistic decisions in head offices. Very few of the surviving journalists have beats, so many reporters really don't understand what they're writing about. That's especially true among the new generation of young reporters hired—even in print media—because they look good on TV and Internet video streams. Most of those kids have never worked anywhere else and have no idea of life outside of school and their fresh media jobs. There aren't enough bodies around, even in the Ottawa bureaus of the CBC and the big Toronto newspapers, for reporters to devote their days to specialized reporting. With fewer people to write hard copy, prepare web content and file film clips for web pages, most Parliament Hill reporters can't take chances on stories that may not pan out. Investigative reporting, when it's done at all, happens when reporters have filed their quota of stories. And reaction to investigative stories can be ugly and expensive, as the *Toronto Star* learned when it took on mayor Rob Ford, was hit by a boycott campaign and saw its sales plunge.

Through the 1980s and 1990s, newspapers, magazines and radio and TV stations had been abandoning Parliament Hill, leaving coverage mainly in the hands of The Canadian Press wire service, and, recently, to the *Ottawa Citizen*, which feeds to Postmedia papers in Montreal, Ottawa, Calgary, Edmonton and Vancouver, the bureaus of the Toronto dailies, and the CBC. In the 1960s, reporters from individual papers, from publications like the *Montreal Gazette, Hamilton Spectator, London Free Press, Winnipeg Free Press, Calgary Herald, Saskatoon Star-Phoenix* and *Vancouver Sun* were the bedrock of the press gallery. By the turn of this century, almost all were gone, the family-owned Halifax *Chronicle Herald* being one of the last holdouts. Where once there had been reporters from news organizations all over the country, looking for regional and local stories, now there were national news bureaus of so-called national media. There are no reporters at all in the Parliamentary

Press Gallery from newspapers or radio or TV stations east of Montreal, except for one journalist from the Halifax *Chronicle Herald*. And there are none from Saskatchewan.

After the 2011 election, only one English-language private radio bureau on Parliament Hill survived, and it had one reporter. News-talk radio stations might claim to offer wall-to-wall news, but none of them would pay for their own Parliament Hill reporter. This change—which had been evolving for years as Canadian newspapers and radio stations were bought up by chains, and which accelerated as newspapers began withering in the late 1970s— radically altered the outlook of the press gallery. Formerly, its members had worked their way up through their own news organizations and were respected reporters in their own communities. Now, many Hill reporters are hired straight out of university, partly because they'll work for almost nothing just for the experience of covering national politics.

The deterioration of Hill coverage has made a difference to the way Canadians vote. Christopher Waddell, chair of Carleton University's journalism school, took a look at the voting patterns of cities whose dominant newspaper had closed their Ottawa bureaus and found an interesting, disturbing pattern. He and David Taras looked at the voter turnout in six Ontario communities over the seven federal elections from 1979 through 2000. Three of those cities—Windsor, London and Hamilton—started the period with a local paper sending a reporter to Ottawa. The other three communities—Niagara Falls, St. Catharines, and Sault Ste. Marie— didn't have anyone in Ottawa reporting for the local paper. By 2000, the Hamilton, London and Windsor dailies had closed their bureaus. Taras and Waddell found voter turnout in the three cities whose newspapers had shut their Ottawa bureaus fell more quickly than the provincial average. Those towns started the period with a much higher voter turnout than the cities without Hill reporters, and, by the end of the period, voter turnout had plunged to the mediocre norm of the rest of Ontario's cities.[35] Why was that? Probably because local MPs and the issues they raise in Ottawa no longer get coverage back home. If issues affecting those cities do make it to the floor of the House of Commons or a parliamentary committee, the news is not considered national and therefore important enough to be covered by national media. The tree falls and no one hears it.

After the mid-1990s, the economic problems of Ontario outside Toronto fell off the agenda in official Ottawa because no one—especially in the media—seemed to care. An unpleasant new shallowness crept into national news coverage, which, even more than it had before, became a sort of sports reporting. The public picked up on it. The media was no longer really part of the public. So it was easy for the media to be identified as elitist, out-of-touch and insular. The Media Party nickname coined by Ezra Levant of Sun News to describe the Hill media is effective because, at the heart of it, there is a substantial grain of truth. Rather than dealing with real people—say, talking to individuals, municipal and provincial politicians, business, church and non-governmental organization leaders, First Nations and others back home—the Ottawa media elite talk to each other and to the new professionals who develop retail politics. This is the selling of voters to parties and parties to voters, paid for with money raised through state-of-the-art donor identification, tracking and fast communications using carefully targeted messages.

These strategists, pollsters and lobbyists work in the high-rises near Parliament Hill and socialize with members of the press gallery. The old National Press Club died a generation before, but the members of this elite, and those who were desperate to join it, haunt the bars on Sparks, Elgin, Queen and Albert streets in downtown Ottawa and find good tables at clubs in the ByWard Market. Now so-called news stories are about polls, party strategy, and winners and losers, not about jobs, health care, and pensions. Those topics may be at the core of some Hill stories, but the issues are not the focus of the stories. Instead, reporters tend to focus on how politicians and their strategists are *seen* to be handling those issues. People don't care about the things Hill reporters find interesting: How did political strategists react to some piece of news? Will there be a cabinet shuffle? An election? Will a leader quit? Is the Liberal Party still split by infighting? Will Stephen Harper be able to hold his party together? One recent study showed that more than half of Canadian federal election news in 2011 coverage was about the way the parties were running their campaigns, rather than about candidates and issues. This cryptic insider coverage may intrigue reporters and the campaign strategists who feed them information, but it must be deadly dull to those who don't know the players.[36]

During the frequent elections of the 2000s, reporters turned their backs on issues and embraced the technology that bound them, ever more strongly, to each other and shielded them from dealing with real people. In 1984, the country had a free trade election. In 2011, it had a Twitter election, after the YouTube and BlackBerry election of 2008 and the blog election of 2004. This came just a few years after the web election of 2000, the first one that featured sophisticated Internet advertising. "Web-based media can narrow rather than expand the information and perspectives available to journalists," Taras and Waddell wrote. "Reporters become so preoccupied with the latest tweets from politicians and each other that they lose sight of what's taking place beyond their own gated community."[37] Elections became so expensive to cover that the big TV networks started relying on pool footage shot by a single camera. The networks chipped in for the pool cameras, which are always trained on the prime minister. That ensures that all the networks are able to get their Harper shot on the nightly news, but the camera doesn't turn toward, say, the Muslim girl being dragged out of a 2011 Conservative rally in London, Ontario, and it doesn't ask questions.

Some papers actually ran winners and losers lists written by reporters who watched to see who was up and who was down. When there was space, they ran insider notebook columns that were read by power players and few other people. Most Canadians, though, seeing their standard of living eroding and unsure of their ability to get their kids through college and retire with dignity, simply did not care about Ottawa's power games.

IT HASN'T HELPED that politics has become progressively more ugly and nasty in the past thirty years. By the time Harper arrived in Ottawa as leader of the new Conservative Party, real discussion and debate in Parliament had pretty much died, electoral politics had become a professional game played by lobbyists and professional campaign managers, and by people hoping to join their lucrative businesses. Running a successful campaign can earn a strategist more than $500,000 a year. Wedge-issue politics, which had been honed in the United States, were brought to Canada by all of the major parties.

"The political parties and the media have created a world in Ottawa in which voters have become outsiders and can't relate to what is being reported," Christopher Waddell wrote. "Too much political coverage means nothing to them and has no impact on their lives. As a result, Canadians tune out until something happens, such as the prospect of an unwanted election that temporarily forces them to pay attention."[38]

Part of the problem lies with the fact that many Hill journalists don't bother reading newspapers. Some print reporters don't even read the publications they work for. News aggregator websites like nationalnewswatch.com are popular with members of the press gallery. These sites do a fairly good job of listing Canadian national news stories and opinion columns, but they're not particularly good at finding important regional and local stories and bringing them to the attention of people inside the Ottawa bubble and they have almost no international news. So, by relying on those kinds of sites for their news, Hill reporters effectively see themselves reflected back.

"This kind of coverage produces a world that people across the country can't comprehend. Canadians don't act that way when they deal with their neighbours, when they are out in the grocery store or riding a bus to work. They do not see any of it as relevant, so increasingly, they ignore it and the national political media as well," Waddell wrote after the 2011 election.

> *Decisions to cut back on reporting staff, close bureaus, and replace reporters from local newspapers and TV stations with national news bureaus and national network reporters have broken the link between the public and the media that has been at the core of political communications. As a result, the media now plays a shrinking role in informing Canadians about politics and public policy.*
>
> *It has replaced its traditional role with an inward-looking, narrowly-focused coverage that concentrates on the issues defined by the parties through their joint sharing with the media of technological tools and their ability to engage reports in concentrating on the artificial world they have collectively created. Instead of using technology to bridge the communications gap between voters in their communities and the media, the media has used it to turn its back on the public, forging closer links with the people reporters cover rather than with the people who used to read, watch and listen to their reporting.[39]*

IT'S HARD TO KNOW the full amount of the damage that's been done to our political system, though we do have some U.S. numbers that may be useful. In August 2013, Pew Research issued a report showing that Americans' public respect for the media on key issues like accuracy, fairness and independence were stuck near all-time lows. Still, the survey showed, a broad majority of those surveyed continued to believe the media has an important role as a political watchdog. And those numbers have held firm for the past three decades. Interestingly, Republicans were slightly more likely to see the media as legitimate watchdogs. Young people, who had seemed apathetic and hostile to media in other surveys, now seemed more supportive of its role. But the media should still take cold comfort from the Pew numbers, which showed a clear break between what people thought the media should be doing and how the public believes media actually behaves. Almost as many people who believed the media had an important policing role in the political system also said news reports were often inaccurate, and more than three-quarters of the people surveyed thought media outlets were biased and subservient to power.[40]

In Canada, the Tories have a foundation myth that the "mainstream media," the "lamestream media" and the "Media Party" oppose them and everything they stand for. They've said it so often that it's believed by many people who don't see themselves as conservative. In fact, through Stephen Harper's career, especially before he won his 2011 majority, he's enjoyed media support, especially among print journalists, that other leaders would envy. Here's what *The Globe and Mail* said in the editorial that endorsed the Tories in 2011: "Only Stephen Harper and the Conservative Party have shown the leadership, the bullheadedness (let's call it what it is) and the discipline this country needs. He has built the Conservatives into arguably the only truly national party, and during his five years in office has demonstrated strength of character, resolve and a desire to reform."[41] *The Globe* was not alone. The Tories, in their hunt for a majority, were endorsed by the *Vancouver Sun, Calgary Herald, Montreal Gazette, Hamilton Spectator, London Free Press, Ottawa Citizen, National Post, Winnipeg Free Press*, the *Waterloo Region Record*, the Sun chain of tabloids in Calgary, Edmonton, Winnipeg, Toronto and Ottawa, and *Maclean's* magazine. The *Toronto Star* endorsed Jack Layton's NDP. Michael Ignatieff and his Liberals did not get the endorsement of any large newspaper in Canada. As well, Conservatives effectively picked the issues in that campaign and received much more coverage than the other parties, continuing a trend that began when the Tories re-emerged as national contenders in 2004.[42]

So, when Harper was elected in 2006, the media was already very, very sick. Isolating and delegitimizing the media and its role in Canadian democracy would be easier than it could have been at any other time in recent Canadian history. The stars had aligned, the media was hobbled, and now, if possible, Harper and his people would push it to the fringe of Canadian politics. At least it wouldn't be alone: scientists, parliamentary watchdogs, and pretty well anyone else who could get in the way would be out there, too.

CHAPTER 3

It Pays to Increase Your Word Power

Four hostile newspapers are more to be feared than a thousand bayonets.
—Napoleon Bonaparte

There was never a truly golden age of the press in Ottawa, some lyrical time when reporters frolicked freely and happily in fresh-mown fields of useful and timely information. Prime ministers and their staff always played favourites and held grudges. Reporters, who should be, and who claim to be, the public's eyes on Parliament Hill, have always been outsiders in the political system. But things are much worse now. Instead of being watchdogs, most of the reporters on Parliament Hill are ciphers, unable to do much more than get reaction to issues that are, for the most part, manufactured by political parties for their own benefit.

Many reporters did try to build bridges to the Liberals during the long decades when Conservative governments were rare and brief. The "natural governing party"—one of the most enduring and successful political machines in the world—and Ottawa media leaders had similar views on Canadian nationalism, economics, federalism and official languages. Through the twentieth century, most reporters, like the people they covered in politics and the bureaucracy, were university-educated first- or second-generation English men from Eastern Canada. They strove to be important actors on Parliament Hill. (The determination to be seen as part of the inner circle may be responsible for the almost comical number of reporters wearing bow ties in the 1960 press gallery "class picture." Lester B. Pearson's influence was obviously sartorial as well as ideological.)

Pierre Trudeau had contempt for the press, even though most Hill journalists fawned over him in the early years of his regime. Brian Mulroney tried to prosecute Global TV reporter Doug Small in 1989 for his scoop on a budget leak. The case was thrown out years later. (The judge called Small's work "exemplary," but Small's career on the Hill was dead.) As soon as Jean Chrétien, who was pretty much incoherent in either official language, took office, he had reporters banned from the government and opposition lobbies behind the benches of the House of Commons. There was very little squawk about that, even though Canadian reporters had had access to them for more than 130 years, and lobby journalists—columnists who write serious analysis—are still key reporters in the United Kingdom.[1] Chrétien also tried to have CBC reporter Terry Milewski fired for his dogged coverage of "peppergate," the police attack on protesters during the 1997 Asia-Pacific summit in Vancouver. Yet most of the media bought the "Liddle Guy" shtick.

In the early 1990s, newly elected Reform Party members were treated like hicks by the media. The satirical magazine *Frank* used the naïveté and talkativeness of several Western rural MPs to set them up for pranks that were sometimes quite cruel. In one, Reform MPs were conned into believing the Chrétien government was giving free Zambonis to tropical African nations (the article was called "Zambonis up the Zambezi"). Reform MPs proved to be easy marks when a *Frank* reporter told them the book *Black Beauty* was being banned as porn.

Hill reporters jumped on Reform Party leader Preston Manning's change of hairstyle and clothing makeover. They, quite rightly, reminded him of a pledge that he had made never to live in Stornoway, the mansion that's the official residence of the leader of the Opposition, and chided him when he moved into the house in 1997.[2]

Then came Stockwell Day, whose brawls with the press gallery usually ended in tears and frustration for the Reform Party. Day and his staff and the media were at each other's throats from the time Day won the leadership of the Canadian Alliance, the party that was crafted from the old Reform movement to unite the political right. Reporters mocked him for holding a press conference on a Jet Ski, gave Day a hard time for the way he handled his Parliament Hill news conferences, and were not kind in the 2000 election, pointing out the many gaffes during Day's leader's tour.

Among the party's executives, organizers and supporters, the bitterness remained, even after Stephen Harper took over. And it was reinforced by a steady message from U.S. right-wing talk radio, newspapers and Fox News that the big TV networks, important metropolitan newspapers and Hollywood were determined not to give conservatives—especially those who, like Day, were religious and social traditionalists—a fair shake.

Day had let his caucus talk. Stephen Harper would not. In 2004, while still leader of the Opposition, Harper demanded all of his MPs let him vet any speeches they made about same-sex marriage after Jason Kenney, one of the party's stars, told Punjabi-media reporters that he believed gay and lesbian people should get married, as long as it was to people of the opposite gender, and then for the purpose of having children. Some of the old Reformers weren't happy with the new rules, which they saw as a break from the party tradition. But this was no longer the Reform Party, it was Stephen Harper's Conservative Party.[3]

Every Conservative leader since R.B. Bennett had faced caucus revolts, and most had succumbed to them. In an undisciplined caucus of Reform MPs who had been elected as populist spokespeople for their predominantly Western, rural constituents, it was easy for reporters to get one policy position from Harper, then find a few backbenchers willing to shoot their mouths off without checking with the leader's office. It had been that way for more than a decade; the party had taken a lot of hits under the leadership of Preston Manning and Stockwell Day, and Harper was determined to stop it from happening. Harper and his senior staff had read *Globe and Mail* columnist Jeffrey Simpson's *Discipline of Power* (1996) and were resolved to make sure that only smart, presentable people who were clearly loyal and who understood Harper's message spoke to the media. Everyone else would just have to be quiet.

STEPHEN HARPER had never been close to the media, even though he did appear on some news network panels during his years in the political wilderness in the late 1990s. Once he was elected party leader, he still kept his distance, although he did show up to a press gallery dinner, where his humorous speech went over well, and at a Christmas party for kids of press members, held on a Saturday in one of the Parliament Building's big committee rooms. Before the 2006 campaign, Harper was somewhat popular with Hill reporters, though most didn't think he had a chance of winning.

But he had some personal reasons to loathe journalists. When Harper went to the 2005 Calgary Stampede, a photographer got an absurd shot of him looking very uncomfortable dressed in a goofy cowboy getup of jeans, hat and a bizarre leather-like vest. The picture has haunted him ever since. Another shot, taken in a summer Parliament Hill press conference, showed Harper's man-boobs through his tee-shirt. (This shot, unlike the Stampede getup, has disappeared from media and public memory, but at the time it generated a lot of hurtful comments about Harper's weight.)

Since the beginning of his mandate, some members of the media—especially journalists working outside of Ottawa—have been among the people who have spread an almost unkillable false rumour that the Harper marriage is in trouble. From time to time, there have been oblique media allusions to the myth. Andrew Coyne hinted about it in an *Ottawa Citizen* column, while Norman Spector, a former Brian Mulroney chief of staff, came out with inaccurate details in a column published, and quickly retracted by, *The Globe and Mail*, which had only carried the piece on its website. The paper replaced the blog post with: "Editor's Note: We have removed the text of an original posting on this blog as it fell short of *The Globe and Mail*'s editorial standards with respect to fairness, balance and accuracy." It's hard to know how much, if at all, the rumour has personally hurt Harper, but the short author biography on his 2013 hockey book, *A Great Game*, says the prime minister "is happily married to Laureen."[4]

His former strategist Tom Flanagan told the *Hill Times* newspaper that Harper's hatred of the press was fixed in stone when the then Opposition leader was hammered in a news conference over an outrageous news release from the Conservative campaign that very strongly suggested Paul Martin tolerated, and maybe even supported, child pornography. On its live broadcast of the scrum, CBC Newsworld showed newspaper reporters huddled together, sharing a voice recording of the Conservative leader's reaction to the uproar. To Harper, Flanagan said, the reporters looked like hungry sharks or wolves. "There's no question, just as a historical comment, that that episode, the child-porn fiasco, represented a turning point for Harper," Flanagan said.[5]

Harper not only dislikes those he sees as liberal journalists, he also has no use for some conservative commentators like Terence Corcoran of the *Financial Post* and Lorne Gunter of the *National Post* (and, later, the Sun chain).[6] Harper drew his inspiration from what might seem to be a strange source, writes Gerry Nicholls, who worked for Harper at the National Citizens Coalition during Harper's hiatus from party politics in the late 1990s and early 2000s. "For Stephen it was all about control. He didn't trust the media to get our message out. And he believed it was a mistake to get too friendly with the press. As he once explained to me, the secret to dealing with the Ottawa press corps was to copy Pierre Trudeau's approach. 'Trudeau,' he said, 'treated reporters with contempt and yet they worshipped him.'"[7]

Tom Flanagan, when he was still in Harper's good books, said Harper's ingrained craving for control fit with the demands of forging a new party that could be taken seriously as a government-in-waiting. "He doesn't repose trust very easily. He's always got his antennae up. His first reaction to anything new is almost always negative. It's a personality trait," Flanagan told author Lawrence Martin. Flanagan says Harper sometimes leaves important details to subordinates, but messaging is always controlled by Harper. "That's where he has taken measures of centralization to new levels."[8]

When Harper became prime minister, the hammer came down. His government would engage in campaigns of information suppression—censorship at source—and propaganda. He would do everything but ignore the media. While Harper's apologists tried to say the media was no longer important and Harper didn't care about journalists and what they thought, the Canadian treasury was paying about 3,800 communications staffers in ministers' offices and federal departments, including 100 in the Prime Minister's Office and Privy Council Office.[9] Those people went to work gagging anyone under Harper's control and reshaping the way Canadians see both their country and its government.

Any MP, public servant, diplomat or military officer who wants to say anything to the media has to fill out a Message Event Proposal (MEP) and submit it to the Prime Minister's Office and the Privy Council Office. The form has headings including Desired Headline, Strategic Objective, and Desired Sound Bite. It asks applicants to describe the backdrop of the event and the type of photograph that the speaker hopes will be taken by the media. It even asks about the speaker's wardrobe. These MEPs sometimes take weeks to process, being the subject of meetings and memos, bounced around between political staffers and senior bureaucrats and sent back to the would-be speaker for revisions. The control isn't just over policy talk. TV reporters who want shots of national parks and historic sites like the Norman Bethune House in Gravenhurst, north of Toronto, are held at bay by staffers until approval comes from the Centre. Ministers' statements and press releases, no matter how seemingly innocuous and banal, get the full MEP treatment. And approval is not guaranteed. When a Parks Canada official wanted to write a press release about the mating habits of black bears, his MEP was turned down. And Canada's financial literacy commissioner won't talk to reporters about financial literacy for kids.[10]

In the winter of 2014, I agreed to write a piece on young people and financial literacy for a trade magazine for credit union managers and executives. Canadian consumers are loaded with unsustainable consumer debt and mortgages. Our big personal debt load scares the hell out of the federal government, to the point that the late finance minister, Jim Flaherty, used to issue warnings, as does the

Bank of Canada. Most Canadians don't spend nearly enough time learning how to handle money. More than half of Canadians don't budget at all, and younger people are the least likely to do any financial planning. It's rare for people to have anywhere near the savings they need for retirement. And, during the 2008 financial meltdown, many Canadians made some pretty poor choices. So after the crash, the Harper government wisely decided to create a committee to learn if Canadians had a clue about money. The results of its study were so shocking that the government hired a national financial literacy commissioner, Lucie Tedesco. You may not have heard of her. Few have. But I wanted to talk to her about financial literacy education for kids for my credit union magazine story. It seemed reasonable to assume that talking to the public about that sort of thing is part of her job. So I sent an email to her office.

Instead of a phone call from the financial literacy commissioner, I got an email from her media handler, who wanted to know about the magazine I was writing for. She wanted a list of the questions I would ask Tedesco. "I would like to talk to her about financial literacy for young people," I replied. Back came the flack's answer: "As the principal spokesperson for the Agency, I would be available for this interview." I replied that I preferred to talk to the financial literacy commissioner, who is, after all, the commissioner of financial literacy, and therefore the go-to person on, say, financial literacy education for young people.

So I wrote back: "Sorry, no. Canada has a financial literacy officer. Will she talk about financial literacy for children? If she will, I will be happy to interview her. If not, I will tell the credit union executives of Canada that Canada's financial literacy commissioner will not speak publicly about teaching financial literacy to children."

I did not hear from the flack again. But the editor's boss did. Someone in the office of the commissioner approached the executives in charge of the magazine to have me yanked from the assignment for pushing too hard to have Canada's financial literacy commissioner talk on the record about the best ways to educate kids on financial literacy. The piece ran without any quotes or material from Canada's financial literacy commissioner. It was just another day in Stephen Harper's Ottawa.

THE RULES OF THIS GAME weren't developed in Canada. The stifling of the media is a worldwide problem. Partly, it's the result of the idea that governments should be run like businesses. To become more "corporate," governments and politicians have turned to media consultants who give them the same advice that corporations get: stay on message, use photo ops, circle the wagons when there's trouble. But governments aren't private companies (at least not yet). They belong to the people, and they exist to serve the public, not make money or build political careers. And it is worse in the United States under the Democrats than it was under George W. Bush. In Washington, photographers have been shut out of many White House activities. Reporters have to clear their questions in advance and feel the president does everything he can to circumvent them. And this is in the White House in a time of hope and change.[11]

In fact, the situation in the United States and the United Kingdom is so bad that Canada sometimes actually looks good. As yet (as far as we know), our government hasn't turned its spy agencies and tax collectors on journalists (unless you count Revenue Canada's audit of the writers' protection group PEN), nor has it thrown any into jail, except for a freelance columnist detained during the G20 police riot in Toronto. When Reporters Without Borders released its annual press freedom report at the beginning of 2014, Canada had actually moved up two spots. It was a hollow victory, though. The previous year, Canada dropped ten points—from 10th to 20th. Still, we were miles ahead of the United States, which fell from 32nd to 46th. The top ten was dominated by central Europe, although New Zealand also made it into the top tier. Finland had the world's freest press, followed by the Netherlands and Norway. (North Korea, Eritrea and Turkmenistan were the worst, with no press freedom at all.) "Since 9/11, the [U.S.] has been torn by the conflict between national security imperatives and respect for the principles of the First Amendment," Reporters Without Borders explained.[12] Probably that was generous. The 9/11 attacks were a great excuse for politicians and security agencies to do what they've always wanted to do.

In her 2007 master's thesis, Calgary television journalist Lynn Raineault explored Prime Minister Stephen Harper's ongoing battles with the Parliamentary Press Gallery. Raineault found most of the Conservatives she interviewed believed Harper was his own worst enemy when it came to getting favourable media coverage. Two factors came up. The high-profile Tories interviewed by Raineault cited Harper's ingrained belief that journalists in the press gallery are ideologically opposed to all conservative governments. Harper's introverted, stubborn, impatient and controlling personality was the second factor supposedly behind the prime minister's decision to alienate and humiliate the media.

Raineault conducted interviews with seven prominent conservatives, including Reform Party founder Preston Manning and lobbyist Geoff Norquay, who had been a director of communications for Harper before Harper became prime minister. Raineault was told by almost all of them that Harper sabotaged his own party by waging war with the media. Manning said Harper is a man who never forgets a perceived slight.

While Harper saw the press gallery that way, almost all the

conservatives interviewed by Raineault believed the press gallery skewed toward the left, but journalists still tried to at least appear to give conservatives a fair shake. Even that was a bit paranoid. In his early years in power, Harper faced a press gallery representing the conservative Canwest chain (*Montreal Gazette*, *Ottawa Citizen*, *National Post*, *Calgary Herald*, *Edmonton Journal* and *Vancouver Sun* and *Province*), the conservative CTV and Global TV networks, and the right-wing Sun chain—which has dozens of small-city and community papers, along with its tabloids. Print was dominated by the centrist *Globe and Mail*, which almost always endorsed conservatives and had pummelled Jean Chrétien over the sponsorship scandal and his real estate dealings. The liberal *Toronto Star* did run plenty of "hidden agenda" stories, but it really was an ideological outlier in the newspaper business. And, when Harper was in opposition, he was able to profit from the fact that criticism makes good copy.

Tom Flanagan, who has spent far less time in Ottawa than Harper, described the bulk of the press gallery as primarily motivated by career ambitions and by groupthink. That's a fairly accurate assessment. Flanagan also told Raineault that Harper's "strong, silent-type approach" can't work when there's a need for someone to explain the government's policies on complicated issues.[13]

Alberta journalist Don Martin, in late November 2006, in the conservative *Calgary Herald*, wrote:

> *The Prime Minister was raised in a Calgary where his party leaders were routinely ground into sausage meat by Ottawa journalists. His DNA is linked to a special chromosome reserved for hating media and he is convinced that any Ottawa communications strategy—be it to babble constantly or stay silent aloof—will generate uniformly negative coverage . . . He will not allow him-*

self to be comically defined like previous prime ministers, who lost their luggage, got disoriented in Jerusalem or slipped on an army helmet backwards.[14]

Tory Senator Marjory LeBreton, who was appointed to the upper chamber by Brian Mulroney, summed the Tories' attitude up quite succinctly: "I am a Conservative and I know more than most that around this town populated by Liberal elites and their media lickspittles, tut-tutting about our government and yearning for the good old days that we are never given the benefit of the doubt and are rarely given credit for all the good work that we do."[15]

Of course, by "media," Harper's spokespeople often mean the CBC. Yet Harper and the CBC have a strange relationship. No one in his government complains when Sun News Network and its winged monkeys in the right-wing blogosphere describe the CBC as the "state broadcaster." Yet, until it lost the revenues of *Hockey Night in Canada* to Rogers in negotiations near the end of 2013, the network came through the media firestorm reasonably unscathed. Andrew Coyne argues the Tories actually need the CBC. Why, he asked in the spring of 2014, haven't the Tories privatized it, shut it down or carved it up? He wrote:

That is what a real conservative government would have done. But as this is not a real conservative government, it has instead simply left the CBC as it is, adrift, purposeless, yet still consuming $1-billion of scarce public funds every year. It does so, for all its pretensions of concern for the taxpayer, because the CBC is more useful to it in its present state: not as a problem to be fixed, but as a platform on which to raise funds, a scapegoat for the party's failures, a diversion for the base's wrath.[16]

Harper's team has never gone after the CBC for far overstepping its mandate by, effectively, running the country's largest online newspaper, one that seriously undermines the ability of newspapers to make money from paywalls. In fact, the CBC has been able to create the publicly funded national newspaper that Tom Kent recommended in his 1981 Royal Commission on Newspapers, but that almost all people ignored at the time because it was believed to be both expensive and rather scary in the hands of a corporation that might someday fit the real description of "state broadcaster."

Ezra Levant, a former communications director for Stockwell Day when he was opposition leader, and now a Sun News Network host, was delighted by what he described as Harper's "marginalization" of the press gallery.[17] Levant wanted to use that tactic to get rid of other watchdogs, starting by "denormalizing" the country's human rights commissions. It was a strategy that would be embraced by the Harper government for most of its information control.

BUT THERE WAS ANOTHER, quite simple reason why Harper picked a fight with the Hill media. Supposedly, Harper is a populist. And populists fight elites. Kate Heartfield, editorial page editor of the *Ottawa Citizen*, a paper that has endorsed Harper in all of his election campaigns, thinks many Conservatives bash the media as part of an elaborate show that is performed for the Tory base, the westerners and rural Ontarians who voted for Reform.

"People cloaking themselves as populists need elites to attack, and conservative populists can't attack the rich and powerful, because some of them are rich and powerful. So we journalists become 'elites,'" Heartfield, hardly anyone's idea of a lefty, wrote.

And then the Conservatives tie themselves in knots to show us how much they don't care about us. They pen reporters at their party convention and yell at them when they walk in the wrong places. They pay, with taxpayers' money, armies of public servants to monitor what we do, to take our questions and pass them around by email like hot potatoes for a few hours, before disgorging approved "lines" that, ideally, have ludicrously little to do with said questions. They spend an awful lot of time and energy to make sure we—and by extension, Canadians—get as little information as possible. And then they spend more time and energy writing aggrieved letters to the editor. They openly mock the press: John Baird's director of communications recently tweeted "The constant whining of the media about access isn't obnoxious at all. Oh wait—it is." A director of communications should hold "access" as sacred as any journalist. His goal, in theory, is exactly the same as the media's goal: to make sure news stories are accurate and informed.[18]

Soon after Paul Martin cleaned out his desk, reporters began to notice Harper did things differently from all of the prime ministers who had come before him. Often, when he walked down a corridor in the Parliament Building, his security guards made sure there were no members of the public, including reporters, around. Instead of arriving at the MPs' door at the front of the House of Commons, Harper began slipping into the building through various entrances, including the Speaker's private door (admittedly a ridiculous holdover from the days when private doors meant something) and even through the loading dock at the back of the building. Dozens of photographs of the prime minister went up on the walls of the large lounges, called lobbies, used by Tory MPs. (They are hidden behind the curtains on the sides of the House of Commons.) The walls of the Langevin Block, which holds the Prime Minister's Office and his hundreds of employees, were also redecorated with dozens of photographs of Harper in various poses, both informal and in official pictures with heads of state and other VIPs. Everywhere he went, his official photographers shot video and still pictures.

Harper came into office believing in the political messaging system of Ronald Reagan and the Gipper's image doctor, Michael Deaver. They believed messages delivered on TV, especially when the leader or candidate looked and spoke directly at viewers, were the most believable. It helps to have a strong visual background. George W. Bush used an aircraft carrier, Reagan chose the Oval Office. Harper liked a lectern placed in front of the main doors of the House of Commons. Talking-to-camera statements allow a politician to cherry-pick facts. Critics and members of the opposition, denied the same direct access and the props of the leader's power, seem not to be in his league.

On the other hand, news conferences and interviews have uncertain outcomes and cannot be scripted. They reduce the leader to the mortal level of his opponents. If interviews have to be done, it is best if the reporter does not normally see the prime minister, is in awe of the office and is grateful for the opportunity. It also helps that many small-town reporters simply don't know much about what's going on in Ottawa.

Sam Donaldson, the venerable ABC reporter, once described the Reagan formula this way: "They are very good at directing the news by making available something on a story that they want out and withholding from sight—remember television—something they aren't prepared to discuss." In the early 1990s, Dick Cheney, who was secretary of defense in the George H.W. Bush White House, said: "I did not look on the press as an asset in doing what I do. Frankly, I looked on it as a problem to be managed."[19]

In the week leading up to the swearing-in of Canada's New Government, as Harper and his people insisted it be called, about thirty people shortlisted for cabinet spots were interviewed by senior members of the prime minister's staff, who summoned them to a downtown hotel. Job candidates were told to keep their mouths shut. If there were any signs of a leak by the prospective ministers or their staffs, they were out. "I think Stephen Harper has placed a great emphasis with this team on discipline," the new immigration minister, Jason Kenney, said. "This is going to be a government that keeps a very tight lid on privileged information. It's a pretty radical difference from the culture of the Martin government, whose modus operandi seemed to be to leak like a sieve." Harper had learned from Paul Martin's government, which was full of freelance cabinet ministers, divided over loyalty between Chrétien and Martin people, and loaded with powerful, vocal staffers with plenty of friends in the media. In the end, a leak of information about the government's plan to get rid of income trusts had brought on a much-publicized police investigation in the middle of an election campaign. That loose talk had probably cost Martin the election. "I think the Martin culture of leaks reached its pinnacle [there]. I think it's just good practice, generally speaking, to be more discreet," Kenney said.[20]

Ottawa Citizen media writer Chris Cobb said Harper's desire to control the message was blatant and obvious, and he would not let the Ottawa press corps get in the way. They might be useful on the campaign trail, but they were dangerous once the election was over. "If Mr. Harper has anything other than an intense dislike of the news media, and distrust of journalists assigned to cover his government, he has done nothing to show it," Cobb wrote. Harper had time to talk hockey on TSN but thought journalists were out of line for criticizing him for appointing campaign strategist Michael Fortier to the Senate and putting Liberal turncoat David Emerson in his cabinet on his first days in office—the kind of things Harper had attacked Paul Martin's Liberals for just a few weeks before the election.[21]

In February 2006, Harper fired William Stairs, his director of communications, over Stairs's handling of the fallout over the recruitment of Emerson. Stairs wanted Harper to level with reporters about why he had accepted a floor-crosser into his cabinet. Instead, the soon-to-be-unemployed communications director learned a quick and tough lesson about Harper's secrecy fetish. Denise Rudnicki, a twenty-year veteran of the press gallery who had worked for Preston Manning (and later was hired as director of communications for Liberal Justice Minister Irwin Cotler), was sharply critical of the new prime minister. "It's clear now why Mr. Harper's media relations are in disarray. It's because he is taking his own bad advice."[22] But Stairs's firing did more than just get rid of someone who seemed too chummy with the press. It sent a message to everyone in the Harper government that anyone who was soft on the press would be driven out. And if anyone didn't get it, all they had to do was watch Stairs's replacement, Sandra Buckler, who had utter contempt for journalists.

By the end of the second month of Harper's regime, whatever honeymoon had existed was over and people were analyzing his throttling of the media. Conservative senator Hugh Segal, a former adviser to Brian Mulroney and Ontario premier Bill Davis, said politicians' communications plans often quickly collided with reality. The new government needed discipline if it was not going to end up a disorganized mess. Harper's team had the perception "that the Martin Liberals had no discipline whatever with their relationship to the media, that they scrummed every 12 seconds somewhere, made another commitment, issued another press release. And in the end, the conclusion of everyone—including the media—was that none of it meant anything at all."[23]

BEGINNING WITH HARPER'S swearing-in as prime minister on February 6, 2006, his media handlers copied the system used at the White House, where the president and his staff, rather than the reporters, decide who asks questions. Reporters said before the prime minister's first-day press conference that they would not follow the new rules, claiming the prime minister or his staffers would ignore reporters who ask tough questions. Instead, the press gallery insisted on using the old system, in which reporters were allowed to ask questions on a first-come, first-served basis. In a typical press conference, a member of the press gallery executive scans the room and writes down the names of the people who have raised their hands. Then those names are called in the order that they were placed on the list. On the morning of April 11, 2006, members of the press gallery were told the prime minister would hold a news conference on the government's showcase accountability legislation. This was the first test of the "list" system.

The conference was held in the small but elegant Commonwealth Room near the rotunda of the Centre Block. As they had done for years at news conferences, reporters lined up at microphones and waited their turn. Instead of using the gallery's system, Harper pointed to freelance writer Tim Naumetz, who was sitting in the centre of the crowded room and was unaware of the lineups at the edges, and called on him to ask the first question. The room erupted with loud complaints from the reporters in line. "Tim, do you want to ask a question or not?" Harper asked the perplexed reporter. The prime minister took two questions from reporters in the gallery's lineup, then left the small room. His staff said he had a tight schedule and needed to leave early.[24]

Calgary Herald columnist Don Martin took Harper to task two days after the botched press conference. Martin, normally fairly supportive of conservative politicians, called Harper Canada's new minister of truth. "In the theatre of absurdity called Parliament Hill, Harper has gone far beyond simply restoring order to the chaotic business of stick-handling the media. He's imposed lalio-phobia—fear of talking—on cowering ministers, MPs, support staff and bureaucrats." Martin described how he had tried to interview Environment Minister Rona Ambrose and had been told by her handlers that the interview would happen if there were no questions on the Kyoto accord and greenhouse gas emissions. When Martin said no, the flack refused the interview. Martin appealed directly to Ambrose, who agreed to do the interview. Five minutes before it was supposed to start, the same flack killed it. "Kyoto? Nope," Martin said, "the Prime Minister's Office abruptly decreed the interview had to be cancelled because it might conflict with the message Harper wanted out this week. Which was, ironically, ACCOUNTABILITY."[25]

A few weeks later, Martin pointed out to his readers that, when Harper spoke, he actually said interesting things. Former prime minister Paul Martin could ramble on at news conferences every week and say nothing. When Harper talked near a microphone, facts and policy ideas rolled out, sometimes to the point where reporters were swamped with stories to write. It didn't help that no other ministers were allowed to say anything interesting or important. "The only other place I've seen media forced onto this sort of single-person reliance is the Alberta legislature, where Premier Ralph Klein unilaterally sets the agenda and delivers enough random quips and quotes to fill up the news hole, often scooping his own ministers in the process," Don Martin wrote. And, he said, it didn't help that Harper's communications team were "evasive, unresponsive, paranoid and unable to wrap their heads around the concept of daily newspaper deadlines." One Tory MP complained that no one could cry about being "out of the loop," since the "loop" consisted of the mind of one man.[26]

That doesn't mean Harper doesn't closely follow the media, or doesn't care about what's written or said about him. For a government that expends so much time and effort trying to define the media as unimportant to Canadian politics, much of the strategy to bury the Mike Duffy housing expense issue, for instance, revolved around how the government's actions would play in the media, and on how to keep Duffy from blabbing to reporters. Attacking the credibility of the reporters who broke the story hadn't worked.

"I met the prime minister and Nigel Wright," Duffy later told the Senate in his swan-song speech. "Just the three of us. I said that despite the smear in the papers, I had not broken the rules. But the prime minister wasn't interested in explanations or the truth. It's not about what you did. It's about the perception of what you did that has been created by the media. The rules are inexplicable to our base."

Anyone who thinks press gallery stories about scandals no longer get traction across the country should take a long, close look at the Duffy case. Certainly, MPs who went back to their ridings in the summer of 2013 heard about it, as did reporters who got out of the Ottawa bubble. And, even discounting the many problems plaguing pollsters, only Harper's most diehard apologists could argue that there were no changes in public attitudes. Polls showed support for the prime minister had started to tumble. There was even talk of him quitting without finishing the first term of his majority.

In another column, *Ottawa Citizen* editorial page editor Kate Heartfield wrote that Harper's obsession with media coverage of the Duffy scandal would hurt the Tories. The prime minister's

weird, pigtail-pulling obsession with the media is partly to blame for the fact that the Senate scandal became a PMO scandal. It's not that he doesn't care what we write. It's that he cares so much,

*he and his staff default to scenarios and talking points. It's become
an instinct. Almost everything Harper's government does—from the
tough on crime agenda to his attempts to make certain senators just
go away—is media strategy. It's fiction all the way down. If there
was ever a political party in Canada deserving of being called the
Media Party, it's the Conservative Party of Canada in 2013.*[27]

Ottawa Citizen media writer Chris Cobb criticized the Tory
media-bashers for their vacuous, knee-jerk assaults on Hill reporters, describing conservative critics within the media and blogosphere as "journalists who seem oddly embarrassed by what they do
for a living, by pseudo-journalists joyfully unencumbered by their
own ignorance and, most troubling, by vocal members of the public who have a perversely negative impression of the news media
and a total misunderstanding of the role journalism plays, or should
play, in a healthy democracy." He singled out callers to the CBC
radio show hosted by commentator Rex Murphy—who had never
worked as a journalist on the Hill and hadn't bothered to do serious research to determine the facts—for congratulating Harper for
whipping journalists into line and asking rhetorically why government behind closed doors is such a bad thing.

Cobb explained something that's obvious to Hill media watch-
ers, but that's lost in all the stereotyping by talk radio blowhards,
open-line hosts, neo-con bloggers and Harper media handlers:
the Parliamentary Press Gallery is very deferential to power, much
more so than, say, the British political press (which is, itself, fairly
cozy with politicians. Its senior members get special secret brief-
ings from top political operative and civil servants). The gallery
rarely mentions the private lives of politicians and powerbrok-
ers. (*Frank* magazine does, but its private-life stories are rarely
matched by the mainstream unless there are serious political over-

tones.) In fact, discretion about affairs, weird habits and addictions that would make the front page of the competitive British papers is part of the requirements of admission to the "insider" culture of the Ottawa bubble.[28]

When Harper visited British Columbia in 2006, local reporters put their name on the Prime Minister's Office list. A national reporter asked a local B.C. reporter to ask her question for her because the national reporters' organization was boycotting the PMO list system. The day after reporters walked out of a press conference about the situation in the miserable Darfur region of Sudan, Harper told an interviewer on London's A-Channel (an outlet that was not exactly famous for its cutting-edge journalism) that he would try to ignore the Parliament Hill media and give preference to media in cities and small towns. "Unfortunately, the press gallery has taken the view they are going to be the opposition to the government. They don't ask questions at my press conferences now. We'll just get the message out on the road. There's lots of media in the country who do want to ask me questions and hear what the government is doing. I have trouble believing that a Liberal prime minister would have this problem. But the press gallery at the leadership level has taken an anti-Conservative view," Harper said.

Yves Malo, who was then the president of the press gallery, objected to Harper's comments. "It's a little paranoid," said Malo, a reporter with the Quebec-based TVA network. Malo had led the walkout over the use of the list. "I'm not anti-Conservative. I'm not pro-Conservative. I'm just a journalist who's trying to do his job."[29]

MANY WRITERS BELIEVED Harper, not the Ottawa media, would win the fight for public support. Columnist Allan Fotheringham, who had left Ottawa years before, told readers of his syndicated column the reason Harper would beat the national media: "Missus Bloggs in Moose Jaw thinks the Ottawa media are overpaid, lazy, drink their own bath water, interviewing each other over beer and [are] into pack journalism," he wrote. "This is a very serious matter, you must understand. If Hogtown Toronto thinks it is the centre of the universe, in Ottawa—the town that fun forgot—the panjandrums of the Press Gallery seriously believe that they hold democracy in their frail little hands." Stephen Harper had been sneered at "for years by the Ottawa pundits as an Alberta yahoo who was going to break up Canada with something called the Reform Party—the Flat Prairie equivalent of Quebec's crazy separatists." The people who had sent Harper to Ottawa had felt the sting of that condescension and were not about to abandon their man.[30]

Conservative columnist Claire Hoy, who had also left the gallery long before Harper's election, said Harper had every right to tell journalists "to take a hike." It wasn't a free speech issue, he said: nobody was being stopped from writing what they wanted, and "a free press does not mean everybody has to co-operate with them [journalists] in any way." The fight was "all about journalistic ego." While, politically, Hoy thought Harper ill advised to "indulge in this silly war with the media," polls were showing the spat was not hurting the prime minister's popularity.[31] A poll by Ipsos-Reid published in June 2006 showed 57 per cent of the people surveyed thought Harper's insistence on controlling who asks him questions is about ensuring friendly questions. About 48 per cent did not think the issue was important at all.

The newspaper chain owned by the Asper family undermined the press gallery's campaign and finally ended it. The Canwest News Service, which fed the *Calgary Herald, Montreal Gazette, Ottawa Citizen, National Post* and several other dailies, along with Global TV, negotiated with the Prime Minister's Office and won an exclusive interview with Harper for two of its reporters after Canwest agreed to submit to the PMO list rule.[32]

In September, the rest of the press gallery caved. It voted to let the prime minister's staff pick the reporters who could ask questions at news conferences. The deal was supposed to be temporary, lasting just thirty days. In fact, it was a complete surrender. The thirty-day trial period has never ended. When the month was over, Harper's communications advisers simply refused to negotiate. A few weeks later, Harper was confronted by a Calgary reporter who said changes to access to information rules unfairly punished inquisitive journalists. "I punish them all anyway," Harper crowed, before breaking into what the journalist described as a "long and sustained laugh."[33]

Eventually, the system evolved on off-the-Hill trips into one in which a Harper press aide tells reporters how many questions they get to ask each day. This system practically ensures a sort of Media Party conspiracy. Because of the small, set number of questions, reporters go into a huddle and decide among themselves which questions will be asked. There are no follow-up questions.[34] The questions are the type that are easily anticipated by the prime minister's staff: very "timely" and "national." Serious, complex questions on, say, business, foreign or regional issues don't get asked because they're not interesting to the national TV and print bureaus.

Reporters have to make sure they get something from these news conferences to make their editors and employers happy, since travelling with Harper in Canada costs about three to five thousand dollars for a few days of stumping through small towns or into the Arctic, with even higher charges for major trips overseas.[35] "In effect, you are paying for access to the Prime Minister," Canadian Press reporter Stephanie Levitz told the *Hill Times* newspaper in 2012. Rather than ignore these trips and simply leave the photo ops unphotographed, news agencies keep signing up for them. It's partly because they need the footage and the bits of text, partly because the news companies and the journalists like the status.

During the trip to the 2014 Francophonie summit in Senegal, Harper answered only ten questions, two of them from Senegalese reporters. In late May 2007, Harper made a second trip to the Afghan war zone. At first, handlers kept the visit secret from the media travelling with the prime minister. During the trip, reporters were kept away from Harper and his officials. What could have been a significant news event, a discussion about Canada's role in Afghanistan, turned into another photo op. "[A] father-knows-best discipline was imposed on a fourth estate Harper clearly considers child-like," *Toronto Star* columnist Jim Travers wrote after the trip.

> *Tough questions weren't answered on the war, the controversial treatment of prisoners, or on Harper's rationale that 'terrorism will come home if we don't confront it here.' . . . prime minister willing to risk his life to the media should have enough confidence in voters to let them sort through the best available information before making political and policy choices. But that isn't in his character.*[36]

Domestic journalists aren't the only ones who are pushed around by Harper's handlers. South African reporters and photographers bitched when officious staff from the Canadian embassy in Pretoria made them move far from Harper's plane so that the prime minister's official photographers and camera operator, as well as Canadian photographers, could have the best view of the prime minister's arrival for the funeral of Nelson Mandela. A few weeks later, Palestinian TV camera crews were forced to give up the spot they'd staked out near the entrance of the Church of the Nativity in Bethlehem to make way for the PMO-paid videographer who records all of Harper's travels. The Palestinian Union of Journalists said that one Palestinian journalist was punched in the face and another was hit with a metal object.[37]

And causes that really could use some positive media coverage can find "help" from the prime minister to be a mixed blessing. Harper spoke at a spring 2014 conference on maternal health issues in Toronto. Reporters spent most of the conference penned up in a media room where they couldn't see or hear anything. Minders escorted them to the washrooms. When journalists were allowed anywhere near the conference, it was usually just as pool reporters, meaning they had to share whatever they learned with the journalists back in the pen. The outcome was predictably bad, both for Harper and the organizers.[38]

SOMETIMES, THERE'S REBELLION, though it never quite morphs into revolution. Just before Parliament resumed in the fall of 2013, a CTV News camera operator dared to shout a question during one of Harper's photo ops. The camera operator wanted to know what Harper thought of Dean Del Mastro (who also had been Harper's parliamentary secretary) being charged under the Elections Act for violating its spending rules. Harper's media handlers barred the CTV camera operator from a trip to Asia, but backed down when other journalists who were supposed to cover the trip said they'd stay home in solidarity.

Soon afterwards, on the day before the 2013 speech from the throne, Harper's office told TV networks that cameras would be welcome inside a Tory caucus meeting to hear Harper give a pep talk to his party's MPs and senators. Reporters were banned. Newspaper and radio reporters hadn't been told about the speech.

When the camera crews arrived at the caucus meeting with reporters in tow, Harper's staff would not let them in. In protest, all of the camera crews, except for Sun News's—who had gone into the meeting through a side door—decided to boycott the event. David Thibault, a Radio-Canada reporter who was president of the press gallery at time, said: "It's important because how can you report if you're not there? A reporter's job is to witness, to listen, to watch."

Reporters, *National Post* columnist John Ivison said, had finally decided to draw a line. "There's a principle at stake . . . that reporters are allowed in to these affairs to do their job," he wrote. "Normally reasonable people decided that this was beyond the pale, and I think they were quite right to do so. It's maybe a fight that the PMO is ill-advised to take on."[39]

Fred DeLorey, the Conservatives' director of political operations, sent a fundraising letter to party supporters explaining why Harper's speech would not be seen on the evening news. "You won't believe what the Press Gallery just did in Ottawa," DeLorey wrote. "Some media decided to boycott an important speech by our Prime Minister—one where he laid out his vision for our country, before today's Speech from the Throne." DeLorey said the Tories needed money to get their message out. "Rather than send cameras to cover the Prime Minister's speech, they attended the NDP's meeting, and were welcomed with cheers and applause. We knew they wouldn't give us fair coverage—but this is a new low for the Ottawa media elite."[40]

At their annual meeting in March 2014, more than seven years after Harper took power, members of the press gallery voted to push back against Canada's New Government. They would dare to ask questions "in all photo-ops and availabilities with the prime minister, cabinet ministers, and all Parliamentarians, to fulfill our functions as journalists in a democratic society." But there would be no boycott. And, in the debate before the vote, many journalists made it clear that they didn't expect the little protest to make a difference with the Harper regime. They just wanted to put a shot over the bow of the next prime minister.

"It's not actually confined to one party," press gallery president Laura Payton, a CBC reporter, said after the meeting. "There are times with all the parties, I think, where we experience that, so we were just discussing about how we have this right to ask a question. It's up to a parliamentarian whether they want to answer the question, but you can't tell us not to ask questions and that's something that we've seen specifically out of the Prime Minister's Office at photo-ops, for example."[41]

During Harper's time in power, personal attacks, including campaigns to get reporters fired, have become common. In January 2013, staff in the Prime Minister's Office put out a statement through the office of Ontario Tory MP Dean Del Mastro, challenging the credibility of Postmedia investigative reporter and political columnist Stephen Maher. The robocalls vote suppression story, in which Tory operatives hired a call centre to send non-Tory voters to bogus poll locations, had been broken by Maher and his colleague Glen McGregor, who works for the *Ottawa Citizen*. The PMO statement, sent to a newspaper in Del Mastro's Peterborough riding, called Maher—who, later that year, would share with McGregor a Michener Award for public service journalism and a National Newspaper Award, among other prizes, for the robocalls series and other stories documenting campaign violations—a "controversial reporter." It went on to remind Tories that Postmedia had corrected one of Maher's stories "because it made false claims against a Conservative riding association."

After the *Peterborough Examiner* ran a story about the PMO statement, Del Mastro made a clumsy attempt to say he, not the Prime Minister's Office, had written it. Gerry Nott, who was then the *Ottawa Citizen*'s editor, said the personal attack on Maher was "quite appalling and surprising. That the PM's office would deal with the issues around the Del Mastro story by looking at concerns they had about a previous story suggests to me they are either trying to deflect or have their eye on the wrong ball." Maher told the *Citizen*: "I don't consider myself to be controversial."[42]

Like the Obama administration, Harper's regime has no qualms about using the tax investigation system against its media critics. In July 2012, a Mennonite church magazine was warned by the Canada Revenue Agency to curb its political activism. The letter was described as a "reminder" to Canadian Mennonite Publishing Service that taking part in "partisan political activities" could cost the organization its valuable charitable status. Without the ability to draw on money from the Mennonite Church Canada and issue tax-deductible receipts to donors, the publisher would have been driven out of business. "It has come to our attention that recent issues of the Organization's monthly periodical, entitled 'Canadian Mennonite,' have contained editorials and/or articles that appear to promote opposition to a political party, or to candidates for public office," the letter said. It reminded the Mennonites that charities are "prohibited (by the Income Tax Act) from engaging in partisan political activities," including "direct or indirect support of, or opposition to, any political party or candidate for public office."

The Mennonites took the letter as a threat. Rather than quietly cave, the church paper posted the letter, along with an angry editorial denouncing it, on the newspaper's website. Canadian Mennonite editor and publisher Dick Benner told a CBC News reporter that the letter was "a chill on speech." Benner said the letter "tells me that I need to be very careful on what I say about government policy and how I say it. That restricts me as a journalist and as a religious commentator."

While the Mennonite paper had, in an editorial published before the May 2011 election, asked its readers to keep in mind the church's policies on social justice, pacifism and environmentalism, it had not endorsed any political party, Benner said. But it had criticized two Tory Mennonite MPs, saying they had distanced themselves from their heritage. And, after the election, Benner had written an article about the killing of Osama bin Laden that condemned the takeover of Canada by what he called "a militaristic Conservative majority government." The tax department also cited stories profiling young Mennonites as they decided who they would vote for, church concerns about an omnibus crime bill, an article on how the death of NDP leader Jack Layton inspired some young Mennonites to get involved in politics, and a story about Mennonite youths who sent paper airplanes to Ottawa to pressure the government to "spend less money on war."[43]

No MATTER WHAT happened between the Harper government and the media, in Harper's world journalists were always to blame. Even the Mike Duffy scandal, in which the Tory senator supposedly overcharged the Senate for his second home and accepted what police would later call a bribe from the prime minister's chief of staff to pay the money back, was the media's fault. In a truly bizarre column published in *The Globe and Mail* during the 2013 Christmas season, Preston Manning tried to blame the Parliamentary Press Gallery for the Duffy scandal, saying reporters should have somehow stopped the gregarious CTV journalist from yearning for a Senate seat.

Manning got his hands on a copy of the gallery's small handbook, which mostly instructs new Hill reporters about things like parking policies and where pictures can be taken. Manning seized on the rule that a journalist can be expelled from the gallery if "such member uses his membership or the facilities of the Gallery to obtain a benefit other than by journalism." Duffy, Manning said, had been lobbying for a seat in the Red Chamber for many years before Harper put the broadcaster (along with Pamela Wallin, who had also been a member of the press gallery in the late 1980s) into the Senate. So, in Manning's world, the press gallery should somehow have stopped Duffy before he schmoozed again.

Manning ignored several key facts. The most glaring one was that, while Duffy did eagerly make his availability known to various prime ministers, both Tory and Liberal, craving a Senate seat is hardly unethical or cause for firing from any job. (Manning's own father had been appointed to the Senate.) The other hole in Manning's argument was that somehow Duffy had used the press gallery's resources to win the job. The only "resource" of any value that Duffy may have co-opted was his job as a host on CTV News channel, since it was that employment that put him face-to-face with politicians. It was up to CTV, not the press gallery, to discipline its employees if they crossed the company's ethical policies.

Manning, who certainly knew more facts about Senate appointments than he let on, was aware—or should have been—that journalists had been appointed to the Senate since Confederation and some had served with distinction. *Globe and Mail* editor Richard Doyle had been given a seat by Brian Mulroney and became one of the hardest-working legislators in the chamber. As members of the Senate's justice committee, Doyle and Senator Gérald Beaudoin, the former dean of the University of Ottawa law school, had, during the Chrétien years, scoured legislation that normally would have been rubber-stamped by the Senate and found many foul-ups and bad laws. Jean Chrétien had appointed, among other journalists, Joan Fraser, who had been pushed out of her job as editor of the *Montreal Gazette* because Conrad Black, who owned the paper, thought she was too liberal. And Manning neglected to say it was journalists, not Senate auditors or the Prime Minister's Office, who raised the issue of Duffy's housing and travel expenses in the first place.

Manning was trying to make the press gallery wear the Duffy scandal, as though the gallery could somehow bar one of its members from accepting a Senate seat or prevent one from being offered. In the press gallery, Duffy had a reputation as an honest man, though one who was difficult to work for. The 2013 allegations of improper expenses were surprising to many journalists who knew him. But no one had been particularly surprised when Duffy got the nod. Author Stevie Cameron described him, during the Mulroney years, as one of the gallery's few stars and, in a piece of prophecy that would turn to irony, wrote in 1989: "If Duffy is appointed to the Senate—the rumour that makes its way around the circuit at least twice a year—not even his fellow journalists, usually an envious lot, will mind."[44] Duffy was a gregarious man, much more friendly and generous with his time and with fans across Canada than most high-profile TV journalists.

Manning might have dropped into the Prime Minister's Office and asked Harper's speechwriters about the ethics of moving from media into political service. Some had been press gallery members. One had been the editor of the *Ottawa Citizen*.

All of this inside baseball and whining does little more than convince people that federal politics is just a game, with patronage as its prize. Many people don't care that the media, one of the watchdogs of the democratic system, can no longer do an effective job. People don't follow politics and they don't vote. They hope that whatever Ottawa does, the federal government leaves them alone, especially at tax time.

Could they be right to ignore the governing of the country? Is it that big of a deal to catch yet another politician in a lie if the present government lies, and the previous governments lied, and if politicians in the provinces lie too? And what if all Western political leaders are shown in news broadcasts, documentaries and Hollywood movies as habitual liars with the ethics of high-functioning psychopaths? "Truth shaving of a serious kind has become so commonplace in politics today that it is expected. In the news business anything that is expected, that happens often, is of declining news value," writes long-time columnist Lawrence Martin, author of the award-winning best-seller *Harperland*.

> And so the media over time has lost its sense of outrage when politicians willfully distort or lie. The media don't hold politicians to as high a standard as they used to. You'll rarely, for example, see a front-page headline saying "Cabinet Minister Caught Up in Baldfaced Lie." Criticism will usually come in the body of the story or the inside pages. Political strategists realize the story will be a one-day wonder, forgotten the next. Big deal.[45]

But when politicians don't lie, and instead speak in self-serving talking points that tell the listener nothing, when they engage in tedious photo ops instead of discussing the governing of the nation with members of the public who actually pay the nation's bills and they still get re-elected, we'll see two things. One is a polarization of politics between those few who are included in the governance of the country and those millions who are excluded from it. And, as happened in 2014, we'll see a public cynicism of political messaging so deeply rooted that an MSNBC TV interviewer can feel free to interrupt an interview with a member of the United States House of Representatives and cut away to coverage of the latest tribulations of pop star Justin Bieber. We'll live in a fantasyland where people pretend our votes and our opinions count. But it will just be an illusion.

CHAPTER 4

Replacing the Media

Journalists make lousy politicians because they
think they always need to tell the truth.
—STEPHEN HARPER[1]

Don Braid, a newspaper columnist who spent a short time in Ottawa
with the *Montreal Gazette* before moving to Alberta, once reflected
on the Alberta/Reform view of the Parliamentary Press Gallery:
"It's now my firm belief that if we replaced the federal government
with the Alberta government, and the Parliamentary Press Gallery
with Alberta's legislature gallery, we'd be better governed and better
informed. Unfortunately, this won't happen because Albertans are
too sensible to allow it."[2]

Braid may have lived to regret those words, not just because
the Alberta legislative gallery is hardly a pack of tigers, but also
in light of the near-death experience in 2014 of a Tory party that
has ruled Alberta since Pierre Trudeau and Richard Nixon were
enjoying their first terms. Canadian democracy needs a vibrant,
strong, brave media covering lawmakers and public policy issues.
Conservatives can argue the media is biased and back their claims
with well-chosen quotes and anecdotes. And many Parliament Hill
journalists aren't particularly good at what they do. But the press

gallery has about 250 reporters (with another 150 support staff like photographers, videographers, producers and researchers). Poke through any group that size and you'll find honest and dishonest people, geniuses, none-too-bright people, and, of course, people with political opinions ranging from the far left to the extreme right. Many of these people don't even like each other, let alone have any desire to conspire.

Preston Manning, writing just before Jean Chrétien took power, summed up the Albertans' view of the media as reckless and hostile, and said they fed on strife and negativity. That, he said with some accuracy, works against meaningful debate and consensus-building:

> *The communications challenge faced by reform movements the world over . . . is this: in the modern communications business, particularly in the case of television, negative is more newsworthy than positive; short-term is more newsworthy than long-term; disagreement is more newsworthy than agreement; emotions-laden critiques are more newsworthy than well-reasoned proposals for constructive change; discord, threats to order, and bad government are much more newsworthy than peace, order and good government.*[3]

He might have added that the typical sound bite in a TV report is just seven seconds long. Ignoring or sidelining the media, however, is not the way to fix its problems.

"Harper ran on a campaign of open and accountable government," New Democrat MP Charlie Angus said. "And the first thing we see him doing is putting plywood up over all his windows and barring access across the doors. My question is why? What is Harper afraid of?" With a straight face, Sandra Buckler, Harper's press secretary, told reporters: "I think this prime minister has been more accessible, gives greater media scrums and provides deeper content than any prime minister has in the last 10 to 12 years." Like so many other conservatives, she appeared to believe Canadians didn't care what was happening in Ottawa as long as the old age pension cheques were mailed and VIA Rail kept to its schedule (and few people really cared about those trains). "I don't think the average Canadian cares as long as they know their government is being well-run," she said.[4]

As Daniel Boorstin wrote in the days of Lester Pearson and John F. Kennedy, "news" is no longer mostly about real events and new facts. This became clear under Canada's New Government. During his fight with the Hill media, Harper's face was still on TV screens as the government rolled out its programs. There were shots of Harper walking down hallways, getting in and out of cars, meeting foreign leaders, and standing at his lectern in front of the House of Commons making announcements. Government press releases and statements were quoted in newspapers as news. Harper's government was on the move, getting things done. At least that's how people outside of the Ottawa bubble saw it, thanks to the fact that pages had to be filled, newscasts couldn't show test patterns, and the Prime Minister's Office was churning out pap and giving it away to anyone who would use it.

Harper picked a great time to take on the press gallery. People were curious and positive about the new government and many Canadians wanted to see a fresh start with an eager young team after the doldrums and indecisiveness of the Chrétien-Martin years. They also knew the Liberals had wallowed in entitlement. In the wake of the sponsorship scandal, Canadians wanted to see a tough, honest new government in action, hopefully applying the high moral tone of the Reform Party to the "mess" in Ottawa. They wanted to know what changes the Tories would bring, and the media, whether on Parliament Hill or across the country, would have to try to tell them. Reporters outside the Ottawa bubble were more than happy to help get the message out, especially if it meant having the prime minister visit their town and give them the chance to ask Harper a question in a press conference free of hollering press gallery reporters. Or, even better, in a once-in-a-lifetime picture-for-the-office-wall sit-down interview.

But Harper and his media advisers still fretted over press gallery's coverage. They decided to create their own TV imagery on Parliament Hill. They'd replace the reporters and the press gallery's control of the Hill's main press theatre by doing their own filming in a government-controlled studio. Sure, it was an idea out of East Germany, but no one could, it seemed, stop them.

In October 2007, *Toronto Star* reporter Tonda MacCharles received plans for a $2 million media briefing room that would be controlled by the Prime Minister's Office. The proposal, which was code-named the Shoe Store Project by the bureaucrats who worked on it, was for a Tory-controlled TV studio and press conference centre. The renovated shoe store would replace the National Press Theatre, which is run by Parliament Hill media. The government planned to convert the empty store on Ottawa's Sparks Street Mall, just a few steps from the Prime Minister's Office and a block from the National Press Theatre, on the public dime to control Stephen Harper's image.

The government justified the plan by claiming the prime minister and members of the cabinet needed tighter security because of post-9/11 domestic terrorism threats. "In the past year, a number of projects have been identified by our [Privy Council Office] Security and Intelligence Secretariat, in order to mitigate the ongoing risks identified with the Threat and Risk Assessment Plan related to physical security provided by the RCMP," according to one heavily censored document released under the Access to Information Act.

The Shoe Store Project would have given Harper's political staff the power to determine which reporters would be allowed into the new centre and who would get to ask questions. They would even use built-in cameras to control the images of the prime minister and edit the film doled out to the major networks. Preliminary plans called for a stage or riser, comfortable seating for forty to eighty people, rooms for bodyguards at the front and the back doors, audiovisual equipment, space for a translator, office equipment and, of course, Canadian flags for a backdrop. The work on the project was so secret that the people involved in the planning decided to leave a For Lease sign in front of the building, which, like most on Sparks Street, is owned by the federal government.

Harper's communications staff cancelled a visit by Public Works planners to the gallery-run National Press Theatre because they were afraid the Shoe Store Project would become public. Many of the details were blacked out in the documents given to MacCharles, with the justification that the censored material was a threat to "international affairs and defence," "security" and cabinet confidentiality.[5] The minority Harper government, which was trying to fend off an election and to generate some positive publicity from a speech from the throne that was read the day after MacCharles's story broke, quickly cancelled the plan.[6]

The Conservative Party media staffers were given a new goal: find ways to get the Harper message out without dealing with the members of the Parliamentary Press Gallery. The press secretaries and public relations people were told to give stories directly to individual radio stations, ethnic media in the larger cities, and reporters on small-town newspapers. This, said the insiders, who included former Reform communications experts like Geoff Norquay and Ezra Levant, Reform Party founder Preston Manning, and Tom Flanagan, was a "gamble" with high stakes. The prime minister's goal was to eviscerate the press gallery. Although there was a large risk of failure, Harper wanted to put a muzzle on the Hill media that was as tight as the ones gagging the members of the cabinet and the Tory caucus.[7]

And what if you can't earn the coverage you want? What if reporters ask annoying questions during photo ops and run embarrassing stories about things like vote-suppressing robocalls? And how do you do an end run around the mainstream media to get your version of the truth out, so that no one hears anything disturbing and troubling about cuts to scientific research, links you to the propaganda pushing the Keystone XL Pipeline, and all the rest of your problems with journalists? Why not have your own TV network?

ENTER THE SUN NEWS NETWORK, a broadcaster that treats Tory spin like gold, has no scruples about putting the gears to Harper's enemies, and can, with a straight face, call the CBC the "state broadcaster." In the early development of Sun News Network (which was quickly labelled Fox News North by its foes and critics), Sun News vice-president Kory Teneycke, a former communications director in Harper's office, and the development team worked with Luc Lavoie, a long-time assistant and friend of Brian Mulroney. Lavoie had left his job as a Parliament Hill TV reporter in the 1980s to be Mulroney's communications director and stayed with Mulroney after he left office. Lavoie was the former prime minister's spokesperson during the years when Mulroney was investigated for supposed involvement in a kickback scheme involving Air Canada's purchase of Airbus jets and strange dealings with German arms dealer Karlheinz Schreiber. Mulroney was never charged with any offence, and Lavoie proved to be an able advocate. Lavoie is known as a tough man, one who does not enjoy being crossed.

Lavoie would work hard to get the Sun News Network onto Canadian TV screens. So would many Tories in Ottawa.

It's hard to know how much pressure the Tories put on the CRTC (Canadian Radio-television and Telecommunications Commission) to license Sun News and get it mandatory carriage, meaning every Canadian cable subscriber would get Sun News and be forced to pay for it. Senator Mike Duffy was among the Tories who wrote to the agency on behalf of Sun. The CRTC shot down mandatory carriage and the cable companies were allowed to decide whether or not they wanted to carry Sun. About half of the cable subscribers in Canada were offered the service, but, understandably, Sun wanted every Canadian cable subscriber to have the opportunity to get their station. They ran into trouble, though, when they pushed for the kind of lucrative deal that the other Canadian news networks receive.

Two years after Sun went live, Saskatchewan Conservative MP David Anderson tried to help Sun get a better deal from the CRTC by writing a letter saying: "Canadians deserve to be presented with a diversity of views when it comes to interpreting the news. Sadly, only specific Canadian newscasters are now being guaranteed a convenient spot on basic cable." Anderson portrayed himself as a keen student of the media. He told the CRTC he had conducted a "media analysis" of the different news networks and was not happy with what he'd found. "We found that although all stations provided approaches to reporting that were useful, it was very evident that for a full variety of opinion and information to be available, all national news providers must be given an equal opportunity to reach Canadians with their coverage."

The market, he said, should decide, even though the network, which was already offered to 40 per cent of the country's cable and satellite subscribers, often drew fewer viewers across Canada than sit in the stands of a college football game. "I would urge you to move to a much more market driven approach to both news and entertainment options, but as that seems a distant possibility, I anticipate a decision that will be based on fairness and will allow Canadians to access a block of stations where all national news broadcasters such as the CBC, CTV news channel, SUN news and Global are all equally accessible on the dial and in cable packages." When he wrote the letter, Anderson was parliamentary secretary to the minister of natural resources. Parliamentary secretaries are considered public office-holders under the federal conflict-of-interest law and aren't supposed to lobby federal regulators. (Finance Minister Jim Flaherty and two parliamentary secretaries, Eve Adams and Colin Carrie, were warned by the federal ethics commissioner in 2013 for breaking the Conflict of Interest Act by writing letters to the CRTC to support radio licence applications unconnected to Sun.)[8]

Sun News Network began with almost 40,000 viewers on its first day. Ezra Levant, former flack for Reform Party leader Stockwell Day, was the most famous face in Sun's stable. Levant spent part of his career on Parliament Hill banned by the Speaker, for one of his publicity stunts, from entering the Centre Block. He revived his career by publishing a collection of Danish cartoons portraying, and often mocking, the Muslim prophet Mohammed. When he was targeted for a complaint to the Alberta Human Rights Commission, Levant was able to turn the case into a best-selling book, with him cast as both victim and hero. As strategist and pundit Warren Kinsella wrote in a 2008 blog post, "Ezra Levant is the kind of guy who begs for crucifixion and complains about the view."

Despite his name recognition as a controversialist, and his

obvious entertainment value as a showman, Levant sometimes drew just 20,000 viewers across the country. (The major networks nightly newscasts usually drew between a half-million and a million viewers. During the day, when the Sun network's shows were hosted by women, the network had as few as 4,000 viewers.

Three days before the 2011 federal election, Sun News had its first major scoop: It shared a story broken by the *Toronto Sun* newspaper that NDP leader Jack Layton, the network said, "was found lying naked on a bed by Toronto Police at a suspected Chinatown bawdy house in 1996." Sun described its story as a "stunning revelation about the current leader of the New Democratic Party" which "comes days before the federal election at a time when his popularity is soaring." The story had been shopped around for years by Liberal political operatives, going back to the days when Layton was running for mayor of Toronto, but no media wanted it, believing it was too old or shabby.[9] Layton, Sun reported, had been found on the second floor of the massage parlour with "an attractive five foot ten Asian woman who was in her mid-twenties." Layton had told the police he didn't know the place was a body rub joint. The NDP, tipped off to the story, quickly produced Olivia Chow, Layton's wife, to deny her husband had done anything wrong. "Sixteen years ago, my husband went for a massage at a massage clinic that is registered with the City of Toronto," Chow wrote. "He exercises regularly; he was and remains in great shape; and he needed a massage. I knew about this appointment, as I always do," she said in an email.[10]

Many reporters covering the federal campaign trashed the story and denounced Sun for running it, though, in fairness, if Harper had been caught in the raid, their reaction would almost certainly have been different. The story should be a case study for media ethics courses for years because of its many nuances: it was old, there were no charges, and there was no real way of knowing what had happened. What is clear is that it was timed to torpedo the Layton campaign. It's difficult to know whether the story and media commentary about it influenced the 2011 election. The NDP's breakthrough in Quebec masked the party's failure to recapture its old Prairie base or add much to its seat count in the rest of English Canada, and the story may well have killed NDP momentum in English Canada. Certainly, the NDP, many Liberals and most members of the media saw the story as a ninth-inning smear.[11]

The network has never had a bigger scoop. Instead, it has struggled on, running its rant journalism and showing ads for geriatric products. It's had to make a few embarrassing climb-downs, especially when Levant worked himself into a lather about Roma people, whom he called "gypsies," and said they were not a real ethnic minority with a separate language, culture and religion. (In fact, they have all three.) Levant urged the government to stop giving them refugee protection, suggesting they were persecuted in Europe because they were criminals. The Roma have "a culture synonymous with swindlers . . . one of the central characteristics of that culture is that their chief economy is theft and begging," Levant told his audience. The head of Toronto's Roma Community Centre called the rant "nearly nine minutes of on-air racist hate speech targeting our community." The Ontario attorney general considered laying charges, then thought better of it. Months later, Levant and Teneycke apologized during one of Levant's shows. "You crossed the line on this one, but I don't think it was done for reasons of malice or any ill motivation," Teneycke said to Levant, whom he called a happy warrior. "I think you were trying to be entertaining, but words matter in this business and I think you crossed the line."

"There were some criticisms afterwards, but I dismissed them as coming from the usual soft-on-crime liberals and grievance groups," Levant told his viewers. "But when I look at some of the words I used last summer—like 'the gypsies have gypped us'—I must admit that I did more than just attack a crime or immigration fraud problem. I attacked a particular group, and painted them all with the same brush. And to those I hurt, I'm sorry."[12] Levant also got a scolding from the Canadian Broadcast Standards Council.

So Sun News Network was a bust. Surely there are other ways to reach over the heads of the national media and talk to people either directly or through friendly filters. Seven years after the Shoe Store Project, the plan for a government-run media centre on the Hill, was shut down, Harper's team came up with a new idea. Why not create an entire TV network devoted to the leader's life? Using public money, four staffers in the Privy Council Office began creating a video record of the prime minister's life. Condensed into dreary three-minute segments, snippets of video—in both official languages—were loaded onto YouTube and several government and Conservative Party websites. Called *24 Seven*, the channel started broadcasting early in 2014, giving the Tories plenty of time to get the bugs out before the 2015 election.[13]

24 Seven features martial music—its theme is a juiced up military band version of the now rarely heard *The Maple Leaf Forever*—videos and still photographs, almost all of them of Stephen Harper. The first installment, which went onto the Internet in early January 2014, showed Harper hard at work on the job, snacking blissfully after work, and enjoying time with his cute family. The show opened with the voice of an eager young woman saying, "Welcome to *24 Seven*, a week in the life of the prime minister of Canada, and more." Later videos showed Harper talking to the Vancouver Board of Trade (protesters who crashed the event were carefully edited out), Harper holding hands with his popular wife, Laureen (after those years of inaccurate and often cruel gossip saying the Harpers had split up), Laureen dedicating the Trans Canada Trail, the prime minister and his son, Ben, at a hockey game, and other candid moments. Or at least they might be candid and private if there weren't a guy with a video camera around all the time. Harper was filmed working in his office, meeting foreign leaders on Parliament Hill, travelling to trade talks in various nations, and flying to Ukraine in the wake of Russia's seizure of Crimea. There were also many, many shots of men in suits sitting in chairs at meetings, conferences, summits and other places where the powerful meet and smile to cameras before they get down to real business.

Pundits said the television show, aired on the prime minister's website and on YouTube, was meant to soften his image. It might have been edited to make Harper look more human, but the program itself was part of the plan by Harper to replace the mainstream media with words and images that are under the complete control of the prime minister and his staff. When Joe Oliver was appointed finance minister in March 2014, to replace Jim Flaherty, media was barred from the swearing-in. (In a rare flash of humour, NDP leader Thomas Mulcair said it looked like Oliver was being initiated into a cult). *24 Seven*, however, got an exclusive interview with the new finance minister, creating a form of TV show that would be familiar to people who live in countries where "state broadcaster" means exactly that.

The Huffington Post said *24 Seven* has a "North Korea" vibe. In fact, Pyongyang does put out a similar video. So, to be fair, does the Obama administration, which issues *West Wing Week*, a program that should not be confused with a now-defunct TV show that actually had some entertainment value. The Obama production, which was launched in 2010, is upbeat and sometimes has slightly interesting programs. In one episode, Obama's science adviser talked about the arctic air vortex that made the winter of 2014 so cold.[14] *24 Seven* has never found the time to tackle this kind of issue.

While those four government-paid camera operators and editors toiled away on the weekly video clips that celebrated the prime minister's accomplishments, no one was watching. In an answer to a written parliamentary question submitted by an opposition MP in the spring of 2014, the government wouldn't say how much it was spending. But it did release YouTube and Internet viewer numbers, and they were dismal. From January 2 to January 8, 2014, 10,172 people watched the English version of *24 Seven* on YouTube and 14,342 saw clips on a government website. French viewership was laughable, with just 21 people tuning in. And after that, the ratings tumbled. From January 23 to 29, just 100 people watched the *24 Seven* clips on YouTube. French numbers remained fairly constant at 19. Even the exclusive "interview" with the newly sworn-in finance minister, Joe Oliver, drew just a few hundred viewers.[15]

A CAMPAIGN STRATEGY paper leaked in early February 2014, just after *24 Seven* was launched, showed the Tories were working hard on plans to thwart the professional media during the 2015 election campaign, tightening their access even more and using the techniques they developed with *24 Seven* to create more fake media coverage on Twitter, YouTube, Facebook, Google and other online sites. News would be "broken" by the party on these websites, and real reporters travelling with Harper would have to follow his campaign's news agenda and be reduced to asking follow-up questions.

Like other Western leaders, Harper has tried to entice publications to use handout pictures. The classic case was the now-famous picture of Barack Obama and his top advisers watching video in the White House of the killing of Osama bin Laden. The picture was taken by President Obama's personal photographer and was photoshopped, but was still used by major mainstream newspapers and TV networks. Harper's public relations people send out far less dramatic photographs that are often used by small-town newspapers, often along with press releases that are often printed verbatim. The Prime Minister's Office's pictures also appear on the prime minister's website and Facebook page. (An analysis of the nuances of the photo handout issue can be found in Chapter 11.)

Harper's Tories, like most politicians, see social media as a cheap, effective way to reach some of their constituents and supporters. At first, the Tories used it to parrot the government's platitudes, but fairly quickly some of the ministers whom Harper trusted started to use social media to give people real news. In 2011, then Industry Minister Tony Clement used Twitter to announce that he was going to overturn a CRTC decision on usage-based Internet billing. John Baird, the foreign minister, told the world in 2013 that Qatar had dropped its campaign to move the International Civil Aviation Organization from Montreal to Doha. A few weeks later, Harper's Twitter account was used to announce the new lineup of his cabinet before the ministers were sworn in at Rideau Hall. And, while some of the prime minister's staff were making sure no reporters got into the Conservative pep rally on the day before a speech from the throne, another staffer using Harper's account was tweeting the speech that journalists were barred from hearing to Harper's 340,000 Twitter followers.[16]

Some journalists welcomed Harper's ministers and staffers to social media, especially to Twitter. Sometimes, ministers or their employees actually used it to answer journalists' questions. Perhaps the responses were short and superficial, but they were still an improvement over the government's usual communication strategy of saying nothing and treating journalists like bacteria. Mostly, though, Twitter was a means of sidetracking the media and keeping questions to a minimum. Harper hadn't invented the tactic. Barack Obama had made social media, including Twitter, an important part of his 2012 re-election strategy. Even Buckingham Palace has a Twitter account, but Her Majesty's public relations people don't pretend that the beloved, elderly monarch is familiar with hashtags or struggles to focus her thoughts into 140-character microblog posts.

Clement's old department, Industry Canada, now headed by James Moore, takes an approach to Twitter that is almost pathological. Teams of bureaucrats sometimes work for weeks to craft and polish an official tweet. The department has a twelve-step protocol. Once the basic concept of the tweet is approved, the department seeks out people in other departments to retweet the now-perfected 140-character message. It's a reciprocal thing. Industry Canada retweets the carefully crafted wisdom of the Business Development Bank of Canada. Dean Beeby, then a reporter with The Canadian Press, who found out about the twelve-step system, illustrated his story with this committee-crafted gem: "Browse the Mobile Protection Toolbox to learn facts & find #tips to protect yourself. #GetCyberSafe," with a link to the department's website. Another one, grabbed at random in January 2014, said: "Are you keeping your cellphone and tablet safe? Share the Mobile Protection Toolbox for the latest tips to stay safe." When short of riveting material like that, staff in Moore's office shake the bushes for other positive tweetables, but, of course, they have to go through the ministerial mill. Insiders told Beeby that spontaneity and humour are smothered at birth by the various clusters of bureaucrats who check Industry Canada's tweets before they're floated out to the 1,500 or so people who wait patiently for the department's little tidbits.[17]

The Harper team has learned that some "ethnic" media tend to be even more deferential to the prime minister than small-town newspapers and TV stations. Like many reporters in rural Canada and in small cities, journalists in the ethnic media see an interview with the prime minister of Canada as the opportunity of a lifetime. They'll lob softball questions and let the prime minister's staff edit scripts, if that's what it takes to get the interview and keep Harper happy. Most small-market publications and stations, including much of the ethnic media, rarely get involved in controversies, and reporters working for them are often used to deferring to authority. Even if they're the kind of journalists who are willing to ask tough questions, they rarely know federal issues well enough to grill the prime minister in ways that Harper's team wouldn't have anticipated. While many ethnic publications are not that well known outside their communities, they're very important to the people who read them: new Canadians whose issues don't get much intelligent coverage in the mainstream media. Conservatives were smart to realize the importance of this media and the voters who depend on them, and to court groups of people whose votes were taken for granted by the Liberals.

The Tory media team doesn't rely on instinct to determine what targeted groups want to hear. The online news publication *Blacklock's Reporter* obtained documents under Access to Information showing the federal government spends millions of dollars to monitor mainstream newsrooms, including *Blacklock's*. It tracks coverage in *Canadian Business* and *Maclean's* magazines; the wire services The Canadian Press, Associated Press, Agence France-Presse, Reuters and Bloomberg financial news; and forty-four Canadian daily newspapers. A Treasury Board study, *Broadcast Monitoring by the*

Government of Canada, which was launched to find ways of saving money on media monitoring, estimated just twelve federal agencies spent more than $3 million in 2012 on transcripts and recordings of newscasts. The Prime Minister's Office spends $276,280 just on its annual Rogers Cable subscription. (That service does not include the Sun News Network, according to a call for tenders released by the government at the end of 2013). *Blacklock's* said the paper trail shows every federal department, agency and Crown corporation, more than a hundred entities, employs an average of seven staff assigned to media monitoring.[18]

From March 2009 to May 2012, the government paid $750,000 to monitor ethnic media, with the public's money being used to pay consultants to assess election events and determine whether people liked Citizen and Immigration Minister Jason Kenney. The contractors looked through the ethnic press "monitoring key words and issues related to the department's mandate," but documents obtained by Canadian Press reporter Bruce Cheadle showed the work was also very political. "A series of interviews and appearances by minister Kenney and his representatives were strong contributors to the upswing in the ministerial image," said one report from May 5, 2010 that was included in the 7,000 pages of documents that Cheadle received from the Immigration Department. That report also had a handy pie chart that showed "Minister Overall Perception."

Those charts arrived at the department every week in the spring of 2010, when the Tories feared the Liberals would withdraw their support of Harper's minority government and force an election. That kind of political monitoring continued through the spring 2011 election campaign. In those weeks, consultants examined ethnic news reports and graded their coverage of Kenney's and Harper's campaign events, and of their political opponents, from "very positive" to "very negative." Just before that election was called, a staffer in Kenney's office used his ministerial letterhead to solicit $200,000 from Conservative MPs for an ad campaign targeting opposition ridings that had large ethnic communities. Reports on that controversy were collected and analyzed by the department's ethnic media monitors.[19]

In January 2014, Harper toured the Lower Mainland of British Columbia. While he was there, he wouldn't take questions from local English-language media or from the Hill reporters who travelled with him, but he did hold a secret press conference on January 6 for ethnic media reporters, or, more accurately, for a few of them. Chinese-language newspaper *Sing Tao*, which is owned by the *Toronto Star*, and Rogers-owned Omni TV, which broadcasts in Chinese, were not told about the session. Of the South Asian newspapers published in the Vancouver area, the *Asian Star* and the *Indo-Canadian Voice* were invited but the *Asian Journal* was not. Harper was accompanied by Tory MPs Wai Young, Nina Grewal and Alice Wong. The "ethnic roundtable" wasn't listed on Harper's trip itinerary and the three local Tory MPs never mentioned it on their websites. Reporters invited to the session lobbed softball questions and took Harper up on his offer to pose with them for pictures after the so-called news conference.

It was during this visit that two left-wing activists were able to sneak into a different event simply by donning aprons they bought at Value Village. While the protesters were able to easily breach security, reporters who arrived late to the Vancouver Board of Trade were turned away by the same staffers who let the protesters slip through.[20]

Harper, who had cancelled his annual Christmas cocktail party for Parliament Hill journalists, held a secret party for ethnic managers in Toronto during the 2013 holiday season. Madeline Zinick, vice-president of Omni, said the Toronto party was described by

Harper's media staff as an "intimate family event." The "media leaders" who were invited were allowed to bring their families, but the session was not to be reported on. "No cameras, no photos, no audio . . . you can't report it in any way. Everyone had to wait in the holding area until Harper and his wife appeared, and there were no questions, just individual photos." And, until Zinick snitched, everyone who accepted the invitation kept the secret. She said it's admirable that Harper finds time for the ethnic media, but she also realized that many reporters and editors of ethnic publications aren't used to dealing with the prime minister and his staff, and are overly deferential, often for cultural reasons and also because the federal government buys a lot of advertising. They should not "humbly accept these photo ops," said Zinick.

"One could say, 'Hey, it's great that they're paying attention to diversity, and having sessions with smaller newspapers and media entities that can have a hard time in a large scrum with traditional or larger ethnic media entities, so you're giving them that opportunity,' but what is that opportunity? It's a very controlled environment where some questions aren't answered . . . They know the ones who ask the hard questions, and sometimes, those reporters aren't invited," Zinick said.[21]

A few days after Harper's visit, British Columbia Premier Christy Clark used the same tactic to try to curry favour with the Chinese-Canadian media, calling an "ethnic press only" news conference to share her insights on the Lunar New Year. (Mainstream Vancouver reporters found out about it and crashed the session.) Bill Chu, chair of the Canadians for Reconciliation Society, wasn't thrilled. He said this soft ghettoization of the ethnic media and the pandering by politicians was a new twist on the old idea that new Canadians and those from non-European cultures were separate from Canada's mainstream. "In the old days they [politicians] treated each particular ethnic community as if they [were] somewhat of second-class citizens. So they would selectively tailor the messages to each community," he said. "So we are talking about remnants from the past. And this is something we should try to get rid of. There shouldn't be a divisive way of somehow saying the Chinese would get one message, the Indo-Canadians would get another message and then other Canadians would get another message. So that's not conducive to country-building. Because in a democracy what I hear should be exactly what you hear."[22]

THERE ARE SOME IDEAS and policies that the Harper team doesn't want to be seen touching. These are trial balloons, ugly little political slurs, anti-Muslim articles and other dirty little stories. From the beginning of his days as leader of the Conservatives, Harper has made use of the Blogging Tories, a collection of dozens of bloggers of varying degrees of integrity, intelligence and skill (see Chapter 11 for more discussion). Tom Flanagan was one of the advisers who spotted blogs as a good way to engage in low-road messaging, and hand-picked bloggers have "broken" several stories that were planted by the Prime Minister's Office. The blogs were used to spread the embarrassing news that the government was paying for Wiccan priests to conduct services in federal penitentiaries and to generate the campaign to get rid of them. When the news broke in 2009 that Diane Ablonczy, then minister of state for tourism, had been smacked down for approving a $400,000 tourism grant to the Toronto Pride Parade, Saskatchewan Tory MP Brad Trost was dispatched to get the message out through supportive blogs like the anti–abortion *LifeSiteNews* that Ablonczy had lost control of the fund as punishment.[23] The episode marked the end of Ablonczy's career as an important minister.

During the 2006 federal election campaign, Paul Martin's communications director Scott Reid yammered on live TV that Harper's promise of $100 a month for daycare was a bad idea. "Don't give people twenty-five bucks a week to blow on beer and popcorn," Reid said while speaking on a news panel. Predictably, Reid was torn apart by Harper and by Rona Ambrose, the Tory critic in charge of the child care file. At the same time, people working in the Conservative campaign floated Reid's expense claims to the conservative bloggers. The expenses were actually quite normal: claims for lunches at pubs with reporters, a New Year's dinner meeting at D'Arcy McGee's pub a short walk from the Prime Minister's Office worth just $22.71. No mainstream media outlet would have bothered with the claims, but once they were posted on Tory blogs, they were somehow deemed newsworthy and found their way into the newspapers and TV broadcasts.[24]

Some members of the Blogging Tories shill for oil, gas and pipeline companies. All of them are skeptical of the link between environmental degradation and climate change. They want human rights commissions shut down (and Saskatchewan, with one of the country's most conservative governments, has obliged). They want the CBC killed off. They want the Parliamentary Press Gallery stifled. And they'd really be happy if the unions were run out of the country. So, if you want to know where the Harper government is going, or would love to go if voters and informed critics weren't in the way, read the Tory blogs. Many people do: the conservative blog *Small Dead Animals*, run by Saskatchewan dog breeder Kate McMillan, is not only one of the most-read blogs in the country, it's one of the most influential and is consistently picked as the country's best blog in reader's choice surveys.

Smacking around the more problematic media, feeding the sycophants and buying glossy coverage is the Harper way of dealing with the media. Creating media of your own is even better. Will Sun News and *24 Seven* catch on? Probably not. But the media is in the middle of a revolution. People who are born a few decades from now may never see a newspaper, except for a few family souvenirs that might be kicking around. It's not clear what media will exist, and anyone who guesses correctly will make an awful lot of money if they invest in winners. This government is determined to be on the forefront of this revolution and control as much as it can of whatever comes out of it. But it's not just a matter of controlling the means of delivery. This government also wants to control content, whether it writes the shows itself on outfits like *24 Seven*, creates its own media studio, or has proxies at Sun News do the work. It also wants to keep a very tight rein on the vast amount of data collected and created by the federal government. That means sorting through the bureaucracy, tracking down potential trouble, and troublemakers, and making sure they stick to the script. From their first days in office, they've gone after the message as well as the messenger, whether in the media or in the public service.

CHAPTER 5

We Don't Govern by Numbers

A student of biology is asked by his professor to perform an experiment on a small animal. The prof gives a frog to the student and tells him to do a dissection. The unique thing about this kind of frog is that they can understand English. So the student takes the frog home, cuts off one of the animal's legs and says to the frog: "Jump!" and the poor frog jumps. The student makes a note of his observation, then he cuts another leg off the frog and says "Jump!" The frog jumps one more time. The student takes note. Then the third leg goes, and the frog is told to jump, and it jumps once again, and the student makes another observation. The fourth leg is cut off. The student says to the frog: "Jump!" and the frog does no such thing. At this time, the student records the conclusion of his experiment, which is: "If you cut off the fourth leg of a frog, it goes deaf."
—Munir Sheikh, former Chief Statistician of Canada

Munir Sheikh is no radical. The Pakistan-born lifelong public servant and math prodigy holds a PhD in Economics from the University of Western Ontario, a well-known hotbed of conformity. He's also a keen student of public policy. The research that he's done since leaving his job as Canada's chief statistician has led him to believe that the country needs to work much harder to make our economy more productive, which is basically the same message that Mark Carney, then governor of the Bank of Canada, gave for many months before hiving off to London. Sheikh steadily rose through the senior bureaucracy, working at key departments like Finance and the Privy Council Office, before he was appointed chief statistician of Canada by Stephen Harper in the late spring of 2008.

There really shouldn't have been any problems. Statistics Canada has collected all kinds of economic data on Canadians for years, through both Liberal and Conservative governments. It runs the national census, which has been taken since the early years of New France. The information it gathers is critical in determining payouts from the federal to the provincial governments, deciding whether or not there are enough minority official language users in a given area (say, francophones in northwestern Ontario) to warrant better bilingual services, and calculating the economic state of Canada's families. It's also used to determine the boundaries of federal ridings. All of the data Statscan collects is useful to government policy setters, and it's valuable enough that many companies will pay for it. The agency used to have a great reputation inside and outside of Canada. And Munir Sheikh did not go into the agency to shake it up.

Sheikh cut staff in his department when Harper's people told him to. He reduced the number of surveys taken by his department, even though he got a lot of complaints from the companies and organizations that used the data. But when Harper decided to get rid of the mandatory long-form census, it was too much. Sheikh argues, and senior bureaucrats believe, that Sheikh had to quit if there was to be any chance of saving Statscan's integrity and reputation.

When Tony Clement told reporters Statistics Canada "operates pursuant to legislation and it does report to a minister who is responsible and accountable to the public," rather than as an arm's-length, objective statistics agency, Sheikh knew he had to go. He believed the agency should operate like the Bank of Canada, doing its job without interference from politicians. If the bank could set interest rates based on data it collects and set its own inflationary targets without arm-twisting from the Department of Finance, why couldn't the statisticians do their work without being pestered by the prime minister and members of the cabinet?

The long-form census had, in its worst moments, been a source of mockery, usually because the form asked people to divulge seemingly bizarre and minor facts like the number of toilets they had in their homes. A relatively small number of people—one in five Canadians—were sent the long form and almost all of them filled it out. They had to, because it was against the law to refuse to divulge the information. And that's not unusual with government statistical agencies. Over the years, parliaments and legislatures have given teeth to legislation that forces all kinds of people and business owners to fill out forms and divulge information. For instance, you can't opt out of filling out income tax returns just because you think the questions are too invasive. Small-business owners get a steady stream of forms from federal and provincial agencies and are required by law to fill them out and send them back on time.

What was Harper's problem with the long-form census? Years later, Sheikh says he still doesn't know. "Only one man knows, and he's not telling."[1]

But hints may be found in the weird corners of the Internet. The National Citizens Coalition, which Harper used to run, has opposed the long-form census for years, but hadn't made it one of their main issues. Brewing in the conservative hinterland was the idea that the 1996 long-form census had introduced the issue of race to the equation. "The Liberal mind-set was revealed when the 1996 Census long form was announced," conservative blogger Dick Field wrote on the Canada Free Press website. "For the first time the Long form asked about racial origin and skin colour. Question #19 asked, is this person: White, Chinese, South Asian (East Indian, Pakistani, Punjabi, Sri Lankan etc), Black, Arab, Filipino, South-East Asian, Latin American, Japanese, Korean? Strange, too, for professional statisticians to be so inaccurate since black and white are skin colours and do not designate origins and South Asian could be any of 85 or so races or cultural identities. Again, 'Canadian' did not get a mention."

The government wasn't gathering these statistics out of curiosity, Field wrote. The bureaucrats had plans to use the numbers to somehow screw white people, just as the Ontario government did when it brought in preferential hiring for minorities a generation ago.

Bob Rae and his NDP socialist-racist group had introduced a racially based hiring policy, known as the Employment Equity Act of Ontario. A job notice went around the Ontario government offices that included a last line that only female visible minority applicants would be considered. The headlines quickly blared, "White Men Need Not Apply." The province was in an uproar. The Federal government did the same. Canada became a racially oriented and skin colour biased state by law. White men and women were marginalized in their own "home and native land" in favour of newcomers. In case you think the powers that be did not intend to discriminate, here is the Statistics Canada announcement that went along with the Long form regarding Question 19: "Question 19 tells us about the visible minority population in Canada. This information is required for programs under the Employment Equity Act, which promotes equal opportunity for everyone." . . . "Equal opportunity for everyone" is doublespeak; you cannot have separate laws for separate groups of people and create "equal opportunity."[2]

On June 17, 2010, the federal cabinet issued an order-in-council killing the mandatory long-form census. Industry Minister Tony Clement, always loyal, carried the ball, saying there would be a complete census, but people would not be forced to answer the probing questions of the long form. Months before, Clement was told by Sheikh and his math wizards that a voluntary long-form survey would get, at best, about a 50 per cent response rate. If the census-takers advertised and won people over, that rate could be pushed up to 75 per cent, but the data would remain statistically worthless. Still, after getting that advice and facing a public backlash for killing the long-form census, Clement hung tough. "We've come up with a way that is statistically valid, that Statscan feels can work," he said in Montreal less than a month after Sheikh warned him that a voluntary system would fail. "I would say to those who are the self-proclaimed experts on this, if you trust Statistics Canada why don't you trust the option that they put forward to obtain the data that businesses and municipalities deem to be necessary?" Clement asked.[3] Meanwhile, the expert chosen by Harper to run Statscan was out of a job.

The day before Sheikh quit, Clement defended the new policy of making changes to the census:

There is no question that we wanted a change from the status quo. And there is no question that if we had not initiated the dialogue with Statistics Canada, Statistics Canada would have gone ahead with the status quo. But there is also no question that, through the dialogue we had with Statscan, that I was able to report to my colleagues that there were ways we could mitigate the risk associated with moving from a mandatory to a voluntary form. But I accepted Statscan's advice with respect to sample size and advocacy [advertising] to mitigate that risk. It's also true that even with the cur-

rent mandatory long-form census there are people who, despite the
threat of jail time, still do not fill out the form: 168,000 of them in
the last census. My position is we are standing on the side of those
Canadians who have an objection to divulging very personal infor-
mation to an arm of government and are subsequently threatened
with jail time when they do not do so. So we are, in my view, speak-
ing to those Canadians while at the same time doing everything in
our power to ensure that the results that are received from the long-
form questionnaire are valid and defensible.[4]

What Clement neglected to say is that it was also illegal to refuse to fill out the short-form census, and that wouldn't change.

So Sheikh quit. On the Statscan website, Sheikh wrote: "I want to take this opportunity to comment on a technical statistical issue which has become the subject of media discussion . . . the question of whether a voluntary survey can become a substitute for a mandatory census. It can not. Under the circumstances, I have tendered my resignation to the prime minister." A few hours afterwards, that note was removed and replaced with this message: "OTTAWA— Statistics Canada is not in a position to answer questions on the advice it gave the Minister in relation to recent statements the Minister has made."[5] The Tories sent out an InfoAlert talking point to their party members: "Our approach is about finding a better balance between collecting necessary data and protecting the privacy rights of Canadians. It is unfortunate that Mr. Sheikh did not share these objectives."[6]

A few days later, the government officially announced that the long-form census would be replaced by a National Household Survey sent out to one in three families. People could fill it out if they wanted to. They would, of course, still be forced to complete the shorter form, too. Tony Clement's office said in an email to CBC that the change was "made to reasonably limit what many Canadians felt was an intrusion of their personal privacy."[7]

A month later, the now-unemployed Sheikh testified at the House of Commons Standing Committee on Science and Technology to explain what had happened. "To go back to the day I resigned, there were stories in the media, particularly in *The Globe and Mail*, which had a headline on page 4 that said the chief statistician supports what the government is planning to do." He resigned, he said, to send a message that, without the agency losing credibility, the head of Statscan could not be seen to agree to such a drastic cut to the agency's ability to gather facts.[8]

The Canadian Association of University Teachers, representing some 65,000 researchers and academic staff at 122 universities and colleges across the country, asked Harper to reconsider. James Turk, the head of the association, said killing the mandatory long-form census would have "disastrous consequences" for research on Canadian society, and "for the ability to make informed decisions about social and economic policies."[9] The Statistical Society of Canada also came out against the decision, saying "in the interests of both cost and retention of the Canadian reputation for the quality of statistical information, the decision to replace the long form by a voluntary survey be revisited, re-informed and reversed."[10] The Canadian Sociology Association pleaded with Clement to reconsider.[11] So did the Canadian Association for Business Economics. "There is no substitute for the census. It is the foundation for our household information set," Paul Jacobson, vice-president of the association, said. The Canadian Bar Association, representing 37,000 lawyers, also complained.[12]

"The census is a vital, even pivotal component of our statistical infrastructure," economists David A. Green and Kevin Milliken wrote in the journal *Canadian Public Policy*.

If the government announced ill-advised technical changes to the power grid or road system, few Canadians might notice or care initially. It is only when their electricity blacks out, or a bridge fails, that the folly of the changes becomes clear. Similarly, the degradation of the Canadian census has impacts that, while perhaps not immediately clear to Canadians, will eventually have large influences on the quality of Canadian society.[13]

Public health clinic managers and researchers argued the information gathered about immigration, ethnicity, language, education, income, employment and transportation are vital determinants of health. People responding to the voluntary census were more likely to be richer and less likely to be new Canadians. Cherie Miller, director of community health at Toronto's Regent Park Community Health Centre, said filling out the new forms would be difficult for many immigrants, if they even bothered to try. But that information was used to show the need for help settling new Canadians. The mandatory long form might have been intrusive and equally difficult, but it "actually gives our folks the chance to have a voice," Miller said.[14] Patricia Martens, director of the Manitoba Centre for Health Policy, was shocked at the news. "Everybody who knew about the long-form census and how it's used, their collective jaw dropped simultaneously," she said.[15]

Paul Hébert, editor-in-chief of the *Canadian Medical Association Journal*, and Marsha Cohen, its associate editor of research, warned:

If this decision is not reversed, Canada will stand alone among developed nations in not having detailed information about its population. The Harper government will appear to have made a decision based on ideology rather than evidence. Worse yet, it has

imposed an uninformed approach to public policy on all other lev-
els of government, health authorities and institutions. The Harper
government will have signaled that it is no longer committed to
accountability.

The two medical authors argued the census's reliability and accuracy made it useful to many scientific researchers. Their search of the National Library of Medicine database using the term "Canadian census" retrieved 7,600 journal articles that discussed the demographic characteristics of the people of this country and the health of Canadians.[16]

Provincial leaders also opposed the idea, with Quebec Finance Minister Raymond Bachand saying: "According to the scientists at the Institut de la statistique, the replacement of the long-form census with a voluntary questionnaire risks depriving Quebec of an important source of information for the development, monitoring and evaluation of public policy, whether it be in social or economic areas. As the minister responsible for the Institut de la statistique, I am worried and I ask you to take into account the concerns of our scientists."[17]

Religious groups weighed in. The Canadian Islamic Congress warned religious prejudice in Canada would become more entrenched if Canadians did not have authoritative census data.[18] The Evangelical Fellowship of Canada wondered, "If a religious group doesn't show up in Statscan's numbers, will they have influence in the public square? Or will their influence potentially go unnoticed?" Rick Hiemstra, director of the Evangelical Fellowship's Centre for Research on Canadian Evangelicalism, said: "The political reality of how money gets allocated is that if you're not visible, you're less likely to have funds allocated to meeting your needs. If you don't show up in the census, there is the risk the government will ignore you when they're developing their social services and programs."[19]

The decision to cut the long-form census didn't even save any money. In fact, in May 2014, the auditor general released a report showing the voluntary household survey cost $22 million more than the old mandatory long-form census.

AFTER HE QUIT his job, Sheikh became quite chatty. But he didn't become a radical. He wrote articles criticizing Canadian industries for not plowing some of their profits back into job-creating investments (which was also a pet peeve of former Bank of Canada governor Mark Carney). He said every one-point reduction in the Canadian corporate tax rate was equivalent to the Government of Canada writing a $500 million cheque to the U.S. government. And even with the U.S. corporate tax rate now double that of Canada's, this country's productivity was lagging and getting worse, which was a drag on Canadians' living standards. But, under all that Chamber of Commerce–friendly wisdom was a deeply held belief that Canadians weren't getting the information they need to make important decisions.

A few months after he resigned, Sheikh wrote:

At a personal level, Canadians make decisions every day based on evidence. They look at mortgage rates before deciding whether, and where, to get a mortgage. They look at food prices to determine what to buy and how much. They look at the job market in various parts of the country to decide whether to move or not. Now imagine all of this happening without citizens and governments paying attention to an evidence-based analysis of the issues: the Bank of Canada not interested in understanding why the inflation target

*is important; the federal government not realizing why it should
or should not cut corporate taxes; and citizens not thinking about
what high mortgage rates, high food prices, and job opportunities
could do to their well-being. Without appropriate evidence-based
analysis, we will all be poorer—in every sense of the word.*[20]

When Statistics Canada released data on languages from the
2011 census, the agency warned that the data couldn't be compared to information from older censuses because the long-form
census had been cancelled. "Data users are advised to exercise caution when evaluating trends related to mother tongue and home
language that compare 2011 census data to those of previous censuses," Statistics Canada said in a warning included in its census
material. Jean-Pierre Corbeil, the lead analyst for the languages
part of the 2011 census, laid the blame at the decision to kill the
long-form census. The language data is important because it tracks
the use of Canada's two official languages, as well as minority languages. Government departments used the information to decide
which parts of the country needed minority language services under
the "where numbers warrant" clauses of the Charter of Rights and
Freedoms and many other federal and provincial laws. A different
style of language question was inserted into the short-form census.

"The only answer we have at the moment . . . [is] it's very likely
that it is related to the changes in the questionnaire," he said in an
interview with The Canadian Press news agency. Corbeil and other
statisticians said the numbers in the 2011 census seemed fishy when
it reported the same percentage of Canadians—58 per cent—spoke
English at home as in 2006, even though 1.1 million new immigrants came to Canada between the two census years. Citizenship
and Immigration data, as well as Statistics Canada's own research,
said 80 per cent of those immigrants did not have English or French

as a mother tongue. Corbeil said between 2001 and 2006, the census found there was an increase of 946,000 in the number of people who claimed a non-official language as a mother tongue. Between 2006 and 2011, that number dropped to 420,000, even though the patterns of immigration had not changed.

As well, the new numbers showed a bizarre increase in the number of people who claimed to be bilingual. In fact, between censuses, hundreds of thousands of people had somehow developed proficiency in both official languages, along with remarkable skills in third and even fourth languages. Doug Norris, chief demographer at Environics Analytics, looked at the numbers and realized they were wonky. "My first thought was 'What the heck is going on?' You've got all these people saying they speak multiple languages, multiple mother tongues plus English, so it really makes it very confusing. You can't do any sensible trend analysis as far as I can see."

In 2013, the Treasury Board hired Eaves Consulting to survey more than eighty users of its Open Data Portal and ask them about the usefulness of government data. Most of the companies said the material was useless because of the data that was missing after killing the long-form census. "At four of the five meetings, large numbers of stakeholders raised concerns about the termination of the mandatory long form census," a report on the consultations, obtained by The Canadian Press under Access to Information, said. "Almost without fail, the single greatest complaint about the Federal Government's Open Data Portal was the quality of its search," the consultant's report said. "Participants talked of searching for datasets they knew existed but could not find without typing an exact phrase or knowing a key term."[21]

Michael Wolfson, a former assistant chief statistician at the agency and now teaching at the University of Ottawa, said Harper had cancelled the long-form census so abruptly that Statistics

Canada was forced to do "last-minute monkeying around with the language question," leaving the federal government with serious problems when the data was needed to set policies and determine what minority language services are needed.[22]

After the 2011 results came in, Sheikh crunched the numbers. Statscan used to believe that if more than 25 per cent of people in a town or city didn't fill out the mandatory census forms, the data from those places was no good. When the Harper government asked people to fill out the new household survey, more than 26 per cent didn't bother. The Ontario non-response rate was 27.1 per cent. "None of the response of the NHS [National Household Survey] would have been published if we had used the usual census criteria," Sheikh said. "That to me is a very strong piece of information to show the worth, or not, of the NHS. They are not usable and not publishable."

Various areas of the country's larger cities had higher and lower response rates. There are 1,096 census districts, called tracts, in Toronto. There were, Sheikh found, big variances in response rates in those census tracts. Sheikh says about 78 per cent of the responses would not have been reported to the public. In Peterborough, Ontario, none of the census data would have been reportable under the old criteria. But the government moved the bar from a 25 per cent non-response rate to 50 per cent, a change that did not impress statisticians.[23]

Could the problems be fixed? Sheikh was pessimistic about the 2011 numbers having any value and believes the situation will get worse:

A census used to be done every five years to ensure that the anchor provided appropriate, up-to-date information in order to adjust data from other surveys. We are now in a funny upside-down world: We're using the old census data to fix the survey results when the objective was to find a new anchor to fix survey results because the old anchor was out of date. This is a vicious circle. The 2006 long-form census will continue to be used as an anchor to adjust other surveys and the longer we use it, the less reliable it will become . . . The only way to avoid this is to restore sanity and bring back the long-form census, but the decision can't wait long. Statistics Canada must start preparing soon if there is to be a long-form census in 2016.[24]

In the winter of 2014, Statistics Canada said it would thoroughly overhaul the way it collects key data about Canadians. The agency plans a "comprehensive review of the potential for administrative and other alternative data sources to replace, complement or supplement" the census and National Household Survey. It also hopes to redesign "major survey programs to ensure their continued relevance and effectiveness." Statistics Canada expected to spend about $380 million in the 2014 fiscal year, down 5 per cent, or more than $21 million, from the previous year.[25]

Former clerk of the Privy Council Alex Himelfarb weighed in to support Sheikh. "Let me be clear about what this was not," Himelfarb said.

This was not a public servant substituting his own judgment for that of the government or in any way being disloyal. Quite the contrary: in the face of criticism from colleagues, Statistics Canada seemed poised to implement the voluntary approach and, in the traditions of public service, Munir was and continues to be publicly silent about his advice. Nor was this an instance of a public servant fighting for turf or more resources. This is not about defending big government or public service jobs as some critics of

government and public service will immediately assume. Indeed,
the voluntary approach will cost more and require more people.
Munir himself played a major role in the past in cost cutting
and reducing the size of public service, and since becoming Chief
Statistician, he has overseen cuts to surveys, cuts which the agency
and some of its clients found very difficult and troubling, but
which he did nonetheless and with no visible controversy. No, it
was none of these things. This was about the integrity of Statistics
Canada and of the public service. The decision to replace the long
form census with a voluntary version put the Chief Statistician in
a difficult position. The way the decision was handled put him in
an impossible position.[26]

And if statistics weren't going to be allowed to get in the way
of the Tory economic and social agendas, facts would not interfere
with its plan to get tough on crime. If a conservative is a liberal
who's been mugged, then a liberal is a conservative who's been jailed.
"Canada's vocation is as the world's great liberal pioneer, to be tough
on crime by treating its causes, reducing the unnecessary and hid-
eously expensive demonization and segregation of the non-violent,
and not . . . to be 'dumb on crime' by stigmatizing and tormenting
trivial offenders, and assuring that greater numbers of young and of
native people are ground to powder in the criminal justice system,"
Conrad Black said after the Tories unveiled their "tough-on-crime"
agenda.[27] Black's opinion reflects that of many Canadians, especially
those who take the time to look at crime statistics.

In the summer of 2010, the federal Finance Department took a
telephone survey of 1,500 Canadians, asking them what issues the
government should focus on. When the government crunched the
numbers, they found just 15 people—1 per cent of those surveyed—
answered "crime."[28] Yet the Harper government has pressed on to

try to remake Canada's justice system into something that resembles the mess in the United States, where millions of people are incarcerated with little or no benefit to themselves or to the public, and at great expense to the people.

No one likes to be a victim of crime.[29] Canadians, especially in larger cities, do put up with a certain amount of theft and mischief, petty crimes such as graffiti and the rifling of cars for change. These crimes are very difficult to solve, and they're seldom reported. But most serious and violent crime—armed robbery, kidnapping, wounding, attempted murder and murder—*is* reported,[30] and government statistics show the rate of those crimes has been decreasing since the early 1990s, after a steady climb in the previous thirty years. The trend has been similar in the United States and other developed countries, and follows the aging of the gigantic baby boom generation, who were in their teens in the 1960s and early 1970s. People, usually men, tend to commit crimes when they are young, and there just aren't as many young men, as a proportion of the population, as there used to be.

Crime rates in Canada—both for violent and non-violent offences—have been trending downward since the early 1990s. The violent crime rate peaked in 1992, and by 2008 had decreased by 14 per cent. Between 1999 and 2008, the Crime Severity Index dropped 22 per cent. People can argue over whether petty crime rates are down because criminals are getting smarter or victims have given up on the system, but everyone reports any murders that they come across. And murder, along with sexual assault, is the crime that gets the most media coverage and generates public fear. Yet the murder rate is far below its peak in the 1970s and hasn't changed much over the past decade. What about Toronto, that Sodom and Gomorrah where even the mayor was on crack? Its crime rate is far below those of Regina, Winnipeg and Thunder Bay. And the guns that gangsters are packing in ever-greater numbers? In 1990, 20 per cent of the people who committed armed robberies were packing guns. That figure dropped to 15 per cent in 2009. (The use of knives in robberies was down by a similar percentage in the same period of time.)

BUT HARPER DOESN'T GOVERN based on statistics and facts, which can be so inconvenient. Nor does he truly embrace law and order and the rule of law, since he believes law should be what he says it is, and he attacks the justice system if he disagrees with a court decision. Conservative tub-thumpers in the United States worked hard to scare the hell out of people with talk of gangs, high murder rates and the need for even tougher sentences. The Harper government has taken up the cudgel in Canada and has passed law after law to crack down on crime. The campaign has been fuelled by rare, random acts of senseless violence—the murder of post-Christmas shopper Jane Creba, a pretty high school student, by gang members on Toronto's Yonge Street during the 2005–2006 election campaign; the beheading of carnival worker Tim McLean on a Greyhound bus near Portage la Prairie, Manitoba, in 2008 by Vince Li; the murder of five Calgary school students in the spring of 2014 by Matthew de Grood; and the killing of three RCMP officers in Moncton a few months after de Grood's spree. The crimes are memorable and dreadful, but they're alarming partly because they are so rare.

Despite scare stories in the media and tough-on-crime talk from politicians, Canadians didn't used to worry much about crime. A poll commissioned by the Harper government in 2009 and released two years later found that 93 per cent of Canadians felt safe. That was the same percentage as in 2004, when Paul Martin was prime minister. But Canadians are still very much a law-and-order kind of people, judging by a 2010 Angus Reid poll showing 62 per cent of Canadians supported the death penalty. That was up from 48 per cent in 2005. (Death penalty support often blips upwards after a particularly nasty and well-publicized homicide or sensational trial.)[31]

So what feeds the fears of Canadians? Our news media, the makers of TV shows and movies, U.S. journalism, and politicians on both sides of the border have a lot to answer for. The Harper Tories shouldn't have to carry all of the blame for tough-on-crime laws. The Chrétien government had already passed several of them, and during the four election campaigns fought by Stephen Harper, all of the major parties except the Bloc Québécois had their policies to ratchet up punishments, especially for gun crimes. No party wants to be hit with attack ads saying they're soft on crime.

Canadians tend to think the police do a good job of solving crime, but, even after a string of Tory crime bills, they believe that courts are too slow in dispensing justice and that judges hand out sentences that are too lenient. A string of polls shows people are also convinced that prisons do a poor job of rehabilitating prisoners and victims are short-changed by the justice system.[32]

So who was clogging up the courts? Drunks and fools, mostly. The Canadian Centre for Justice Statistics, a part of Statistics Canada, has crunched the numbers. People charged with failing to appear in court, breaking the rules of their probation and other "administration of justice" crimes account for almost a quarter of court cases. In terms of actual Criminal Code cases, impaired driving tops the list, at about 9 per cent. And the number of impaired driving cases has been going down since the 1970s as people's attitudes change. (An unscientific poll conducted by the author showed many teenagers today are flabbergasted by the idea that, forty years ago, people often drove around with a beer held between their knees.) Common assault is the only violent crime on the list of the top five offences (at about 8 per cent). So almost half of the people on the court dockets in this country are in trouble for driving drunk, getting drunk or high while on parole or probation, hitting people, or not showing up for court. Murder, the crime that gets so much ink and air time, accounts for 0.04 per cent of the crime that's reported in Canada.

In 2006, the Harper government appointed the Correctional Services Review Panel to examine the justice system and recommend ways to tighten it up. It issued a *Roadmap to Strengthening Public Safety* that was condemned by academics and even by Conrad Black, a man who had seen American justice at unpleasantly close quarters and emerged convinced that it was a wasteful, cruel system that neither protects the public nor reforms criminals. He warned the Canadian government that, if it followed the *Roadmap*, it was heading down the wrong path: "The crime rate has been declining for years, and there is no evidence cited to support any of the repression that is requested. It appears to defy a number of Supreme Court decisions, and is an affront, at least to the spirit, of the Charter of Rights . . . It is painful for me to write that with this garrote of a blueprint, the government I generally support is flirting with moral and political catastrophe."[33]

The government reacted to the criticism by closing its eyes. Starting on April 1, 2014, the Justice Department chopped $1.2 million from its research budget. That's about one-fifth of the money that was spent on legal scholarship in a department, which, in 2014, had a budget of $662 million. Even more troubling, the department tightened control over its experts to make sure their work helped justify the government's law-and-order agenda. Previously, the results of legal research in the department sometimes caught senior officials "off-guard . . . and may even have run contrary to government direction," according to a report written by Justice staff for deputy minister William Pentney. "The review confirmed that there have been examples of work that was not aligned with government or departmental priorities," says the October 2013 document, obtained by The Canadian Press under Access to Information. The report said some Justice research projects "at times left the impression that research is undermining government decisions."[34]

The Harper government has also made it tougher to get a pardon, even when the convicted criminal has lived for years without reoffending. New laws reduced the credit for "dead time," the weeks or months that prisoners serve in provincial jails before they go to trial. House arrest and conditional sentences were abolished for many crimes. The faint hope clause, which gave people convicted of first-degree murder a chance to prove they had reformed enough to warrant an early parole hearing, was done away with. White-collar criminals are supposed to get tougher sentences. Judges were ordered to impose mandatory minimum sentences for some drug and gun crimes. People on bail were subject to random drug tests. Telecommunications companies were ordered to provide information on their customers to the RCMP. The young offender law was toughened, though courts have more discretion to keep delinquent kids out of jail.

These laws have taken up a huge amount of Parliament's time. In the minority government years of 2006–2011, between 20 and 30 per cent of the legislation being debated in the House of Commons and the Senate at any given time dealt with crime.

Parliamentary Budget Officer Kevin Page said, during Harper's second minority term, that the tough-on-crime legislation that had already been passed would cost the government about a billion dollars a year, doubling what Canadians already spend on Corrections Canada. "They knew that the real figures wouldn't come out for years as people made their way through the system, and that it would be hard to get them because the costs are paid by different levels of government. It costs a lot to keep people in jail, and there's no way that you can increase the number of people who are incarcerated without it costing hundreds of millions of dollars," Page said.[36]

Governments pay $85,000 a year to keep a person in a provincial jail. That's a steal compared to what Canadians spend to jail a woman in a federal prison: $385,000. The cost of keeping a man in maximum security is $224,000. It drops to $140,000 for medium security. And even someone on parole costs, on average, $40,000. "Together, the Truth in Sentencing Act, the Serious Time for the Most Serious Crime Act, the Eliminating Pardons for Serious Crimes Act, and other acts packaged with provocative titles will see the cost of our criminal justice system rise by tens of billions of dollars over the next 15 years," lawyer Edward Greenspan wrote in *The United Church Observer*. "By then, the values and assumptions that underlie this legislation will have been proven wrong by the social and fiscal costs they incur. We will have to admit that tragic mistakes were made and that our generation made them. It will be impossible to unravel and undo this government's mistakes."[37]

Between 2006 and 2013, the prison population rose by 7 per cent. All of the increase, and more, came from First Nations and visible minorities. In spite of the tough-on-crime agenda, the number of white people in federal prisons actually went down. Howard Sapers, the country's ombudsman for federal prisoners, detailed these interesting figures in his 2013 report: 23 per cent of federal prisoners (serving sentences of more than two years) were Aboriginal people, though they made up just 4.3 per cent of the population. About 10 per cent were black. That was up 80 per cent in the previous decade. And the racialized often get harsher treatment than the rest of the people in prison. "These groups are over-represented in

138

maximum security institutions and segregation placements," Sapers told a meeting in a Toronto church in the fall of 2013. "They are more likely to be subject to use of force interventions and incur a disproportionate number of institutional disciplinary charges. They are released later in their sentences and are less likely to be granted day or full parole."[38] In response to Sapers's speech, then Justice Minister Peter MacKay's press secretary, Paloma Aguilar, wrote in an email: "We make no apologies for standing up for victims' rights, and ensuring their voices are heard in our justice system." She had nothing to say about Sapers's figures.

In the spring of 2014, the government announced it would no longer pay for eighteen Aboriginal Circles of Support across Canada. The circles used large numbers of First Nations and non-Aboriginal volunteers to help high-risk sexual offenders reintegrate into society, while at the same time holding them accountable for their offences. The program cost $1.5 million a year and gave support to 185 high-risk offenders. Dan Haley, who oversaw the program in Peterborough, Ontario, said he didn't think the circles could raise money on their own. "Stand on the corner and collect dollars and cents from the public to support your local sex offender? Give me a break," he said.[39] The Harper government also closed the prison farm at Joyceville, Ontario, and at other jails, even though working with animals and producing their own food did the prisoners a lot of good. It also cut funding for prison nursing homes, where lifers went to die.[40]

While the Criminal Code is a federal responsibility, anyone sentenced to less than two years serves the time in a provincial jail. The tough-on-crime bills have cost provincial governments hundreds of millions, perhaps billions of dollars, for new jails and to feed and guard all the extra prisoners, even though the provinces have no say in the laws they enforce.

Lawyers Adelina Iftene and Allan Manson argued in the *Canadian Medical Association Journal* that Harper's crime laws will cause prison overcrowding that will seriously harm inmates. Cases of HIV spread by prisoners sharing needles are on the rise in federal prisons. The epidemic is worse because the government can't solve the trafficking of illegal drugs in prison and will not mitigate the problem with a needle exchange program. The tough-on-crime laws also produce ex-cons with serious psychological problems along with their addictions, since, "by incarcerating more people, exposing them to an increased potential for violence, and keeping them in prison longer, the system will further foster an environment of mental, emotional and physical degradation," Iftene and Manson wrote.[41]

Exposure to drugs while inside the country's jails and penitentiaries makes things even worse for addicts who are locked up, rather than treated, for their drug problems. While some U.S. states have legalized marijuana without incurring serious social problems, Canada has toughened its pot laws, along with penalties for other drugs. This mimics the United States' "war on drugs," which has been an abject failure. Drugs are still easy to get in America. Organized crime has made out like bandits under what's turned out to be a stimulus program for drug lords and vicious criminals in North America and, in even more extreme ways, in Latin America. The Global Commission on Drug Policy released a report in 2011 denouncing the drug war and recommending drug policies based on "solid empirical evidence."[42] It seems the lessons of Prohibition will have to be learned again.

Prison guards protested in front of Harper's constituency office in Calgary in September 2012, saying the tough-on-crime agenda puts them at risk. Kevin Grabowsky, Prairies regional president of the Union of Canadian Correctional Officers, said, "the government is locking up more inmates in fewer prisons while giving us less resources to rehabilitate them. This is a recipe for disaster. We have requested to sit down with the government to find a solution but so far we have heard nothing." By the spring of 2014, the guards were mobilizing to fight Harper in the next election.[43]

While Canadian federal and provincial governments are building more jails and prisons, they're cutting back on psychiatric hospital beds and fast-tracking mentally ill people out of institutions, after which they often become a problem for the police and the public. Part of this is a shell game: provinces want violent offenders to be locked up in federal penitentiaries, because provincial governments pay for psychiatric hospitals while Ottawa writes the cheques for prisons. More than one in ten people arrive at prisons with, or develop, at least one serious mental illness. About 30 per cent of female federal prisoners and 14.5 per cent of men had already spent time in psychiatric hospitals before being jailed. In his 2010 report, Howard Sapers, the correctional investigator of Canada, said: "Federal penitentiaries are fast becoming our nation's largest psychiatric facilities and repositories for the mentally ill. As a society, we are criminalizing, incarcerating and warehousing the mentally disordered in large and alarming numbers."[44] Canadian prisons have a bad record of keeping mentally ill patients in solitary confinement for long periods of time. Our jails are overcrowded, putting even more stress on mentally ill prisoners, and therapy available for mental illness lags far behind the needs of inmates.[45]

The Canadian Psychiatric Association struck a committee just after the Conservatives won their majority in 2011. It looked into the scarcity of psychiatric care for prisoners and recommended Corrections Canada revamp its mental health system to deal with the problem. "The burdens of stigma and discrimination faced by people with serious mental illness are accentuated in the criminal justice system," the panel said in its report. "People with mental illness, not necessarily well-equipped to live on the streets, are even less likely to function within correctional settings. Untreated, they are often placed in segregation cells for extended periods of time."[46] Stephen Hucker, one of the country's most respected forensic psychiatrists, Noni MacDonald and Paul Hébert, editors of the *Canadian Medical Association Journal*, summed up the situation: "Having people with treatable mental health disorders fall into the criminal justice system serves neither society nor the individual. That so many inmates in jails and prisons have mental health disorders—often untreated—is an indictment of society's values and understanding of mental health disorders."[47]

Shortly after Manitoba's Criminal Code Review Board, which determines the fate of people who are found not criminally responsible for crimes because of serious mental illness, decided to give greater freedom to bus passenger–beheader Vince Li, the Harper government brought in amendments to make it tougher for the people formerly called "criminally insane" to be released from institutions. Previously, provincial review boards, headed by judges and including psychiatrists and lawyers, decided whether people found not criminally responsible for offences because of a mental disorder could get day passes, be transferred to a less-secure institution or released. Now, courts are able to label these people "high risk." The review boards won't have control over those high-risk psychiatric patients. The mentally ill prisoner-patients will have to ask the courts for any changes to their security status.[48] Instead of having review boards look at their cases every year, high-risk patients will have to wait three years for a hearing.

"So Mr. Harper's minister is recommending that reviews take place only every three years," lawyer Edward Greenspan and criminologist Anthony Doob wrote in an opinion piece published by *The*

Globe and Mail. "It doesn't matter that it is in the public interest to release people when they can be safely released—not before and not years after. It doesn't matter that the hospitals are full and that the cost of detaining these patients mean that services are not available for others who need them. Nor does it matter whether the patient has been successfully treated."[49]

Justice Richard Schneider, chair of the Ontario Review Board when the new law was introduced, said the government was playing to people's prejudices and was ignoring reality. "If you want to enhance public safety, all the data is saying turn right and we're going left," he said. The law didn't address the fact that many people can't get mental health treatment, the judge said. Li and several other high-profile mentally ill offenders sought help before committing their crimes, but didn't get effective treatment.[50]

So what's going on? Why, instead of levelling with Canadians that their streets are, in fact, safe and their kids can play outside, does the Harper government insist on scaring the hell out of people with a fake problem, then offering a solution that causes both human misery and higher government spending? Because scaring Canadians elects Conservatives. That's why the facts aren't allowed to get in the way of Tory truth, and why the Harper government works so hard to make Canadians believe their streets are swarming with criminals. When pressed in a parliamentary committee by NDP MP Libby Davies to explain why the Tories keep pushing for an American-style justice and prison system, then Justice Minister Rob Nicholson said, "We have the mandate of the Canadian people and they have told us this is what they want to see us move on."[51] In reality, says former top bureaucrat Alex Himelfarb, "This turn to 'tough on criminals' makes Canada a meaner—not safer—place."[52]

Many of the laws that have been passed under the Tough on Crime banner have been struck down by the courts. In the fall of 2012, Ontario Superior Court judge Alan Bryant killed the "three strikes" provision of the 2008 omnibus crime bill, saying that the law's requirement that criminals prove they are not dangerous creates a reverse onus that is an infringement of principles of fundamental justice. In November 2013, the Ontario Court of Appeal struck down the mandatory three-year minimum sentence for possession of a loaded handgun. (The mandatory sentence was part of the same 2008 crime bill as "three strikes"). In January 2014, the Supreme Court of Canada heard an appeal of the Truth in Sentencing Act, which took away sentencing judges' discretion to award prisoners two-for-one days' credit for the time they were held in pre-trial custody. This formula had become common practice as a way to credit prisoners—who have not been convicted and are, legally, considered innocent—for spending time waiting for trial in overcrowded and grim provincial jails. The Truth in Sentencing Act allowed judges to give 1.5 days' credit "if circumstances justify it." In hundreds of courtrooms across the country, judges routinely found that circumstances did, indeed, justify the extra credit, and lawyers began making arguments that the law is unconstitutional.[53]

In February 2014, British Columbia provincial court judge Joseph Galati struck down the one-year mandatory sentence for drug traffickers who had been convicted of selling drugs in the past ten years. "The circumstances related to convictions for designated substance offences run the gamut from very serious cases to more trivial ones and offenders range from career criminals . . . to small offenders," Galati wrote in his judgment. "Many offenders are of Aboriginal heritage and their respective personal circumstances would otherwise warrant particular attention."[54] Higher courts, including the Supreme Court of Canada, have upheld most of the decisions of the lower courts.

But the Harper team will soldier on, convinced that contempt for evidence resonates with what they believe is Canadians' anti-intellectualism. Ian Brodie, then Harper's chief of staff, nailed the Harper mindset—not just on crime, but also on science and evidence-based policy-making, while speaking at a political conference in Montreal. "Every time we proposed amendments to the Criminal Code, sociologists, criminologists, defence lawyers, and liberals attacked us for proposing measures that the evidence apparently showed did not work. That was a good thing for us politically, in that sociologists, criminologists and defence lawyers were and are held in lower repute than Conservative politicians by the voting public. Politically it helped us tremendously to be attacked by this coalition of university types."[173]

CHAPTER 6

Harper and History

He who controls the past controls the future.
He who controls the present controls the past.
—GEORGE ORWELL, *1984*

In the 1930s, a railway worker who spent his spare time prospecting for gold near the northern Ontario town of Beardmore found a cache of Viking weapons. Jimmy Dodd's sword and battle-axe were real early medieval hardware, and his story was so convincing that the Royal Ontario Museum paid him $500 for his stuff.

Southwest of Lake Superior, in Minnesota, someone had already found a rock covered with what looked like ancient runes describing the massacre of Vikings exploring the region in the 1300s. James Watson Curran, editor of the *Sault Ste. Marie Star*, made it his life's work to publicize the discovery that Vikings had sailed and walked deep into northwestern Ontario. Farley Mowat built a book around the theory—*Westviking*, which was published in 1965. By then, Dodd's son had admitted that he'd seen his father plant the Viking weapons. Yes, they were real, but the older Dodd bought them from a Scandinavian man who had brought them with him to Thunder Bay, Ontario. (The carved stone found in Minnesota was also exposed as a fake.)

No one was really hurt by the Beardmore hoax. It didn't even seriously damage the reputation of the museum curator who bought the collection, and $500 was a pretty small loss, compared to what some art galleries have paid for fakes. *Westviking* is still a good read, and, other than waste his own time, Curran did no harm by publicizing the Beardmore Relics and pushing his theory. And a few people believing a fairly common old coin, found in a weird place, can be used to rewrite the history books is no big problem. Where it gets tricky is when Canadian journalists and the rest of the public get sucked into big questions, like whether the War of 1812 really was Canada's War of Independence, whether Vimy Ridge was the place where Canada became a nation, and whether Pierre Trudeau gave us our rights in 1982 when he pushed through the Constitution.

History isn't just a pastime, like metal detecting. All history is important to someone. It underlies the way we see ourselves. It often becomes the foundation of public policies. It can be manipulated—as Hitler did with the myth that leftist politicians, not military failure, caused Germany to lose World War I—to win power and to justify war. When a government gets into the act of trying to remake the way its citizens see their country by rewriting its history, bad things tend to happen.

Canada no longer carefully passes its history from one generation to another. While history has always aroused passion and controversy, it's now also ammunition in the culture war. History is used as a wedge, a way of separating Canadians into us and them, with the underlying message that those who do not adopt the Harper government's bombastic, militaristic and strangely colonial version of history are not patriotic. Of course, the Harper government is not alone in using interpretations of history to shape people's views on modern events. Liberal historians have, for generations, succeeded in interpreting Canada's political history as a long struggle against

British, then American, dominance as a way to promote Canadian nationalism. In Quebec, according to a recent book by Université Laval history professor Jocelyn Létourneau, the separatist Parti Québécois and nationalists in the provincial education ministry have entrenched the idea that Quebec history is an unhappy litany of defeat, subjugation and exploitation that can only end with independence. In a ten-year study, Dr. Létourneau found: "A large proportion of young Québécois [around 40 per cent of the answers collected] hold to a melancholic or sad vision of Quebec history and a perspective in which the history of Quebec is depicted as a struggle." While some students argued that the invention of poutine was the culmination of Quebec's long struggle against time, space and evil outsiders, more serious answers showed students who had taken the province's mandatory Quebec history high school course held negative accounts of history. The number who believed Quebec had a sad and sorry past rose to 40 per cent from 22 per cent after taking the course. Those offering positive accounts dropped to 16 per cent from 24 per cent. Neutral statements dropped to 16 per cent from 29 per cent.[1]

Over the years, Quebecers have been convinced to shed their old self-image as Roman Catholic people of the land, content to farm in the St. Lawrence Valley, and embrace the idea of belonging to an oppressed nation struggling to survive despite a determined campaign by foreigners to assimilate them. If the Quebec "nation" could craft such a powerful new version of history, so could the Harper Tories, who despise the liberal definition of Canadian history as a struggle for economic and political independence, a fight against British imperialism and American dominance that has led us to seek a Third Way of peacemaking and peacekeeping. Right now, that image is being recrafted, sometimes in very bizarre ways.

NOTHING HAS BEEN more strange than the Conservative obsession with the War of 1812. It was an ugly little war, fought by the Americans, British soldiers who were stuck in colonial duty during the Napoleonic Wars, citizen soldiers in what's now Ontario and the Montreal area, and First Nations warriors. None of the battles were particularly interesting, or, even for the times, very large. In fact, far more people were killed in the three days of manoeuvres leading up to the Battle of Waterloo than died in the entire War of 1812. Much of the war was a campaign against civilians. York—now Toronto—was burned. So were numerous villages and farms along Lake Ontario and Lake Erie, in the Thames Valley and around Sault Ste. Marie, along with Washington, D.C.

To sanitize and remember the War of 1812, federal money was thrown at war re-enactors who cleaned up and recreated the bloody little battles for children's entertainment and downplayed real blood and pain like the kind seen by William "Tiger" Dunlop, a twenty-one-year-old British surgeon's assistant who was the only medic on the scene after the Battle of Lundy's Lane. He seems to lack the government's enthusiasm for the war. His observation was lost on official Ottawa, which didn't want to hear about limbs shattered by musket balls:

"I had 220 wounded turned in upon me that morning," he says in his autobiography, with the lack of gratitude that comes with youth. "It would be a useful lesson to cold-blooded politicians, who calculate a war costing so many lives and so many limbs as they would calculate on a horse costing so many pounds—or to the thoughtless at home, whom the excitement of a gazette, or the glare of an illumination, more than reconciles to the expense of war—to witness such a scene, if only for an hour."

And this proto-peacenik had the nerve to quote an American woman who came to the battlefield under a flag of truce to find her sixty-year-old husband, who had been shot in the gut and leg and had been left to die in agony: "O that the King and President were both here this moment to see the misery their quarrels lead to—they surely would never have gone to war without a cause that they could give as a reason to God at the last day, for thus destroying the creatures that He hath made in his own image." Now, this was obviously a woman who did not realize the heroic implications of this incredible war. And she had the nerve to drag the Almighty into her bleating.

Despite all the hype and the money thrown around to create a homegrown War of 1812 mythology and a new glorification of "Canada's War of Independence," very little of the Canadian literary effort came close to Alan Taylor's best-selling *The Civil War of 1812*. Taylor, a Pulitzer Prize–winning American historian, produced a solid piece of scholarship, with a quarter of the paperback version consisting of footnotes and bibliography.

Taylor saw the war as a minor and somewhat comical set of military actions that pitted the amateur—but eager to be taken seriously—American army and navy against a professional British military and the settlers living on what's now the Canadian side of the Great Lakes. Those farmers, many of them first- or second-generation refugees from the American Revolution were, and saw themselves as, British subjects, not Canadians. It was a war between American citizens and British subjects.

And the people who lived in the Canadian part of the war zone—a relatively small part of the present-day border region, roughly from Sault Ste. Marie to Lake Champlain—were not always anti-American. People on both sides were torn by loyalties to the land where they were born, usually the new United States. They saw Britain, the mother country, as the leader of the world's greatest empire and a symbol of stability in a world torn by the

French and American revolutions and the mayhem of Napoleon. The First Nations had loyalty to neither country and were simply trying to survive. They, for the most part, backed the British because Whitehall promised them their own territory. If it was a war of independence for anyone, it was for these people, and, in the end, they were cheated.

The British ruthlessly crushed civilian opposition in their colonies, seizing the land of hundreds of men who had fled military service. In the London district, Upper Canadians who opposed the war looted farms, rustled cattle and kidnapped militia officers. When sixteen of these people were captured, the British decided to treat them as traitors. John Beverley Robinson, the attorney general, believed killing these men would "overawe the spirit of disaffection in the Province by examples of condign [well-deserved] punishment by the laws of the land." Nineteen men went on trial (the government tossed a few local malcontents in with the marauders) at the town of Ancaster, on the Niagara Escarpment inland from Hamilton.

Eventually, eight of the "traitors" were singled out to be hanged, drawn and quartered. They were strangled on makeshift wooden gallows that was so shabby that one beam collapsed, killing a spectator. Their guts were cut out and burned, their heads chopped off and stuck on posts, and their bodies hacked into quarters. Three more died of disease in squalid Canadian jails. The rest were sent to penal colonies in Australia. And their families were turned out into the woods when the government seized the convicts' land.[2] This heritage moment has not been re-enacted by the history buffs subsidized by the Harper government. Like any other conflict, the War of 1812 was a nuanced affair, with some heroism but much more suffering, with most people simply hoping the war would pass them by.

THE MODERN ALLURE of the War of 1812 seems lost on both the United Kingdom and the United States. In October 2012, *The New York Times* ran a story noting that the Canadian government had put a "spotlight" on the war and had cast the Americans as the villains. Reporter Ian Austen watched war re-enactors at Dunvegan, southeast of Ottawa, and filed a story that challenged the Harper government's framing of the conflict as Canada's War of Independence. He told the *Times*'s influential readers that the Canadian government "is devoting surprising attention to the bicentennial of the conflict, which it describes bluntly in a new television commercial as an act of American aggression against Canada." Austen mentioned the $28 million that the Canadian government had set aside for commemoration of the conflict at a time when Ottawa was cutting budgets for national parks and historic sites—the ones that weren't connected to the war. And Austen seemed surprised that the federal propaganda had a distinctly anti-American message at a time when Harper boasted that he's improved relations between Canada and its superpower neighbour.

"Two hundred years ago, the United States invaded our territory," a narrator says over dark images and ominous music in a government commercial that was described by Austen. "But we defended our land; we stood side by side and won the fight for Canada." The editors of the world's most prestigious newspaper were so lacking in awareness of this great struggle for continental dominance that it was called "The War of 1912" in the headline on the newspaper's website. A day later, someone caught the error and corrected it.

Journalism professor and amateur historian Andrew Cohen, the founding president of the Historica-Dominion Institute, which promotes awareness of Canada's history, told the *Times*: "The War of 1812 is part of our history, and that's fine." But, he added, "it's turned into a form of propaganda, and it seems to have married the government's interest in the military with its interest, some would say obsession, with the War of 1812. It's clearly, to me, part of a campaign to politicize history." David J. Bercuson, a professor at the University of Calgary and one of the country's top military historians, was also perplexed about the Harper team's overly keen interest in a rather obscure conflict. "I'm scratching my head for the last year and asking myself: 'Why is the government placing so much emphasis on this war?'" he said. James Moore, who was then the heritage minister, answered by saying: "Canada was invaded, the invasion was repelled and we endured, but we endured in partnership with the United States. It's a very compelling story."

Actually, "Canada" had not been invaded, many historians pointed out. Taylor, whose book far outsold anything published in Canada on the War of 1812, made a clear and compelling case that the war was between the great military power of Britain, the troubled new American republic, First Nations people fighting the last big battle in the Great Lakes region against colonialism, and the tiny civilian settler population, mostly American-born, in what is now southern Ontario. The country of Canada would not exist until 1867, some fifty-five years after the war started. The border would not change, and the people living in the war zone would not come out of the conflict with any more political or civil rights than they had when the war started. If anything, the war entrenched anti-American attitudes that survived in Canada well into the twentieth century. A Liberal government was defeated in 1911 for advocating free trade with the United States, and a Conservative government had to fight to survive in 1988 after negotiating the first Canada-U.S. Free Trade Agreement, partly because of resentment over this war and later border raids.

Whatever the reason behind the Canadian government's enthusiasm for the war, the Americans did not share it. Congress killed a bill to create a United States commission to mark the bicentennial of the war and celebrate the one recognizable artifact that survives, the "The Star-Spangled Banner." The U.S. Navy, Coast Guard and Marines staged low-key commemorations and some states held celebrations paid for with money that was raised privately. The *Times* noted that New York's governor, Andrew M. Cuomo, vetoed a bill to establish a War of 1812 commission. The state, which saw the brunt of the fighting, allocated $450,000 for commemorations. By contrast, the *Times* notes, the Canadian government spent $6.5 million on television commercials alone.

The government did much more than just throw money around. Its advertising, described as "more Jerry Bruckheimer than Canadian Heritage Moment," was intensely micromanaged.[3] The Heritage department called the shots on the bombastic tone of the ad "Fight for Canada," and, as *Globe and Mail* reporters Daniel Leblanc and Stephen Chase learned from documents they obtained through the Access to Information system, the commercial was inspired by the trailer for Sylvester Stallone's 2010 action film *The Expendables*. The ad agency that made the commercial had to put up with a lot of meddling from officials at the Heritage Department. The Heritage people passed on thoughts from the Centre. Laura Secord looked too drab. Her costume needed more colour. The ad agency replied that they wanted to avoid "making her look like Little Red Riding Hood!"

After many weeks of quibbling over the colour and fabric of Secord's clothes ("No two-tone velour! Brown exterior and beige interior!"), attention focused on diversity. The Centre wanted to know why there were no black soldiers in the rough cut of the commercial. "Urgent: can you ask Heritage why they were no black [people] in the British Army cast? Apparently there were some. This needs to be addressed," a senior Privy Council Office official wrote to the ad agency. That dispute became a numbers game. Two historians were consulted: one said the number of soldiers of African descent who fought in the war may have been as high as 1 per cent. "There were five black soldiers in the Glengarry Light Infantry out of a total of several hundred," the historian wrote in a memo to the Privy Council Office that was obtained by Chase and Leblanc. "The 104th Regiment had a black drummer and perhaps other black musicians . . . but the line infantry was all of European stock." The question got bounced to the Heritage Department, where a bureaucrat argued against casting black actors. "I think if we include one black soldier in a group of 10 it would look like 10 per cent of soldiers were black and I don't think that was the case."

Then the bureaucrats argued among themselves about the computer-generated ships that were digitally menacing the British side of the Great Lakes. They didn't seem to be moving fast enough. There wasn't enough action in the sails. A Heritage bureaucrat who may have spent some time around actual sailing ships said the images looked to him like real tall ships. The sails weren't supposed to move much, and the American flags were fluttering, which was pretty much all you'd expect to see in a brief glance of schooners and brigantines on a calm lake. The Centre, landlubbers all, wanted more action: "With regards to the ships being parked, I'm being asked if the sails should be down then?" And, in the end, the ad shows the ships sitting on a calm lake with billowing sails.

The government managed to come up with $700,000 to buy a collection of War of 1812–era letters, maps and artifacts belonging to Sir John Coape Sherbrooke when they went to auction in 2013, at a time when the national archives had stopped collecting documents written by modern Canadian authors and public figures.[4]

And it planned a fifty-square-metre monument on the northeast corner of Parliament Hill that will dominate a nearby statue of Sir Wilfrid Laurier and be easily seen from the National War Memorial across the street. Meanwhile, veterans of the Afghanistan war complained that no one planned a monument for them. When they asked to have the years of their war carved into the National War Memorial, they were, at first, turned down.[5]

The Harper government had a tough row to hoe. Few Canadians knew much about the War of 1812, and—especially outside of Ontario, where almost all of the major fighting happened—no one really cared much. A poll and focus groups commissioned in early 2012 showed few people could remember the name of the war, although some people were able to figure it out when tipped off that the questions were about the two hundredth anniversary of *something*. Polling showed apathy across the country, and people who lived in the areas where the toughest fighting took place, such as the Niagara Peninsula, really didn't care much more than anyone else. People in the focus groups said they thought it was a good idea to do some sort of commemoration, but the company that did the research said that few "focus group members could clearly articulate why celebrating or marking such events is important."[6]

They weren't alone in their confusion. Peter MacKay, who was then the defence minister, made a riveting speech at the 2012 celebration of Bastille Day at the French embassy in Ottawa, telling his hosts: "Suffice it to say in the 200th commemoration of the War of 1812, had the French not been here fighting side-by-side, we might be standing here next to each other in a new light."[7] In fact, in 1812 Napoleon was fighting the British in Spain and leading the French army into Russia, not Canada. The $4 million that the government spent on advertising the war in 2012 didn't seem to increase awareness much.[8]

WHY DID THE GOVERNMENT put so much time and energy into commemorating a forgotten little conflict, one that was just a sideshow to the Napoleonic Wars and that ended with almost no change to anything? There were other wars that could be commemorated. The 250th anniversary of the Battle of the Plains of Abraham, one of the world's most decisive battles, fell during Harper's first term. And the government could have celebrated the 250th anniversary of the Treaty of Paris, which transferred most of eastern Canada from French to British control. Or the 250th anniversary of the Royal Proclamation, a document that has tremendous historic value, since it says, in effect, that governments cannot steal land from Aboriginal people. No federal government, even one led by the Tories, would go near those with a barge pole. But it's not just controversial military history that's ignored. Senior public servants wanted to throw a party in the spring of 2012 to celebrate the thirtieth anniversary of the proclamation of the Charter of Rights and Freedoms. Heritage Minister James Moore nixed the idea. Instead, the government issued a very brief press release.[9]

In his 2012 book *What We Talk About When We Talk About War*, Noah Richler analyzed the remaking of Canada into a warrior nation. He described the hyping of the Vimy Myth, the idea that Canada was forged on a World War I battlefield when, for the first time, all of the Canadian soldiers in Western Europe fought together and took an important hill defended by well-entrenched, determined Germans. Propaganda from the time doesn't fit with the Vimy Myth. Back then, Canadians were portrayed in official films and on posters as junior partners of the British Empire, often shown as one of the lion's cubs. And it's arguable that Canada actually showed its first signs of independence during the long-forgotten Chanak Crisis of 1922, when, for the first time, the Canadian government said *no* to a British request for troops.

The image of Canadians as partners of the British, with special military and political links to the empire, was still strong a generation later, when Canada joined the war against Hitler without hesitation (rather than following the lead of the United States, as we probably would now in a similar crisis). We fought as junior partners of the British in an army that, in Western Europe, covered the left flank of Field Marshal Montgomery's British forces.

Gen. Sir Arthur Currie, who led the Canadians well in World War I, didn't seem to see himself fighting for Canada's independence. In the introduction to *Canada's Sons and Great Britain in the World War* by Col. George C. Nasmith, published just after the war, Currie used most of his space to describe the heroic acts of Canadian troops who had won the Victoria Cross.

> *Sergeant [Hugh] Cairns, with his Lewis gun, and two others broke open the door and entered the yard, Cairns firing his machine gun from the hip. About sixty Germans threw up their hands. Their officer passed in front of them, and when close to Cairns shot the latter through the body with his revolver. He sank to his knees but again opened fire with his machine gun. The fighting became general, the enemy picking up their arms and opening fire. Sergeant Cairns was shot through the wrist, but he continued firing inflicting heavy casualties.*

Currie could have chosen anything to say. He chose to frame his stories as patriotism of Canadians fighting at the side of the mother country. Currie's introduction ends with Ewing Buchan's lyrics of "O Canada":

> *O Canada, our heritage, our love,*
> *Thy worth we praise, all other lands above.*

From sea to sea, throughout thy length
From pole to border land,
At Britain's side whate'er betide
Unflinchingly we stand.
With hearts we sing, God Save the King.
God bless our Empire wide we do implore,
And prosper Canada from shore to shore.[10]

These lyrics, long supplanted and erased from our national conscience by those of Robert Stanley Weir, are hardly a rousing declara-
tion of independence from our colonial overlords. But no matter. To
the myth-makers, Vimy and the rest of World War I symbolize glori-
ous sacrifice, not independence. The Vimy Myth is about strength.
And it ascribes some sort of meaning to a war that, especially after
the passing of a century, seems like such an utter waste of blood
and money.[11] But the Vimy Myth is really the conservative antidote
to the Liberal-era worship of peacekeeping and peacemaking. The
Tories like it so much that they removed Bill Reid's sculpture *The
Spirit of Haida Gwaii* from the back of the $20 bill and replaced
it with an image of the Vimy Ridge memorial. The peacekeeping
troops on the back of the $50 bill also quietly disappeared.

Noah Richler attributed the phrase "Vimy Myth" to former
chief of the defence staff Rick Hillier, an officer who was never
mistaken for a social worker. He coined it in 2007 and used it at
the Conference of Defence Associations and on the speaking circuit. The phrase was so catchy that Hillier employed it in his 2010
book *Leadership: 50 Points of Wisdom for Today's Leaders*. Hillier
used Vimy as a sort of magic moment in which Canadian soldiers
performed admirably and Canada's wartime officer corps, so often
trashed by their British colleagues in both world wars, shone. After
Vimy, Canadians had a seat at the big war conferences and got to

sign the Treaty of Versailles, which formally ended that war (and set the stage for the next one). Vimy, Richler said, was used by Hillier to create a model for the new, fighting Canadian Forces that had previously "meandered aimlessly, perceived as essentially just another department of government."

So it really wasn't independence that Canadians were fighting for. It was international influence. And, in Tory mythology, that influence had to be paid for constantly. Canada had made that payment in World War II, but in the postwar years failed to pull its weight in the North Atlantic Treaty Organization. While liberals liked peacekeeping, being part of international missions to dangerous places like the Balkans in the 1990s, it made no impression on our allies or enemies. The country needed a fighting force, especially after the attacks of September 11, 2001, after which Canada went to war in Afghanistan.[12]

The Vimy Myth, as Richler points out, was one of the cornerstones of a new Canadian self-image. One of the best examples of this mythology finding its way into the arts was the movie *Passchendaele*, filmed in Alberta in 2007. It was a remarkable film that won several Canadian awards. The film gathered up and reused World War I mythology, including a variation of the story of "the crucified Canadian," a tale that motivated many Canadian units to stop taking prisoners on the Western Front. In the culminating scene, Sgt. Michael Dunne (played by writer-producer Paul Gross) dies after saving a man who had been flung by an exploding shell onto a cross of debris erected in no man's land. Dunne drags the injured man back to the Canadian lines as German soldiers watch in silence, their rifles and machine guns stilled. (In the actual wartime myth, a Canadian was spiked to a barn door with bayonets by leering German sadists. The story cropped up in both world wars and was believed by many Canadian soldiers, with nasty consequences for the Germans.)

The Historica-Dominion Institute used the movie as a teaching aid, issuing material to go along with the film as part of its "*Passchendaele* in the Classroom" education program. "Of all the Allies, the Canadians were the most feared," Gross wrote in the material sent out with the film, repeating the popular view that the war represented the country's "coming of age" and that "our notion of what it means to be Canadian was forged in the crucible of the Western Front."[13] Gross received an Order of Canada soon after the Passchendaele project.

The conservative Canadian military clique—with its media boosters like former *Alberta Report* history writer Christian P. Champion (who went on to become an adviser to Citizenship Minister Jason Kenney), prolific author and former Canadian War Museum head Jack Granatstein, PMO history adviser Roy Rempel (who ran the War of 1812 commemoration), and other professional and amateur historians—is a formidable group, as social historians and journalists who have crossed it have learned. On his own, Granatstein was able to start a war among historians with his 1998 bestseller *Who Killed Canadian History?* which set the country's left-wing social and gender historians against political and military specialists.

For all the talk of the media, especially the CBC, being left-leaning, Granatstein is still, even in retirement, the most famous historian in Canada, and the go-to guy for Peter Mansbridge and other media leaders. He remains critical of the shift in academic history, and he understands the threat the social historians pose to Harper's (and his) view of history: "Obviously I am generalizing, but historians are all NDPers, they hate the Tories with a passion, and they're all social historians, so they think any government that's going to commemorate the War of 1812—which they have all said is unimportant, which is just silly—is a war mongering government," he said in 2013. And he believed Harper was not spending enough to commemorate World War I.[14]

Yet in Europe, historians abandoned the myth of a heroic World War I long ago, and the United States pretty much ignores the entire conflict as a sort of military-political train wreck. (Countries that have seen big wars close-up tend to want to move on. As for the Napoleonic Wars, of which the War of 1812 was a sideshow, most of the countries involved in the killing and dying have ignored the bicentennial). Canada clings to the glory of the trenches because the country's leaders believe we need war heroes. And, over the past century, we've made many more heroes, with the help of the Canadian media. After Canadians began fighting in Afghanistan, journalists set out to make two groups of heroes. One group was the journalists themselves, who tried to portray themselves to readers and viewers back home as being as swashbuckling as the great nine-teenth-century colonial correspondents who filed from that same nasty little corner of the world. The other heroes were the dead.

With the same propaganda constructs that Lord Beaverbrook and Lord Northcliffe used so well for the British in World War I, the Canadians killed in Afghanistan were not—as confidential mil-itary reports of World War I called them—"wastage." And they were not "killed." They "offered themselves" as "sacrifices." During the Afghanistan war, the stretch of Highway 401 in southern Ontario leading from the big air base at Trenton to the media capital of Toronto was renamed the Highway of Heroes, and people stood on bridges over the highway not to see the triumphant return of living conquerors and brave warriors but to honour the dead.

Noah Richler parsed out then *Globe and Mail* columnist Christie Blatchford's casting of the death of Capt. Nichola Goddard, the first Canadian woman to die in combat in Afghanistan, as "heroic."

"Her death," Blatchford wrote in May 2006, was "not a tragedy at all [but] an honourable death, a soldier's death, in the service of her country and of another, Afghanistan, she had come to admire and love." There could be no questioning of this new definition of heroics.[15] There would be no decoration ceremonies to remind the Canadian people of killing. Instead, the government wanted people to see each dead soldier as a sort of payment for our nationhood.

In 2005, a new war museum opened in Ottawa, mainly because of the lobbying of Granatstein.[16] The road built beside it was, of course, called Vimy Place. At the same time, the Vimy Myth crowd went to work to dismantle what was left of the country's self-image as a peacekeeper. The new heritage minister, James Moore, began quoting Granatstein by his first name, "Jack," in many of his speeches and often cited Granatstein's *Who Killed Canadian History?* Sean Maloney, a professor at Kingston's Royal Military College, attacked Canada's "feel goodism" and the "hollow façade" of peacekeeping's "myth-making exercise." Canada may have been involved in peace-keeping for years and had even built a now-ignored monument to it within sight of Parliament Hill, but what Canada really needed to do to be a real player was to link itself to the hard power of NATO.[17] The attacks of 9/11 helped move that along. The Canadian Forces began recruiting infantry, changing its ads to focus on combat rather than on peacekeeping, learning trades and leadership.

Richler wasn't the only writer worried about the rebranding of the country's history. "Canadian history has been conscripted," Queen's University history professor Ian McKay said in a 2011 lecture, "The Empire Fights Back: Militarism, Imperial Nostalgia and the Right-Wing Reconceptualization of Canada." McKay, who, along with Jamie Swift, wrote *Warrior Nation: Rebranding Canada in an Age of Anxiety*, warned that the prime minister has a narrow, war-obsessed version of Canadian history anchored in the writings of Granatstein and Bercuson.

James Loney, a peace activist who was kidnapped and held prisoner by insurgents in Iraq in 2005 until he was rescued by British Special Forces, wrote in 2014:

As we approach the hundredth anniversary of the First World War, we must think carefully about how we remember and understand war in our history. Is it central to who we are as a nation, the necessary anvil for the forging of a collective identity? I don't think it is. At the very least, it is a lopsided perspective that ignores the quiet, largely hidden and unsung creative work of nonviolence that undergirds everything. A gun or a tank can't build a road or a hospital or a communications network. The warrior nation is a partisan project. By turning soldiers into heroes, our political spin masters are seeking to shield themselves against dissent . . . My experience as a hostage is a window into the psychology of violence. Every act of violence seems to have a pointing finger behind it, an accusation, a narrative that explains and justifies it.[18]

In October 2012, Foreign Affairs Minister John Baird used the backdrop of the newly rebranded Canadian Museum of History to show off the Harper government's new passports, which played up a triumphant view of Canada's history. To prevent forgery, the government had imprinted images on every page of the redesigned passports. They showed the Fathers of Confederation, the driving of the Last Spike on the Canadian Pacific Railway in 1885, Mounties performing the musical ride, the Parliament Buildings, the *Bluenose*, the Rockies and Niagara Falls. Along with those innocuous scenes were images of Billy Bishop, who won the Victoria Cross during World War I for his one-man raid on a German airfield, the warship HMCS *Sackville*, and of course, the Vimy Ridge memorial. "These images showcase Canadian history and the building of our great nation," Baird told reporters.[19]

LONG BEFORE the run-up to the 2015 election, Harper's government was trying to find ways to work Canada's military past into the celebration of the country's 150th anniversary in 2017. (There had been few celebrations in 1917 because Canada and its allies seemed to be losing World War I and the people were split on whether young men should be drafted to fight overseas. A celebration on Parliament Hill seemed out of the question, since the Parliament Building had burned down in February 1916.) Strangely, as it planned its sesquicentennial celebrations, the Harper government chose to honour quite a few battles that Canada lost. The Battle of Ridgeway, part of the Fenian Raids of 1866, was won by the precursor of the IRA. The 1916 Battle of the Somme was not only lost by the British, but also defined World War I in the public mind as a futile waste run by incompetents and buffoons. The 1917 Battle of Passchendaele reinforced that line of thinking. The Battle of Hong Kong at Christmas 1941 resulted in a Canadian surrender and the imprisonment of hundreds of our soldiers by the Japanese in filthy, brutal conditions. The Tories also honoured the Dieppe Raid fiasco of 1942, and, of course, Vimy Ridge, the Canadian success story in the Battle of Arras, a battle the British and her allies lost. These battles would be celebrated along with the 200th anniversary of the birth of Sir John A. Macdonald and the centennial of the National Hockey League (though not hockey itself, or the Stanley Cup, which are older).

What about the veterans who are still with us? Sometimes, they make good props, too. Months before the last Afghan vets arrived home in 2013, the Prime Minister's Office wanted them honoured as part of Operation Distinction, said to be one of Harper's pet projects. It's a series of high-profile commemorations and events with World War I, World War II and Afghanistan themes leading up to the celebration of the 150th anniversary of Confederation in 2017. In May 2014, the Harper team parked military helicopters and tanks on Parliament Hill to celebrate a National Day of Honour for Afghan war vets. The head of the Royal Canadian Legion was enraged when it became known that Harper wanted vets to give him the flag that flew over the Canadian headquarters in Kandahar. "Governor General David Johnston is the commander-in-chief of the Canadian Armed Forces," Gordon Moore explained to *Maclean's* magazine's John Geddes. "He and he only should be receiving the last Canadian flag that flew in Afghanistan."[20]

At first, families of the soldiers killed in Afghanistan were expected to pay their own way to the National Day of Honour. The Department of National Defence sent out a form letter to the next of kin of all 158 Canadians killed in that war, signed by the military's director of casualty support management, describing the event as a way "to commemorate our service and our sacrifices in order to achieve the security and stability we brought to Afghanistan." But recipients were told, "your attendance would be at your own expense." Some of the families were horrified by what they saw as a slap in the face by an ungrateful government. Others thought all of the money spent on the event should have gone toward helping injured and wounded veterans.[21]

The original plan was to hold the big parade on Canada Day, when Ottawa's downtown was crowded with tourists. Documents that were released to the Liberals through Access to Information show military officers were worried that there would be embarrassing political questions raised by a big Afghanistan commemoration, ones that could vex the government and the Canadian Forces. "While it is clear that this decision was made deliberately, the fact that it is so heavily weighted towards Afghanistan may be problematic given GoC [Government of Canada] expectations," an August 12, 2013, army briefing note said.[22]

Instead, the government held a parade on the first Friday after VE-Day 2014. Armoured vehicles were parked on the lawn of Parliament Hill, along with a Chinook helicopter. Although spring was a month late that year, the weather was fairly decent. The Afghan veterans marched from the war museum to the centre of the capital, where they heard speeches by the Governor General and Prime Minister. The Governor General got the Kandahar flag.

The point of all this commemoration is not to change Canadians' views of history, but to change history itself. Since the days of Lester Pearson, Liberals and New Democrats had portrayed Canada as a "middle power," a force for good in a world full of trouble. Our diplomacy and our peacekeepers were said to be part of the country's quest for social justice. Jean Chrétien explained the concept in a 2000 speech, "The Canadian Way in the 21st Century," at a conference sponsored by Germany's left-leaning Social Democratic Party. Chrétien described Canada as being in the forefront of developed nations that married progressive social and foreign policies with sound fiscal management. He claimed that Canada had invented the Third Way politics that were very popular at the time. This, he said, had "always" been the "Canadian way."[23]

This kind of framing of diplomacy (and history) linked the prevailing national identity to the Liberal Party, with some justification. The Liberals, in their day, had erased the idea of Canada as an active and important part of a vibrant British Empire. Canadians' view of their place in the world is startlingly different from the prevailing view as late as the 1960s, when *God Save the Queen* was still sung in the country's schools and Canadians still saw themselves as having a special bond with what was called the "mother country." Under Harper, the military has been used—as have sports—to change Canadians' view of their country from one of consensus builder to a competing nation ready to fight to exert power and influence in the world.

Some well-meaning citizens have joined the campaign. Toronto businessman Tony Trigiani, in 2013, came up with the idea of a huge monument on the East Coast to honour Canada's war dead. The Harper Tories jumped on the idea, while the people who would have to look at the gigantic statue girded themselves for battle. "Mother Canada," a ten-storey image that evokes images of Stalinist war art like the Red Army's monument at Stalingrad, may be built on the Cape Breton Island coast in time for Canada's 150th anniversary in 2017. Parks Canada is supposed to assemble the Never Forgotten National Memorial at Green Cove, on a rocky point jutting out into Cabot Strait. A gigantic statue of a grieving woman modelled on one of the images on the Vimy Ridge memorial in France, staring out to sea, may take shape at what's said to be one of the most beautiful places in Cape Breton Highlands National Park. Local opponents of the statue say that it, and a parking lot for three hundred cars, will ruin the look of that part of the park. They also think the statue is ugly and wonder why the government thinks people would want to see a statue of a woman from the back. (To see the front, they'll need to get into a boat.) Hector Murphy, a local opponent of the plan, told *The Globe and Mail*'s Jane Taber that he believes Cape Breton deserves the monument. He just doesn't like the idea of putting it at Green Cove. "If they put it down at Green Cove," he says, laughing, "all you're going to see is her arse."[24]

So WHEN WE THINK about Canada, we should think about our wars. The government made its position quite clear in the fall of 2013, when it closed the Ottawa-based Pearson Centre (previously called the Pearson Peacekeeping Centre), which had been created by the Chrétien government in 1994. The centre trained Canadian and foreign soldiers, along with staff of non-governmental agencies, in peacekeeping. The Harper government had been starving the agency of money for several years, causing the centre to close its office in Cornwallis, Nova Scotia, and to lay off some of its staff at its headquarters in Ottawa. In 2012, the Harper government stripped the Pearson Centre of its last $4 million in federal funding. "They did a hell of a good job training police officers, females in particular, in Africa," retired Gen. Lewis MacKenzie, a former Tory candidate and board member of the Pearson Centre, told the *Ottawa Citizen*'s military specialist, David Pugliese. "That was a very cost-effective organization."[25]

At the same time, MPs fanned out with government cheques for local museums and war re-enactors. The National Capital Commission (NCC), the federal agency that runs most tourism programs in the capital, rewrote the sound and light show on Parliament Hill to highlight some of the country's wars. "Mosaika" is a light show projected on the main Parliament Building on summer nights. It's backed up with a booming sound system. In 2013 the thirty-three-minute show was remade to stress the War of 1812 and Canada's participation in the peace conference that ended with the signing of the Treaty of Versailles in 1919. The two World Wars were already part of the show, but parts dealing with Canada's defence of human rights and early relations between European settlers and First Nations were cut to make room for material about Canada's wars in Korea and Afghanistan, dangerous operations during the 1990s Balkans War, and peacekeeping in Cyprus and other countries. "There's a very emotionally touching moment with the Highway of Heroes," NCC spokesperson Denise LeBlanc said.[26]

But, while the Harper government was projecting more war onto the Parliament Building, it was making deep cuts to the Department of National Defence's Directorate of History and Heritage. It is headquartered in a non-descript building in suburban Ottawa and does much of the country's most accurate and detailed military research. It drafts official histories, advises the government on protocol on decorations and battle honours, and also handles public inquiries about medals and decorations. Probably its most important job is to protect a large military archive, much of it secret, that is used by historians, genealogists, researchers looking for sites in Canada that might contain unexploded bombs and artillery shells, and the odd journalist. But just before Christmas 2013, historians were told they had to get permission from senior staff of the minister of defence before they could answer questions from reporters. The staff of historians, most with PhDs and superb expertise in military history, was cut from fourteen to twelve during the first year of the commemoration of the War of 1812, with more cuts to come.

The directorate ran afoul of the Prime Minister's Office in 2012 when it resisted a PMO plan to give battle honours to modern regiments that had, the historians believed, no real connections to units that fought in the War of 1812. For instance, PMO staffers demanded battle honours for the Royal 22e Régiment (the Van Doos) for the Battle of Chateauguay, even though the Van Doos were created during World War I. Prime Minister's Office staffers pushed the military historians to find connections between modern units and the regiments that fought in the War of 1812. The Van Doos chose not to add honours for Chateauguay to their military colours, insisting that no one from their regiment, which earned a reputation for courage and skill in the wars of the twentieth century and Afghanistan, had fought in the War of 1812.

The Vimy Myth supposedly explains how Canadian boys fought for the country's independence on a French hillside in World War I and made Canada a real country, with the respect of all the belligerents. But the acceptance of the myth by the country's Tory policy-makers does not explain why the Harper government did so much to turn the clock back to colonial times. It has gone out of its way to remind people that Canada is a monarchy. Pictures of Elizabeth II went up in government buildings and embassies. You can write to any Tory MP and receive a poster of the Queen, free of charge. Early in the Tory regime, the government ordered the "Royal" to be put back into Royal Canadian Air Force. The navy got the same treatment soon afterwards.

Then the clock was turned back for the army. In the summer of 2013, then Defence Minister Peter MacKay announced the army would replace the Maple Leaf rank designations on the shoulder boards of officers with the traditional "pips" and crowns worn back in the days when Canada followed British rank-designation traditions. In effect, the government was unwinding some of the changes made when Pierre Trudeau amalgamated the Canadian Forces in 1968. Ranks of non-commissioned officers were renamed. The rank of "private" was virtually eliminated in this new rank system, replaced with trooper, bombardier, fusilier, rifleman or guardsman. "This takes nothing away from the Maple Leaf," MacKay said. "There are other places in which the Maple Leaf is honoured. On the uniform, for example, our officers who accepted the [German] surrender, were wearing pips and Crowns. This in no way diminishes Canada's identity, and I would suggest we are returning to the insignia that was so much a part of what the Canadian Army accomplished in Canada's name."[27]

When it came to the military, the government talked a good fight. While it wrapped itself in the flag and said it supported the troops, veterans and soldiers serving in the Canadian Forces were killing themselves in numbers that were truly shocking. Veterans who tried to talk to Julian Fantino, the hapless minister who had been placed in charge of their affairs, were treated like dirt. Soldiers who had been wounded in Afghanistan were effectively bought out with one-time cash payments that might have been tempting to young soldiers but were nowhere near enough to help carry the vets through the decades. Military budgets were slashed after the troops left Afghanistan. The Canadian Forces are stuck with dangerous old helicopters, ancient trucks, and fighter planes that are near the end of their lifespan. People in the military complained about the discrepancy between propaganda and reality, between celebrating the glories of the past and letting down today's soldiers and vets.

In the fall of 2012, Harper took aim at another national historical institution, the Canadian Museum of Civilization. The government announced that it would now be the Canadian Museum of History. Heritage Minister James Moore told reporters on Parliament Hill that "this is not left wing or right wing but the right thing to do, to build an institution that will span all of Canada and represent all of Canada's rich diverse issues." Mark O'Neill, president of the Museum of Civilization, said the museum needed a revamp if it was to tell the story of Canada and the ethnic groups that make up the people of this country. "Look around," he said. "You will learn virtually nothing about Ukrainian Canadians. You will learn nothing about the first Canadian internment camps. You will learn nothing about the Ukrainian community today."

Most historians and museum fans agreed that the Canada Hall did need serious work. Its displays were lifeless and somewhat hokey. Most of the artifacts really said very little. There was an exhibit on the Acadian settlement of Bay of Fundy salt marshes, but it showed almost nothing about their expulsion in 1755. Another 1970s-style diorama showed a Quebec City square with no historical context. A Red River cart sat somewhat alone and told almost nothing of the story of the Métis and their struggle to survive on the Prairies.

Robert Rabinovitch,[28] a former director of the museum and now an adjunct professor at Queen's University, asked: "Why would you abandon the word 'civilization'? Why would you reduce so significantly the mandate of the museum, from expanding critical understanding of human creations, civilizations, cultures, and instead frame it as focused on the study and popularization of Canadian history?" The following year, the government launched what it called a "thorough and comprehensive review of significant aspects in Canadian history." Conservative MPs were assigned to investigate courses taught in schools. They were told to concentrate on the way school children learned about Canada's wars. It didn't seem to matter that education is the constitutional responsibility of the provinces, not Ottawa. And the politicians began to poke around the heritage and history programs of all levels of government. They also visited what the Heritage Committee called "relevant national museums" and summoned executives of the CBC and National Film Board to explain how they portray history. The committee said its final report would "highlight best practices, new methods and potential opportunities to preserve, protect and enhance Canadians' knowledge of our history while recommending ways of improving access to our historical collections." New Democratic MP Andrew Cash commented, "They're obsessed with reframing history and rebranding it in the image of the Conservative party."[29]

The government also rewrote the citizenship test handbook to fit the warrior nation narrative. The guide now says military service is "a noble way to contribute to Canada and an excellent career choice . . . Young people can learn discipline, responsibility and skills by getting involved in the cadets." In the new guide, Louis Riel, who led two armed campaigns against non-Native settlers on the Prairies, is called "polarizing." Jason Kenney, the minister of citizenship and immigration, said of the old handbook that it had two pages about garbage recycling "but not one single sentence on Canadian military history . . . Nowhere does it indicate what the poppy represents as a Canadian symbol. This is ridiculous. This is indicative of a completely insipid view of Canada."[30]

ANYONE LOOKING FOR CRITICS of the government's expensive commemoration fetish would not have to go too far. They are as close as the local Royal Canadian Legion, and you can find quite a lot of them near your community's war memorial on Remembrance Day. The Legion and the Veterans Ombudsman's Office have come out against lavish spending on commemorating World War I. Sure, they say, it's important that people remember it, but the speeches and ad campaigns should start after all of the real war veterans have been looked after. "I understand our role on the world stage and what we should do to commemorate the fantastic deeds that have been done in the past," said deputy veterans ombudsman Gary Walbourne. "But I don't know if we need the Library and Archives Canada version for every event. Yes, there's a need and a place [for commemorations]. But there are bigger needs and requirements that are needed today, that are urgent today." Instead, the government earmarked an extra $70 million for Canadian Heritage in 2014, partly for World War I commemoration. While much of the rest of the government was being cut, the National Battlefields Commission got an extra $5 million.[31]

Because, for all the talk about sacrifice, and about war as the driving force of nation-building, the government has been pretty cheap with the vets. The Legion asked the government to show vets the budget for the World War I commemorations so they can compare it to the cuts that Harper's government made to veterans support programs. Veterans Affairs Canada lost hundreds of employees when the Conservative government cut nearly $130 million from its budget during the same years that it was hyping the War of 1812. Another $132 million is scheduled to be cut 2016. In early 2014, the government closed nine Veterans Affairs offices across Canada to save about $4 million per year.[32]

Gordon Moore, who was Dominion president of the Royal Canadian Legion when a parliamentary committee started examining the veterans' benefit system in the fall of 2013, says veterans' advocates want three major changes. They want more money for retirees from the regular forces, more generous help for soldiers who have been wounded or injured in the line of duty, and a fair deal for reservists who served in Afghanistan. "They like to have those veterans in the photos," he said, "but you won't see too many from after the Second World War and Korea."[33]

The veterans thought they had a deal. They'd go overseas and put their lives on the line. If they got killed, we'd support their families. If they got seriously hurt, we'd make sure they always had a comfortable living. If they needed doctors or psychiatrists, physical therapy or job training, we'd make sure they got it. Then, veterans claim, they found they didn't have a deal after all. Since the passing of a New Veterans Charter in 2005, the rules have changed. Veterans say they've been gouged and can expect to spend their retirement years in poverty. They've become much more militant. There are 700,000 of them, and they're getting very good at embarrassing the government and building popular support.

Many veterans argue we have a much, much longer way to go than just hiring a few more therapists. They say modern warriors are not treated with anything like the generosity that the country extended to veterans of World War II. They resent the Harper Conservatives' military history commemorations—in 2014, marking the hundredth anniversary of the outbreak of World War I, the seventy-fifth anniversary of the beginning of World War II, and the seventieth anniversary of D-Day—saying the money should go to wounded and injured soldiers. In the end, to the chagrin of some people in the military, Laureen Harper, rather than the Governor General, the defence minister or a prominent soldier represented Canada at some of the 2014 D-Day commemorations in Normandy.

Only about 10 per cent of the 700,000 veterans of the Canadian Forces get any help at all. Of that small number, only 1 per cent get lifetime help as Totally and Permanently Incapacitated (TPI). To qualify as totally disabled, a soldier has to lose both legs above the knee or both arms above the elbow, suffer psychological damage that leaves the veteran bedridden, or a combination of factors that make the veteran unable to work.

"It is beyond my comprehension how the system could knowingly deny so many of our veterans the rights and benefits that the people and the government of Canada recognized a long, long time ago as being their obligation to provide," says Lt.-Col. Pat Stogran, Canada's first veterans ombudsman, who lost his job in 2010 after criticizing Harper and Fantino for the way veterans are treated. He was one of the watchdogs hired by Harper. For years, the Tory campaign platform had called for a better deal for veterans. In April 2007, the minority Conservative government passed the Veterans Bill of Rights, and, six months later, Stogran was appointed by cabinet to be veterans ombudsman.

Stogran was a combat veteran in the Princess Patricia's Canadian Light Infantry in Afghanistan and suffered post-traumatic stress disorder (PTSD) from his experiences in the Balkans in the 1990s. "One of the reasons I became interested in this position was because I was working with the Legion about a year ago because I recognized that 15–20 years from now we're going to have a whole bunch of veterans who, if they had a problem coming out of Afghanistan, are going to have a bigger problem 15 or 20 years down the road," Stogran told *Esprit de Corps* magazine. "In this day and age the way we do these interagency operations, whole of government, the comprehensive approach, there's going to be a lot of hurting civilians too suffering from the traumas of war . . . With that sort of strategic perspective I was eager to get in this job because I think I might be able to shape that situation for them."

After fighting in Afghanistan, Stogran had several job offers from "defence industries and that sort of thing" and felt he would be prostituting a reputation that he'd gained with his troops if he accepted one of those offers. "You know . . . I can't think of a better job for a soldier to fade away to."[34]

He has a martial arts black belt, and he decided he would fight hard for the veterans. Firing Stogran didn't shut him up: he immediately became a vocal critic of the government, saying it was not living up to its obligations and promises. He says the administrators of the veterans' pension program had a "penny pinching insurance company mentality." Stogran said:

We started to put pressure on. They basically told me to pound salt. It became clear they weren't going to co-operate. It was a waiting game for me to leave . . . My ministers were as thick as three short planks. They were completely dependent on their deputy minister. Julian Fantino is a classic example. He's one of Harper's yes men who says the government is backing vets and is pouring money into programs to help them. At the same time, you have federal government lawyers saying in British Columbia that the government has no legal or moral obligation to the veterans. I argued against the lump sum. I said it was wrong to give people who were physically and emotionally traumatized a lump sum of money and then tell them 'have a good day.' Harper never did anything to back me up . . . I despise Harper personally. He's pushed politics to another level.[35]

In early 2012, Stogran repeatedly criticized the Harper government for its treatment of veterans, saying the bureaucrats at Veteran Affairs and in other government departments were making it very difficult for him to do his job. Soon afterwards, Auditor General Michael Ferguson backed Stogran, complaining Veterans Affairs' red tape makes it "difficult to access services and benefits in a timely fashion." The next summer, Stephen Harper refused to renew Stogran's contract. After he left his job, Stogran started receiving a new round of treatment for PTSD, which, he said, was caused by his treatment at the hands of the Harper government.

Sean Bruyea, another young veteran with distinguished combat experience in the Balkans and the Gulf War, is one of the more vocal critics of Veterans Affairs. He filed a lawsuit against the government in 2006. Three years later, Bruyea, an airman with fourteen years' service, learned that his medical file had been made widely available to government bureaucrats. Some of them had made crude and cruel jokes in emails that Bruyea was able to get through Access to Information.

Someone in Veterans Affairs cut off payments for his treatment for PTSD. When Bruyea appealed, Veterans Affairs told him to get a psychiatric assessment, and it was that report that was passed around and laughed at. Jean-Pierre Blackburn, then veterans affairs minister, apologized to Bruyea, but the government had made a very articulate enemy who has loudly attacked the system ever since. Pat Stogran also believes his information may have been improperly used, the way Bruyea's was. In 2010, he applied to the privacy commissioner to find out why his Veterans Affairs file had been accessed hundreds of times.

The attack on Bruyea won him support from Gulf War and Afghanistan veterans. Military historian Jack Granatstein wrote in the *The Globe and Mail*: "The Kafkaesque breaches of faith in VAC are a blot on the department's record and a stain on Canadian government. If the public's confidence is to be restored, if veterans' confidence in the department of government created to assist them is recreated, there must a genuine investigation with real punishment for those who tried to smear opponents."[36]

Bruyea says he believes veterans won't get a fair shake until they stop being polite. One way, he says, is to put veterans' issues front and centre as the government commemorates the centennial of World War I and other military history milestones. "A big focus of the Conservatives is military commemoration. They get a big PR bang for a relatively little buck compared to what it costs to look after a veteran. Those commemoration plans are absolutely cynical," he said.[37]

During World War I, Prime Minister Robert Borden promised veterans they would be looked after by Canadians. It took more than twenty-five years for that to come true, and the World War II veterans got help with jobs, education and paying for houses. Soldiers who were wounded in the last fifty years want the same deal as their parents and grandparents. Six veterans filed a class action lawsuit against the federal government in the British Columbia Supreme Court in 2012, saying the New Veterans Charter violates the Constitution and the Charter of Rights. All of them served in Afghanistan and were injured. The cornerstone of their lawsuit is the social contract that they claim exists between Canadians and the veterans.

Federal lawyers denied any social contract or covenant can be found in this country's laws. "At no time in Canada's history has any alleged 'social contract' or 'social covenant' having the attributes pleaded by the plaintiffs been given effect in any statute, regulations, or as a constitutional principle, written or unwritten," the government's submission says. So much for Sir Robert Borden's promise that Canada would always take care of its war veterans.

Why bother with this stuff? It all seems so nitpicky, so insider. Historians can be pretty tiresome people, and that's one reason why their fights aren't televised on sports networks. But there's method in meddling with a country's history, especially if you want to change the very nature of the nation. Harper and his government have a view of Canadian history that's based on a foundation of deference—to order, to the monarchy, to a British world view in which progress is perpetual, people accept their lot in life, and civilized white people tame the wild land and "savage" people. It is a world of Christians converting heathens, of darkness pushed back, of simple stories of heroics, where men are men and women know their place.

"At the heart of our relationship is the golden circle of the Crown, which links us all together with the majestic past that takes up back to the Tudors, the Plantagenets, habeas corpus, petition of rights and English Common Law," Harper said when he took office in 2006.[38] That's a call to a sort of counter-revolution to the democratic turmoil of the last two hundred years. It's also a view of history that embraces the kind of paternalism that breeds institutions like the Canadian Senate. It washes away struggles for gender and racial equality, the fight of working people for decent wages and working conditions, the survival of French culture in Canada, and the need to set things right with the country's Native people. It works against real democratic reform in this country. And it's strange coming from a government that has done so much to undermine the country's most important institutions.

CHAPTER 7

The War on Brains

Of all national assets, archives are the most precious.
They are the gift of one generation to another and the extent of our
care of them marks the extent of our civilization.
—Sir Arthur Doughty, former chief archivist of Canada

When we think of silver, we think of something valuable. Money used to be made out of it. Silver is still used in jewellery, tableware and plenty of other pretty things. And electronics factories use a lot of it. You shouldn't eat it—but you do.

Chris Metcalfe, a Trent University scientist, got an $800,000 federal grant to test the effects of nanosilver pollution on the environment. Those are silver particles and ions that are so small you need a powerful microscope to see them. They range in size from one nanometre, comparable to a DNA molecule, to a hundred nanometres, the size of a blood cell. Nanosilver particles are a by-product of several manufacturing processes, and they're found in the weirdest places. Scientists have detected them in more than 250 consumer products. They're used in new clothes to kill odour, but they also show up in machines, toys, cosmetics and many other things. They end up in the sewage system when people wash their clothes. Once they get into the environment, they kill microbes at

182

the bottom of the food chain. And, if you think the loss of some bacteria is no big deal, there's also strong evidence that nanosilver can be carried into your brain, a place where silver does not belong.

Scientific research like Metcalfe's—as well as accurate history—has little value to a government that makes policy based on its appeal to a rural, Western, anti-intellectual base where, for many people, PhD stands for "piled higher and deeper" and science is seen as a threat to the resource boom. Environmental science has taken a direct hit from a government that has an obvious chip on its shoulder when it comes to expertise of all kinds. So what we have is a war on expertise. It's not just a matter of killing the messenger. It's a war on the message itself. There can't be a public debate on issues like climate change without scientific information. When a government wants to put an end to serious public discussion of science or history, it stifles scientific research and muzzles archives. Allowing the public access to scientific information means surrendering a lot of control over information. Fully aware that control of information is the key to power, the Harper government has worked hard to make sure people stay uninformed.

Metcalfe's research on nanosilver pollution—paid for with a grant from the Natural Sciences and Engineering Research Council of Canada, a respected federal agency—and the work of many other biologists and environmental scientists, was put at risk in 2012, when the Harper government decided to close the Experimental Lakes Area. It's in the Canadian Shield of northwestern Ontario, near the Manitoba border.

Metcalfe was partway through his experiments. He needed an entire lake for one of his projects, and the only place where there are whole lakes available for environment experiments is the Experimental Lakes Area. "We're currently investing billions if not trillions of dollars in the development of various nano-materials.

Why not take a look also at what the potential impacts might be on the environment?" Metcalfe asked, with a touch of naïveté. "I think what will happen is that there will still be questions about whether nano-materials—and specifically nanosilver—are potentially harmful to the environment or not." Metcalfe believes Canadian regulatory agencies won't have enough information to make informed, fair decisions about the development and uses of nano-materials unless work like his continues.[1]

C. Scott Findlay, associate professor of biology at the University of Ottawa and visiting research scientist at the Ottawa Hospital Research Unit, spoke for many scientists when he talked about the importance of the Experimental Lakes Area: "Evidence-free decisions are merely uneducated guesswork. Scientific evidence is a form of insurance, a comparatively inexpensive yet effective way to ensure that much larger investments in government programs are not wasted, that opportunities are not squandered, and that others will not have to shoulder the burden of (whoops!) undesired and unanticipated consequences. In other words, scientific evidence forms the basis for true public accountability. And isn't accountability the horse on which Harper rode into Parliament?"[2]

By mid-July, 2012, nearly three thousand people, including cottagers who believe the research helps protect their lakes and scientists working in labs and universities around the world, had signed petitions urging the government to change its mind.[3] A poll commissioned by the Council of Canadians found three out of four Canadians opposed the closing of the Experimental Lakes Area. Some 60 per cent of Conservative voters were against the idea.[4]

Experts estimated it would cost $50 million to wrap up the Experimental Lakes Area. That was twenty-five years' worth of its operating budget. Eventually, the Experimental Lakes Area was saved through a deal between the Ontario government and the

Winnipeg-based non-profit International Institute for Sustainable Development, with no help from Ottawa.

After the 2012 federal budget, the National Research Council, whose research had helped the Allies win the Second World War, chopped about a hundred scientists. It was told to spend its time and money developing marketable products instead of basic science directed at public policy issues. The National Research Council started calling itself a "concierge service" for businesses to "find high-quality, timely advice to help them innovate and accelerate their growth." The council surveyed its scientists after the change in mandate and found that 63 per cent were opposed to the National Research Council's change of direction. Just 2 per cent said they "strongly agreed" the National Research Council was making the right decisions; some 15 per cent said that they "agreed."[5]

LIKE MOST OTHER EXPERTS employed by the federal government, scientists have been gagged by strict rules laid down at the Centre. The Prime Minister's Office has crafted an information control system that ensures no one in the government speaks without permission. Tory politicians and the public servants in the bureaucracy can't do media interviews unless the Prime Minister's Office approves the Message Event Proposals that lay out the content of the interview, the length, and the visuals that may be used.

Until 2007, reporters could simply call up scientists. Usually reporters were interviewed after they had published a paper about a discovery they'd made. But starting that year, according to respected Postmedia writer Margaret Munro, one of the handful of Canadian journalists who specialize in science, the system changed. Environment Canada started ordering scientists to refer media enquiries first to government media handlers—people who were not scientists—who would help write responses to the questions.[6]

Scientists say these rules have muzzled them. Their complaints began when Environment Canada climatologist Mark Tushingham booked the National Press Theatre in Ottawa, which is operated by the Parliamentary Press Gallery, for the launch of his novel *Hotter Than Hell*. Harper's officials told Tushingham to cancel the event, even though *Hotter Than Hell*—which is based on the idea, unpopular in Tory circles, that climate change is caused by humans—is a work of fiction.

In March 2012, the journal *Nature*, one of the world's most prestigious science magazines, came down on the side of the muzzled scientists. In an editorial, *Nature* told of the problems faced by its own reporters who had tried to write about Canadian science policies. Since President George W. Bush left office, the United States had reversed many of his restraints on government-employed scientists. At the same time, Canada had tightened them. "The Harper government's poor record on openness has been raised by this publication before . . . and *Nature*'s news reporters, who have an obvious interest in access to scientific information and expert opinion, have experienced directly the cumbersome approval process that stalls or prevents meaningful contact with Canada's publicly funded scientists," the editorial said. "Policy directives and emails obtained from the government through freedom of information reveal a confused and Byzantine approach to the press, prioritizing message control and showing little understanding of the importance of the free flow of scientific knowledge."[7]

Scientists at the American Association for the Advancement of Science's annual conference in Vancouver in 2012 signed a letter to Harper asking the prime minister to let federal scientists speak. They said they were proud of their work. "Why are we suppressing really good news to Canadians, that is, successful science being done in federal government labs?" Andrew Weaver, a climate scientist at the University of Victoria, said during the session. "Why don't we open it up? There's nothing to fear but success." The letter that the scientists drafted was short. In part, it said: "Despite promises that your majority government would follow principles of accountability and transparency, federal scientists in Canada are still not allowed to speak to reporters without the consent of media relations officers."[8]

At the same conference, science journalist Margaret Munro told scientists about reporters' frustration in January 2011 when flacks wouldn't let them interview Kristin Miller, a biologist with Fisheries and Oceans Canada. Miller was the lead author of a study published in the journal *Science* that examined the decline of salmon stocks on the west coast. At first, media handlers in the fisheries department had told reporters that they could talk to Miller. Harper's department, the Privy Council Office, stepped in and blocked all interviews. The prime minister's communications wizards said they were worried Miller might say something to influence the ongoing judicial inquiry into the decline of sockeye salmon in the rivers of British Columbia.

A few months earlier, reporters tried to interview Edmonton-based Environment Canada researcher David Tarasick about the things he'd found while researching the state of the hole in the ozone layer above the Arctic. Tarasick's article "Unprecedented Arctic Ozone Loss in 2011" was published in *Nature*. Tarasick found one of the largest ozone holes ever discovered above the Arctic, covering two million square kilometres. He warned that the ultraviolet light that penetrates the atmosphere through the ozone hole is a threat to plants and animals. Predictably, the *Nature* article got a lot of attention from the world's media.

Media handlers in Tarasick's own department gagged him for two weeks, until reporters either found other sources to talk about the problem or lost interest.[9] When a Canadian reporter asked for an interview, Tarasick wrote back in an email: "I'm available when Media Relations says I'm available."

Media Relations was no more helpful. "While an interview cannot be granted, we are able to provide additional information on the paper . . . You may attribute these responses to Dr. David Tarasick, Research Scientist, Environment Canada." The department, it seems, wanted to interpret the scientist's findings and write them into its own words, then put those words into Tarasick's mouth.

Documents released under the Access to Information regime show everyone was in the information loop except Tarasick. Spin strategy went all the way up the information food chain to the assistant deputy minister. One of the media handlers told Tarasick, "I just wanted to let you know that proposed responses are with the ADM [assistant deputy minister] for review right now." Apparently not having had any involvement with the preparation of the proposed responses, Tarasick replied to his handlers, "I haven't given you any proposed responses." So whatever the spinners were giving out, it wasn't science, and it wasn't written by anyone who had anything to do with scientific research.[10]

Although then Environment Minister Peter Kent said in the House of Commons, "We are not muzzling scientists," Kent told a parliamentary committee that "circumstances simply did not work out" to allow Tarasick to give interviews about his ozone hole study. Whatever circumstances were at work, none of them seemed to involve Tarasick, who was more than willing to chat.

Tarasick couldn't talk because, just after Harper won his majority, the Prime Minister's Office, in an effort to control the environmental message, had made it clear that loyal communications wizards would decide what information went out of the Environment Ministry. In most cases, it turned out, there would be a written response to media questions crafted by grads of journalism schools and veterans of Tory campaigns, rather than the words of scientists. Previously, reporters had simply called up scientists to ask about their work.

TARASICK WASN'T the only scientist caught up in this strategy. At an Arctic science conference in 2012, Environment Canada researchers were told to let a minder know if they were approached by a reporter. The angry scientists leaked that email to the media.[11]

At first, Environment Minister Kent denied issuing any gag order on the Arctic scientists. Emails obtained by reporters showed otherwise: senior managers in the environment department approved of Tarasick talking about his research, but Kent and the Prime Minister's Office said no. Kent, a former anchor of CBC's nightly news show, *The National,* and lead anchor at Global TV—and a member of the Canadian Broadcast Hall of Fame—had developed a strong disdain for his former colleagues and their profession. "There is an element in all of this controversy, second-hand information and criticism from the scientific community abroad responding to a few, a very small number of Canadian journalists who believe they're the centres of their respective universes and deserve access to our scientists on their timeline and to their deadlines. And it simply doesn't work that way," Kent said. "Where we run into problems is when journalists try to lead scientists away from science into policy matters." And when the assistant deputy minister said she was willing to speak at a Vancouver conference on the subject of unmuzzling scientists, she was forbidden to speak at the session.

Globe and Mail columnist Lawrence Martin wrote about the environment ministry's internal censorship: "The controls aren't all that far afield from what I used to deal with once, long ago, while covering the Kremlin as a correspondent in Moscow. Never thought I'd see it in 21st century North America."[12]

Federal geologist Scott Dallimore was forbidden from talking about his research on a massive flood that swept over northern Canada thirteen thousand years ago. This catastrophe sent enough glacial melt water into the Arctic Ocean to change the climate for a thousand years. Scientists had spent a long time looking for evidence of such a flood to prove a theory that this influx of fresh water effectively restarted the last ice age. Dallimore discovered the flood poured through the Mackenzie River Delta, a place that was unexpected. When news of the discovery was published, American researchers, not Dallimore, got the credit.[13]

Maybe the muzzling of climate scientists did pay off for Harper and Tories who didn't want Canadians to spend too much time thinking about the climate: from 2007 to 2012, the volume of media coverage of climate change issues fell by 80 per cent.[14]

When the Harper government held closed-door meetings to talk about ways to cut Environment Canada's budget by $60 million in the 2012 federal budget, Harper's team made sure communications specialists were in the room. Records labelled "secret advice to the minister" were part of five hundred pages of briefing material prepared for a new deputy minister when she arrived at Environment Canada a few months after the meetings. "Strategists from the communication branch were involved in Environment Canada's deliberations on its contribution to the deficit action reduction plan from the beginning," said the records, released through Access to Information. They also showed that Environment Canada's human resources branch managers stayed in touch with both the Prime Minister's Office and the Privy Council Office.

"That sounds a bit backwards to me," Gary Corbett, president of the Professional Institute of the Public Service of Canada, which represents about sixty thousand government scientists and professionals, told Postmedia journalist Mike De Souza. "It's wrong for communications people to be involved in deciding what decisions to make. Communications people are there to communicate the decisions after they're made. It seems the government is just being political rather than [doing] what's in the best interests of Canadians."

The Harper government is especially sensitive about any scientific research that shows the extraction of oil from the bitumen sands of northern Alberta is a threat to the environment or to people. Environment Canada researchers Derek Muir and Jane Kirk agreed with findings by University of Alberta scientists Erin Kelly and David Schindler that contaminants are accumulating in snow near the oilsands quarries. While the university scientists could discuss their findings with the media, the government scientists could not.

The University of Alberta scientists' report was presented in November 2011 at a conference in Boston of the Society of Environmental Toxicology and Chemistry. "[Environment Canada's] research conducted during winter 2010–11 confirms results already published by the University of Alberta that show contaminants in snow in the oilsands area," an Environment Canada memorandum admitted, but the authors of the document warned: "If scientists are approached for interviews at the conference, the EC [Environment Canada] communications policy will be followed by referring the journalist to the media relations . . . phone number. An appropriate spokesperson will then be identified depending on journalist questions." The document was obtained through Access to Information by Postmedia's Mike De Souza, who had been bird-dogging the government on its cover-up of data that might cause trouble for oil extraction companies. (Their problem was solved when De Souza was laid off in 2014, when Postmedia shut down its Ottawa bureau. The Postmedia chain no longer has a full-time environment reporter on Parliament Hill.)

Environment Canada scientists were told to say, "I am a scientist. I'm not in a position to answer that question, but I'd be happy to refer you to an appropriate spokesperson." The official line was: "We are comparing the levels of contamination we found in our work to other studies and find that other studies report both higher and lower levels. These efforts will allow us to better understand deposition patterns and levels of oilsands related contaminants with a view to better identify their sources and ecological risks."[15]

By the sixth year of the Harper regime, most scientists knew it was foolish and dangerous to try to buck the system. The *Index on Censorship* took a survey of four thousand Canadian scientists in 2013. Only 14 per cent said they felt they would be able to share a concern about public health and safety, or a threat to the environment, without fear of retaliation or censure from their department or agency.[16]

Once the Harper government had scientists under its control, it went after their research libraries. First, Health Canada turned over its interlibrary loan system to a company called Infotrieve. Every time a researcher wanted material from a scientific journal article, a book from a university library or a publication from a federal or provincial agency, Infotrieve billed the scientist's department. To save money and aggravation, some research scientists started borrowing university library cards from co-op students and friends who taught in universities so they could get the interlibrary loan material for free. Others had to ask friends working for private companies to get government-owned research material for them.

Health Canada's head office library was shut down. The books and journals, essential for serious research, were sent to the National Science Library on the Ottawa campus of the National Research Council in 2013. Rudi Mueller, who left Health Canada in 2012, says the department simply did not want it to be easy for scientists to use libraries. "I look at it as an insidious plan to discourage people from using libraries," Mueller said. "If you want to justify closing a library, you make access difficult and then you say it is hardly used." Scientists like Mueller were not just kept away from books. They were also unable to get help from trained science librarians who know how to track down publications that are obscure, rare or hard to get. Health Canada had forty of these librarians. In April 2013, it had six. "A librarian is far better at doing a literature search than I am," Mueller said. "It's their profession." Mueller said the research support system had become absurd and, by the end of his career with Health Canada, he believed he wasn't able to do his work properly.

At least one Health Canada scientist started his own library, squirrelling away 250 feet of shelf space worth of books and journals in his basement. Friends who work for the department email him with requests, and the scientist tracks the material down and brings it to work.

If the plan was designed to save money, it's been a failure. Health Canada Library Services had a staff of thirty-six and a budget of $1.75 million in 2008–2009. In 2013–2014 there was a staff of six and the cost had risen to $2.67 million. On top of that, each time a Health Canada scientist needs a document, the department has to pay a $25.65 retrieval fee plus the courier bill from the National Science Library. Scientists are charged $9 for a scanned, emailed document.[17]

Former Green Party activist Katie Gibbs, who holds a PhD in biology specializing in conservation science, organized the Death of Evidence marches in 2012. She believes the Harper government doesn't want to hear from scientists, even those who work in the federal bureaucracy. "I think there are multiple ways to avoid using scientific evidence in policy development. One way is to not collect it and get rid of historical documentary information," Gibbs said.

"A picture does say a thousand words. You see pictures of dumpsters full of books. It's alarming. You see lots of examples of private companies picking up these books. I've heard from so many scientists who took the material home because they couldn't stand to see this material thrown out. Scientists are sending out emails to each other saying what they have stored away. It's having an impact on the ability of scientists to do their job," she said.[18]

HISTORIANS HAVE FACED the same kind of cuts. In Harper's Canada, history comes from the Centre, not from the work of the professors and authors who depend on easy access to the vast collection of documents and pictures at Library and Archives Canada (LAC). Inside its Ottawa building, just a block from Parliament Hill, services have been slashed, employee morale is dismal and visiting scholars are angry.

The words "dusty" and "archives" are usually used in the same breath by people who don't understand that history is a living thing that can, and often is, remade to suit political agendas. History is also often hidden by governments that want to write their own narrative of what a country's about. The archives is so poor that it's missed out on important historical letters, a collection of narratives from fugitive slaves in Upper Canada from 1856, and letters from British colonial officials on the state of First Nations in eastern

Canada during pioneer times. In 2008–2009, Library and Archives Canada spent $385,461 on historic documents. In 2011–2012 it spent nothing. In Washington, the Library of Congress's acquisition budget was between $18 million and $19 million annually from 2009 to 2012.[19]

In the early years of this century, Library and Archives Canada started working on a project to make its collection accessible to everyone. First, Prime Minister William Lyon Mackenzie King's diary and documents from New France were posted on the Internet. Probably the department's heart was in the right place, but the plan has been a failure. Six years into the digitalization project, there was very little to show for it except frustration, with LAC staff and managers unable to get the system running properly and Canadians finding it not very helpful.

When people have asked for material that is politically sensitive, Library and Archives Canada, prompted by its overseers in the Heritage Ministry and the Prime Minister's Office, has dug in its heels. Since 2005, Canadian Press reporter Jim Bronskill has been trying to see the RCMP security service file on one-time federal NDP leader and Saskatchewan premier Tommy Douglas, who died in 1986. The file is 1,149 pages thick, but Bronskill received just 400 heavily censored pages when he filed his first request. Library and Archives Canada released another 300 pages of the file just before Bronskill's case was heard by the Federal Court, and Bronskill got some more of the file after the court ruled in his favour.[20] The material that has been released shows the country's national police force tailed a mainstream elected politician for almost sixty years and watched him long after he retired to see if he was involved with communists, members of the peace movement or anyone else identified by the police as a danger to the state.

The federal government outsourced some of the archives' work to ancestry.ca, a for-profit website used by genealogists. People can go to the archives building and use this service without paying, but if they to want use census material from the comfort of their home, they'd better have their credit card handy.

To do the job right, a national archives still needs archivists—many of them skilled historians—to help professional and amateur researchers who come to Ottawa to use the collection. But rather than increase Library and Archives Canada's budget so it can do its job, the Harper government has cut it. It may scold Canadians and immigrants for not knowing their history, but it has made it much harder for people to study and write about the past. Along with preventing the archives from adding to the nation's collection, cuts have manifested themselves in reduced hours, slower service, lack of access to important documents, and slashing of staff. The ones who still have their jobs often seem overwhelmed and overworked.

In May 2012, more than two hundred people, many of them experts with unique skills and years of experience, lost their jobs. People who arranged for loans of material in the collection, specialists who preserved microfilm, digital experts and reference librarians were tossed out. Training was cut. Half the LAC circulation staff who dealt with analog material—what the rest of us call books and documents—were fired.[21] The library also killed its interlibrary loan program. In its last year in the interlibrary loan system, the national library lent twenty thousand books to people across the country, often in isolated communities.

Morale among the surviving staff, which was never very good, has tanked. Rather than deal with the lousy work environment, Daniel Caron, the former head of Library and Archives Canada, simply gagged his employees. He was trained as an economist, not a librarian or archivist, and his tenure saw a rapid deterioration in services and morale. Like other managers in the Harper government, Caron wanted to put the screws to employees who might gripe to the public.

Caron and his management team came up with a code of conduct banning librarians and archivists from setting foot in classrooms, attending conferences and speaking at public meetings, whether on the institution's time or their own. The twenty-three pages of rules, called "Library and Archives Canada's Code of Conduct: Values and Ethics," came into effect in January 2013. Employees could get special dispensation from their bosses, but the fine print of the gag order made it unlikely that permission would be granted. The rules called public speaking, whether to university students, genealogy groups, historians and even other archivists and librarians "high risk" activities that could create conflicts of interest or "other risks to LAC." The code stressed federal employees' "duty of loyalty" not to history or to Library and Archives Canada, but rather to the "duly elected government." Employees breaking the code could find themselves reported to LAC managers by colleagues who turned them in on what James Turk, executive director of the Canadian Association of University Teachers, called a "snitch line."

"As public servants, our duty of loyalty to the Government of Canada and its elected officials extends beyond our workplace to our personal activities," the code said. It reminded librarians and archivists, many of whom do not consider themselves public menaces, that they must maintain awareness of their surroundings, their audience and how their words or actions could be interpreted (or misinterpreted). They were warned not to fall into the trap of social media. And LAC employees were warned that teaching a class or speaking at a conference put them at special risk, since "such activities have been identified as high risk to Library and Archives Canada and to the employee with regard to conflict of interest, conflict of duties and duty of loyalty."[22]

In March 2013, Harper's hometown paper, the *Calgary Herald*, editorialized: "The code appears overly concerned with what an employee might say about the federal government. Speaking at a conference about the role of archivists, for example, cannot by anyone's wildest imagination be construed as disloyal. This unwarranted dictate severely limiting the librarians' and archivists' freedom of speech is intolerable and must be reversed."[23]

Caron was one person who was allowed to speak out. "Library and Archives Canada's Code of Conduct for its employees is wholly consistent with the values of the Public Service of Canada," he wrote in a letter to the editor of the *Ottawa Citizen*. "Library and Archives Canada's Code of Conduct does not prevent Library and Archives employees from engaging in external activities. However, for all public servants, the right to freedom of expression must be balanced with their responsibility to remain impartial and effective in their professional duties. This is commonly applied in the private and public sector."[24]

That chattiness came to an abrupt end in May 2013, after Caron was called into Heritage Minister James Moore's office to explain why Library and Archives Canada's leader billed the government nearly $4,500 for Spanish lessons.[25] Soon afterwards, the New Democrats released a document outlining what the party's heritage critic, Pierre Nantel, called Caron's "titanic expenses." The publicly available figures show Caron filed $87,000 in expense claims in each of 2011 and 2012. Moore's own expenses were about $46,000 in each of those years. Caron submitted expenses for business lunches in Ottawa's best restaurants and the private Rideau Club, and for rooms in expensive hotels in Quebec City and Puerto Rico, along with trips to Toronto, Europe and Australia.[26] Suddenly, Caron was out of a job.

Just a month after Caron left, the archives finally opened its wallet to buy some Canadiana. It was obvious Library and Archives Canada had learned a lesson on how to serve its masters in the Prime Minister's Office. Library and Archives Canada chipped in with the Canadian Museum of Civilization (now the Canadian Museum of History) to spend almost $700,000 on a collection of documents and artifacts belonging to Sir John Coape Sherbrooke. It fit with the War of 1812 fetish. The collection was described as "the largest and most complete collection of War of 1812 documentation ever" in the government's announcement, which was made by Heritage Minister Moore.[27] Library and Archives Canada would carry on, at least for War of 1812 buffs, but its staff would continue to tread very, very carefully.

CHAPTER 8

Frat Boys and Cheerleaders

A government is like a sausage. You want some shit in it, but not too much.
—NAZI COLLABORATOR AND FUTURE FIRING SQUAD TARGET
PIERRE LAVAL, PREMIER OF VICHY FRANCE

Arthur J. Finkelstein is proud of being called America's Merchant of Venom. He is one of a growing army of professional strategists who have changed politics from a profession to a game. Politics has never been a calling for the thin-skinned and the empathic, but it used to have some moral standards. And, in the end, people seeking political office did tend to take public service seriously and act as though they were responsible for a sacred trust. Not all of them were as conscientious as Harry Truman, who saw all of the trappings of presidential power as baubles lent to the citizen who holds the job that must be returned upon leaving, but ministers did use to resign in shame for transgressions as minor as being caught in a strip club. People like Finkelstein changed that.

Nowadays, honour is seen as a sign of weakness and honesty is construed as possible disloyalty to the team. Finkelstein, one of the people who is supposed to have inspired Stephen Harper's combativeness, made his reputation helping Ronald Reagan and the two Bush presidents get elected; he was also one of the strategists who put Benjamin Netanyahu into power in Israel. He first showed up in Canada as an adviser to the National Citizens Coalition, helping with its advocacy ads in the early 1990s, before Stephen Harper was hired to run the mysterious pressure group. Finkelstein, like many other modern political strategists, advocates tough attack advertising against opposing candidates as they appear on the scene, so that their reputation can be poisoned in the public mind before voters get a chance to get to know them.

At least one writer credits Finkelstein with changing the public meaning of the word "liberal" from one of generosity and open-mindedness to recklessness and weakness. It didn't matter that nineteenth-century liberals favoured free markets and decent wages and working conditions, or that in the twentieth century liberals had led the United States through the two world wars and the Korean War and had got the country mired in Vietnam. They were appeasers, and, when a highly decorated Democrat ran for president, the neo-cons brought out other veterans to ruin his reputation. Nor would the public remember that liberals had led them out of the Great Depression, passed the Civil Rights Act and presided over the transition of the American wartime economy into a consumer-driven behemoth that raised millions of people out of poverty, not only in America, but also all over the world.

Starting in the Reagan years, Democrats would flinch at the word "liberal," and middle-class voters who had become the wealthiest working people in world history would spit the word out as a political profanity. Liberals would now, in the public mind, be considered wastrels, cowardly in the face of foreign enemies, soft on illegal immigrants, and adopters of pretty much every loony idea that comes along. Unfortunately, some liberals came to believe it, too.[1]

Finkelstein was in and out of the National Citizens Coalition through Harper's tenure, working as a political consultant. But, as

201

happens with many of Harper's close advisers, the two men had a falling out. In the 2002 Conservative leadership campaign, Finkelstein was courted by Stockwell Day but, after talking to National Citizens Coalition staffer Gerry Nicholls, turned Day down. Considering an offer by Day—even though Harper was not yet officially in the race—was, in Harper's eyes, a grotesque betrayal. He would never work with Finkelstein again, but Harper had already learned a lot about hardball politics.[2]

Karl Rove—who was, at various times, called the "Architect" and "Turdblossom" by President George W. Bush, but who will likely be best remembered as the father of the modern attack ad—was another influence on Harper and the Canadian right. Rove is a proponent of the politics of deception. He engineered the "Swift boat" campaign that transformed Democratic presidential candidate John Kerry from a decorated war hero to a punch line. "Swiftboating," the use of outright lies and half-truths backed by a massive amount of advertising and trumpeted by biased media, has become a verb in the political world.

Frank Luntz, a pollster and strategist who prides himself on manipulating language (he was able to remake "inheritance tax" into "death tax" and "health care reform" into "government takeover of health care") came to Ottawa in 2006 to speak to the right-wing Civitas organization, then delivered a campaign-style tub-thumper to the Conservative caucus on how to win a majority in the next election. Harper told reporters he had known Luntz "for many years," but denied his party employed the controversial pollster.[3]

HARPER USED the manipulation of language very well during the 2008–2009 prorogation controversy, when the Liberals and New Democrats sought to form a coalition government, with cabinet ministers from both parties and parliamentary support by the Bloc Québécois. What was a legitimate constitutional option was remade into an attempted *coup d'état*. "Coalition" became a political obscenity. When used against political opponents it puts candidates on the defensive. Governor General Michaëlle Jean's decision to shut down Parliament at a time when the prime minister obviously did not have the confidence of the majority of MPs was a huge setback for the supremacy of the elected legislature. It flew in the face of the precedent set in the King-Byng Affair of 1926 when the Governor General forced Prime Minister King to face the music in the House of Commons.

As constitutional scholar Andrew Heard wrote of the Harper-Jean showdown, "By granting prorogation, the Governor General not only allowed the prime minister to escape almost certain defeat in a confidence motion, but she also set the stage for every prime minister to follow suit. With this precedent, any prime minister can demand that the governor general suspend Parliament whenever he or she believes a successful vote of no confidence is imminent." The whole thing may sound academic, but, for example, Joe Clark would have been able to save his government in 1979 if he'd been able to get the Governor General to shut down Parliament. Instead, he lost a confidence test by just six votes, and Pierre Trudeau was returned to power in the election that followed.[4]

Harper would shut down Parliament again in December 2009, partly to allow the government to work on security for the 2010 Winter Olympics in Vancouver. The prestigious *Economist* observed with appropriate dry wit that Canadian parliamentarians "cannot, apparently, cope with Parliament's deliberations while dealing with the country's economic troubles and the challenge of hosting the Olympics."[5]

Harper is not an easy man to work for. Gerry Nicholls's description of toiling with Harper at the National Citizens Coalition is most people's idea of working for the boss from hell. It appears Harper's people-handling skills have not improved much. The Prime Minister's Office has a revolving door. Chiefs of staff, who run the day-to-day operations of the PMO, don't stay long. Directors of communication hold on for about a year. William Stairs, Harper's first communications director as prime minister, lasted less than a month. He was forced out when he asked the prime minister for more leeway to deal with the hostile reaction from the media and the public over Harper's decision to entice former Liberal cabinet minister David Emerson to cross the floor of the House of Commons for a Tory cabinet seat. Stairs believed the bad publicity over Emerson's appointment had dragged on for weeks because Harper had kept Emerson away from the media, and neither Harper nor Emerson had come close to giving the public a reasonable excuse for what seemed to be an overly cute move. Stairs had set up a phone-in press conference to try to clear the air. Emerson hadn't shown up, pleading he'd been caught in traffic. A media storyline of a minister-in-hiding turned into one of a minister who supposedly didn't have a cell phone.[6]

Harper had eight directors of communications in his first six years in office. For many of them, their biggest problem was that Harper does not actually take communications advice from anyone, except maybe his wife. The prime minister does set the tone, though, for the crowd of frat boys in short pants who work in his office. And they live in a world where, as they walk through the halls covered with pictures of their leader, they are reminded that it's his will that must be done.

These staffers are not very popular, even in their own party. Keith Beardsley, former deputy chief of staff for issues management to Harper, noticed a distinct distaste among Tory backbench MPs for taking orders from what he called "the boys in short pants." Even cabinet ministers could not convince the Prime Minister's Office to reconsider its position on an issue once it had been settled in the boardrooms of the Langevin Block and the talking points had been written by Harper's people. And there was not a lot of respect on the Hill for Harper's staffers. "There has been more than one instance within the government of an applicant being interviewed for a junior position in a minister's office, and being turned down for lack of experience, only to be hired by the PMO and put in charge of the people who had rejected them," Beardsley wrote in the fall of 2012. "That doesn't make for a lot of confidence on the ministerial side."[7]

Some observers—such as former Harper confidants and staffers Gerry Nicholls, Tom Flanagan, Bob Plamandon and Bruce Carson— have described a prime minister prone to ugly depressions and to frightening and unpleasant mood swings. "He can be suspicious, secretive, and vindictive, prone to sudden eruptions of white hot rage over meaningless trivia, at other times falling into weeklong depressions in which he is incapable of making decisions," Flanagan wrote in *Persona Non Grata: The Death of Free Speech in the Internet Age*. Nicholls was a little kinder, telling a reporter, "I would see Stephen sometimes get morose and sad but it never affected his ability to do his job. Yes, sometimes he would get depressed, but he was always a hard worker and always doing his job."

Bob Plamondon wrote of periods where Harper had "gone dark," and in *The Longer I'm Prime Minister*, journalist Paul Wells describes ugly moods that last several hours. Wells quotes an anonymous person who worked with the prime minister saying, "He comes into the office sometimes in a bad mood and that will affect how he sees things throughout the day. And if he comes in a good mood no one can do anything wrong." The classic example of Harper's moodiness came during the 2009 prorogation controversy, when Stéphane Dion seemed on the verge of cobbling together a governing coalition. Harper was almost immobilized with shock and depression until Dion made the tactical mistake of including the Bloc Québécois at a press conference announcing the coalition. Harper realized how English Canada would see that, and quickly regained his feet.[8]

Jason MacDonald, Harper's communications director in 2014, denied claims that the prime minister had been treated for depression, or that his funk, however it manifested itself, seriously affected his ability to lead the country. "It's odd that after not having worked on the Hill in almost a decade, and in the context of defending his own outrageous comments on child pornography, Mr. Flanagan comes forward with these ridiculous allegations," MacDonald said in an email to Parliament Hill reporters. "As the public knows, and as the Prime Minister's record shows, he's had no difficulties making decisions in good times or bad."[9]

But Harper's combative nature and his need to pick fights, whether fuelled by depression or by his own personal wiring, could well be the political death of him, Flanagan believes. Taking on people who run the country's institutions and attacking the officers of Parliament, the Supreme Court, and others who seem to get in his way could eventually cost the Conservatives power. "That narrative is largely built, it's already there," Flanagan said at an Ottawa book launch in the spring of 2014, "and that's pretty dangerous to your continuation in power."[10]

POLITICS, POLITICAL PARTIES and elected representatives are pawns in the game. So are the segments of the population that Harper wants as friends and needs as enemies. For, in this type of politics, enemies are important: the base wants to see the destruction of enemies like the media, unions and the courts, and it wants to see some damp scalps. Winning arguments is not enough.

That means the Conservative Party—and, to be fair, the Liberal Party and the New Democratic Party, since they, too, have embraced hardball politics—is a vehicle that is used to win office for a new governing clique. It doesn't matter what a party stood for in the past. And quite often, it also doesn't matter what the party stands for now. It's a machine for raising money, attracting volunteers and hiring people to run a national leader's tour and country-wide ad campaigns. In a national survey of 1,807 Canadians conducted by the public-interest think tank Samara in 2013, the majority of those polled said political parties exist mainly to get candidates elected. The parties aren't there to listen to members' views on how the country should be governed.

Poll respondents weren't happy with that. They believed "recruiting candidates and competing in elections" should be the least important job for political parties. Only 4 per cent of them ranked it the number one priority, so they're unlikely to join one. Samara argues that the poll result shows that the focus of political parties on winning elections comes at the expense of real grassroots democracy. Some 69 per cent of respondents agreed or strongly agreed that "candidates and political parties are interested only in people's votes, not their opinions." If the poll results are extrapolated, more than half of Canadians believe political parties' first priority should be "reaching out to Canadians," but the parties were awarded the lowest grade for that work.

Earlier research from Samara showed that Canadians believe a member of Parliament's most important job was also to "represent the views of constituents," and again, awarded MPs a failing grade for performance in this area. Together, these two findings send Canada's political leadership—regardless of party—a dire message:

Canadians want to be heard and represented by parties, and they firmly believe this is not happening.[11]

By and large, the people polled by Samara are right. Political parties are no place for old ladies in tennis shoes who want to dabble in politics. They are magnets for sociopaths attracted by money and power. During the Nixon years, the frat boys who tried to screw their political enemies by both legal and illegal means were called "ratfuckers." Quite a few still wear that label with some pride.

But to crush your opponents these days, you need money. In the 2006 election, which pitted the wounded government of Paul Martin against a Tory machine that, after years in the wilderness, now saw itself with a shot at power, the Tory campaign managers came across a way to do an end run around election spending rules. The extra money that they raised was used to saturate the country with nasty ads.

This "in and out" scheme was a complicated way to launder money and to allow the Conservatives to outspend Paul Martin. The Tories did not invent it. In 2002, the Bloc Québécois developed a system to cook local riding campaign books to make it look like candidates spent more money than they actually did. Elections Canada then reimbursed about half of that money. With both the Tories and the Bloc, money was paid out to "volunteers" who then donated it back to the party. That way, it looked like the local campaigns were spending, and raising, far more money. The scheme was exposed when the Bloc was stiffed by former MP Jean-Paul Marchand.[12] During his failed re-election campaign, he had agreed to push $66,000 through his local bank account and redirect the money to the party's headquarters. When Marchand didn't go through with the deal, the Bloc sued him for breach of contract, demanding $36,000. The party won the case, but the judge knocked $20,000 off the debt, leaving Marchand owing just $16,362.[13] The Martin government, seeing how the scheme worked, tried to bring in a law against it, but the bill died when the government fell in 2006.

During that election, the Conservatives raised so much money that they couldn't legally spend all of it on national advertising and campaign staff. The party distributed the cash to riding associations, who kicked it back to headquarters to use it the same way the Bloc had. The Tories took $1.3 million of the $18.3 million they raised, gave it to local candidates, and those candidates then flipped the money back to the national headquarters to use on "local" ads. In fact, they were really national ads, but with a tag line saying the ad was "paid for by . . . (insert local candidate's name here)." Elections Canada became suspicious when most of the "local" ad invoices were billed by one firm in Toronto. Under questioning from an Elections Canada investigator, ad executives said they had never worked for local candidates, talked to them or billed them. The Tories denied falsifying documents but would eventually admit to "alterations" to divide up the invoices to be billed to riding associations.

Just a few months into Harper's first term, Chief Electoral Officer Marc Mayrand said his agency would not pay almost $800,000 in refunds that the riding associations had billed for. The Tories filed a lawsuit for the money, but eventually, Elections Canada won the case. In April 2008, the RCMP and Elections Canada investigators raided Conservative Party headquarters in Ottawa. Someone, likely an Elections Canada staffer, tipped media about the raid, and Tories were horrified to see it on the television news networks. A House of Commons committee began an investigation of the "in and out" scandal, but the Tories engaged in a series of stall tactics. The committee chair, Tory Gary Goodyear (a future Harper minister), was so dedicated to not getting to the bottom of the scandal that his fellow MPs passed a vote of non-confidence against him.

On February 24, 2011, four Conservative national strategists were charged with overspending over one million dollars in the 2006 election. They were also accused of submitting "false or misleading" documents to Elections Canada. Just over a year later, they made a plea deal in which the Tories agreed to repay $230,000 in taxpayer money and pay $55,000 in fines in return for the dropping of charges against individual party strategists. To the Tories, this was "vindication," despite the fact that Elections Canada had proven that the party had cheated in the election that brought it to power. The fact that Elections Canada had investigated the scheme added yet one more reason for Harper to hold a grudge against the agency and its head, Mayrand. Eventually, accounts would be settled.

BUT OTHERS WOULD FEEL the sting first. KAIROS is an international aid organization run by the Anglican Church of Canada, the Evangelical Lutheran Church in Canada, the Presbyterian Church in Canada, the United Church of Canada, the Quakers, the Mennonite Central Committee of Canada and several Roman Catholic bodies including the Canadian Conference of Catholic Bishops. Those churches chipped in to pay and manage KAIROS's good works in poor countries. Near the end of September 2009, the president of the Canadian International Development Agency recommended KAIROS receive $7,098,758 to help pay for its foreign aid work. Two months later, Bev Oda, the minister responsible for CIDA, signed the recommendation, but supposedly changed it to say KAIROS should "not" get the money, and a few days later signed a letter to KAIROS telling the church group that its foreign projects would not get funding.

KAIROS's supporters said the agency was under attack because the Harper government believed it was anti-Israel. Jason

Kenney, the minister of citizenship and immigration, had told an Israeli audience in the fall of 2009 that the Harper government would stop giving money to any group that was anti-Semitic. In KAIROS's case, Kenney told the Israelis, the group was engaged in the boycott, divestment and sanctions campaign against Israel, an accusation KAIROS denied. Over the next year, Oda's claim that she had denied KAIROS funding because the agency didn't meet CIDA criteria fell apart. CIDA officials confirmed that they not only approved the grant, but wanted to increase the amount KAIROS got from the government. In 2010, testifying at a parliamentary committee, Oda denied adding the word "not" to the CIDA document. House of Commons Speaker Peter Milliken ruled that the document had been deliberately tampered with by mysterious and unknown persons. The issue dragged on through parliamentary hearings, where Oda denied the document had been changed by Kenney or someone in the Prime Minister's Office. Then, in February 2011, Oda admitted she had told someone in her office to alter the recommendation.[14]

If that's confusing to you, don't be alarmed. Dozens of people who are paid to understand this stuff could not keep the lies, half-truths, semi-denials and spin straight, either.

The government also went after the women's group MATCH, which operated in the Third World, and an organization called the International Centre for Human Rights and Democratic Development, which was attacked by the PMO for its stance on Israel. A few hours after one particularly nasty meeting in January 2010, Rémy Beauregard, the organization's president, died of a heart attack. Two years later, Harper shut the agency down.

Academics also came under fire from the PMO and the Tories. Two University of Ottawa law professors who wrote critical newspaper opinion pieces believe the Tories were responsible for Access to Information requests probing their university expense accounts. (The University of Ottawa refuses to divulge the names of the people who asked for the data.) And when a University of Ottawa history professor wrote an op-ed piece opposing Harper's "Quebec is a Nation" resolution, Marjory LeBreton, the Conservatives' leader in the Senate, wrote a letter to chancellor Huguette Labelle demanding the professor be brought to heel. The university told LeBreton to take a hike: "Universities have faculty members who are outspoken on a whole range of issues," David Mitchell, vice-president of university relations, wrote to LeBreton. "And they have the freedom to do so." So LeBreton wrote a nasty letter to the *Ottawa Citizen*, which published it.[15]

And Harper's team doesn't like artists much, either, especially when they get in the way of the agendas of big corporations. Lobbyists in Ottawa make more money from arguing the case of big business on copyright law changes than from any other issue. In 2011, the Canadian Conference of the Arts learned that its $390,000-a-year grant from the federal government would be cut. It was about 75 per cent of the arts group's income. The Canadian Conference of the Arts asked the Harper government for a one-time grant of just under $800,000 to help it set up a fundraising system to ease it through the transition to a privately funded agency. The Department of Canadian Heritage offered about one-quarter of that amount, telling the arts group to use the money to wind up its operations. Why was the group, which cost very little, was praised by bureaucrats for being careful with its money and represented a wide swath of the arts—including the National Ballet of Canada; Royal Conservatory of Music; Alliance of Canadian Cinema, Television and Radio Artists; and the National Theatre School— effectively put out of business? Partly, said observers, because the Canadian Conference of the Arts opposed changes to copyright law that, it said, would cost its members and other Canadian artists $126 million a year.[16]

In 2010, the government pulled funding from the Toronto theatre and music festival SummerWorks because it booked a play that was attacked by pro-government bloggers and conservative journalists for supposedly glorifying terrorism. SummerWorks was hit hard by the yanking of its grant, since money from the federal government covered about 20 per cent of its expenses. (The federal grant was restored in 2012.)[17]

Protesters saw the nasty side of the Harper government during the June 2010 G20 heads of government meeting in Toronto, when more than 1,100 people were arrested and held in pens at a fetid makeshift jail on Eastern Avenue. It was the largest mass arrest in Ontario history. Police even went into areas that were, supposedly, set aside for peaceful protest. Alok Mukherjee, chair of the Toronto Police Services Board, believes the RCMP took over Toronto that weekend and, along with 10,000 Ontario Provincial Police officers who arrived in the city on the second day of the protests, used the G20 protest as a pretext to sweep the streets of people. Several journalists were arrested, as were bystanders. The police were given extra powers under a secret regulation drafted by the Ontario Liberal provincial government. In the end, 800 people were released without charge after spending hours or days locked in pens. It was one of the post-9/11 police actions, like those in Ferguson, Missouri, in the summer of 2014, that caused people on both sides of the political spectrum to worry that the police have become too militarized and politicized. In the end, the gross violations of Torontonians' civil rights likely contributed to the police chief, Bill Blair, losing his job in 2014.

And the Harper frat boys don't always hide behind the cops. At the 2006 Liberal leadership convention, Tories tried to make sure that the man they most feared, Bob Rae, was not elected leader of the Liberal Party. James Moore, the long-time citizenship minister, was put in charge of screwing Rae. He showed up at the convention to hand out buttons saying "Make Bob the first NDP prime minister" and "Vote Bob. Who needs Ontario?" He later told reporters, "There's a reason we handed out so many of these. The Liberals don't know how to play poker." Doug Finley, one of the campaign strategists who would soon be charged in the "in and out" money laundering scandal, forged a fake Conservative memo that was leaked to newspapers. The note said the party was terrified of Michael Ignatieff and wanted Bob Rae to win. (In the end, the Liberals chose Stéphane Dion.)[18]

But if you really want to anger this government, try blocking one of the oil industry's projects. Opponents of the Keystone XL oilsands bitumen pipeline between Hardisty, Alberta, and Steele City, Nebraska, and the Northern Gateway—a $6-billion, 1,200-kilometre pipeline between Bruderheim, Alberta, and Kitimat, B.C.—say these pipelines would harm the environment.

Northern Gateway opponents have been targeted by Canada's police and intelligence agencies. The National Energy Board is supposed to be an objective tribunal that listens fairly to all sides of the pipeline debate. Sheila Leggett, who was heading a panel studying the feasibility of the Northern Gateway pipeline, had the RCMP and CSIS investigate environmental and First Nations opponents of the plan. She did it even though she had already been told by the RCMP that there was no evidence of lawbreaking by any of the Northern Gateway opponents.[19]

CSIS and the RCMP spied on the Sierra Club, the Forest Ethics Advocacy Association and the Council of Canadians. The National Energy Board's security division, the RCMP and CSIS agents poked though YouTube videos, Facebook accounts, and monitored websites such as rabble.ca and genuinewitty.com and

Twitter users like poormansmedia. What's even more outrageous, they even spied on Green Party leader Elizabeth May, telling the National Energy Board that she had spoken at a rally of Northern Gateway opponents.

"This is not what you do in a free society," May said in an interview with the online publication *Blacklock's Reporter*, which broke the story of the Energy Board's spy campaign. "Nobody is threatening them, but the National Energy Board is still acting as though legitimate public participation in their hearings represents some kind of threat. That's deeply troubling. The implication of the National Energy Board contacting the RCMP and CSIS because these people may interfere with hearings is disturbing and anti-democratic," May said. "A regulator is supposed to be independent of one interest group or the other. A regulator is supposed to have an open mind. A regulator should not be concerned with groups that oppose a proposal—especially when the RCMP tell them there is no security threat."[20]

She is convinced the country's intelligence agencies were spying on her, and other environmentalists, long before Stephen Harper became prime minister. "I always assumed so," she said, when asked whether she knew CSIS was watching her. "And I assumed so before Stephen Harper, and I'm trying to get access to my CSIS file because I believe it would be interesting. I assume that anyone who does any public activism in this country, given the scope of the anti-terrorism laws passed after 9/11, is being watched." May said the British newspaper *The Guardian* got briefing notes written for the energy companies by CSIS, the RCMP and the Communications Security Establishment Canada (CSEC), which is only supposed to spy on people outside Canada. "That means they're also doing foreign spying, as well as domestic spying, probably spying on environmentalists and Indigenous groups in other countries," May said.[21]

In February 2014, the B.C. Civil Liberties Association, on behalf of the groups targeted by CSIS and the RCMP, filed complaints against the investigators. Josh Paterson, executive director of the civil liberties group, said, "There are things in the documents that are very suggestive of covert means being used. We can't conclude that because there's things blacked out . . . That's why we're asking for an investigation. What we're hoping here is to find out more about what's happening."

Paterson said the spies passed on the information to Enbridge, the company that wants to build the pipeline. The civil liberties group was leaked an agenda for a "classified briefing for energy and utilities sector stakeholders" that was held by Natural Resources Canada, with presentations by RCMP and CSIS representatives. The BCCLA charged that the information that CSIS and the RCMP gave to the National Energy Board could "compromise these groups' ability to participate fully and effectively before the NEB."

Tory cabinet minister Joe Oliver tried to run interference for the government. "The safety of Canadians is a priority for our government. As part of its commitment to safety, the National Energy Board may conduct a security assessment prior to a regulatory hearing," he said. "The NEB will often work with the RCMP to protect the safety of everyone involved. Neither I, nor any member of my department, gave instructions to any federal agency in this matter."[22]

The government tried to strengthen its case with a memo, written to the National Energy Board by Tim O'Neil, senior criminal intelligence research specialist with Federal Policing Criminal Operations at RCMP headquarters in Ottawa, that warned it was "highly likely" oilsands opponents would break the law or threaten regulators. Strangely, O'Neil added, the Mounties couldn't find evidence of a "direct or specific criminal threat."

The O'Neil memo, dated April 19, 2013, was released to the media through Access to Information. The memo continued:

> *Opponents of the oil sands have used a variety of protest actions to draw attention to the oil sands' negative environmental impact, with the ultimate goal of forcing the shutdown of the Canadian petroleum industry. The anti-petroleum and anti-nuclear movement has attempted to interfere within the federal regulatory hearings and have used coordinated/mass interventions that have at times bogged down the regulatory hearings. In response, the federal government has instituted new regulatory procedures that will limit who may make formal presentations at the National Energy Board's public hearings . . . It is the focus of attention by many anti-oil sands, anti-Canadian petroleum and anti-petroleum pipeline operations, and it is highly likely that the National Energy Board may expect to receive threats to its hearings and its board members.*[23]

Pipeline opponents were not really too surprised that the National Energy Board was in bed with CSIS and the RCMP. They knew an oil lobby group co-founded by Douglas Black, a Tory senator from Alberta, wrote the 2012 law that requires people who want to speak at National Energy Board hearings to prove they have "relevant information or expertise" and are "directly affected" by a proposed development. Clayton Ruby, counsel for the Forest Ethics Advocacy Association, said the wording of the amendments to the National Energy Board Act buried in the federal budget omnibus bill looks just like a passage in a 2012 report by the Energy Policy Institute of Canada. Enbridge, Imperial Oil, Rio Tinto Alcan, and Canadian Energy Pipeline Association were founding members of the Energy Policy Institute.

"The government is totally in the hands of the oil industry,"

Ruby said in the fall of 2013. "They are two sides of the same face." His client sued the federal department National Resources Canada in Federal Court, saying that the rule change violated Charter-protected free speech. The Forest Ethics Advocacy Association wanted the right to argue against Enbridge's Trailbreaker project, a pipeline that would carry Alberta bitumen from Sarnia, Ontario, to a refinery in Montreal.[24]

Natural Resources Minister Joe Oliver then went after James Hansen, a former NASA scientist, for saying expansion of Alberta oilsands projects means "game over for the climate." Hansen had also called the Harper team a desperate and "Neanderthal" government. Oliver, on a trip to Washington to lobby for the Keystone XL pipeline, warned Hansen would regret his comments.

On CBC Radio's Saturday morning political show *The House*, Hansen lashed out at Oliver for saying scientists who oppose oilsands expansion are "crying wolf." Hansen, unlike many Canadian scientists, refused to be muzzled. Oliver, he said, was "beginning to get worried because the [U.S.] secretary of state, John Kerry, is well-informed on the climate issue and he knows that his legacy and President Obama's is going to depend upon whether they open this spigot to these very dirty, unconventional fossil fuels. We can't do that without guaranteeing disasters for young people and future generations. The current government is a Neanderthal government on this issue, but Canada can actually be a leader." Hansen said British Columbia's carbon tax is a positive step. "I have hopes that Canada will actually be a good example for the United States but the present government is certainly not. They're in the hip pocket of the fossil fuel industry, as you can see, but that doesn't mean that the Canadian people are," Hansen told the radio audience.[25] These were just the kind of comments that would cause apoplexy to such oilsands cheerleaders as Harper's

Prime Minister's Office, the Canadian Association of Petroleum Producers, the Sun News Network, and *Ethical Oil* author Ezra Levant. He and his fans started an association with the same name to push the idea that Canadian oil was not only safely available to the United States, but that the profits from our oil do not go to fund oppression and war. Opponents on both sides of the border said the environmental damage and the risk of pipeline spills did not outweigh the national security benefits of Canadian oil.

WHILE CSIS and the RCMP don't give opponents of the Harper government the full bare-light-bulb-and-electrodes secret police treatment, Ottawa does have ways of making their lives miserable. For one thing, they can audit critics' tax returns, take away any charitable status and intimidate donors. Normally, the Canada Revenue Agency audits about 10 per cent of the country's charities, about eight hundred groups, every year. Under Canadian law, charities can't use more than 10 per cent of their money for advocacy or politics. Those charities that can't give tax deduction receipts have a very hard time raising money. In the 2012 budget, Finance Minister Jim Flaherty set aside $8 million to pay for extra audits of environmental groups to determine whether they should be stripped of their charitable status. If they lost that status, the environmental groups would no longer be able to issue tax deduction receipts to donors, which would severely hurt their ability to raise money. The audits targeted the David Suzuki Foundation, Tides Canada, West Coast Environmental Law, The Pembina Foundation, Environmental Defence, Équiterre, the writers' group PEN Canada and Ecology Action Centre. Also targeted were OXFAM and Amnesty International, two foreign aid groups that many Tories consider too left-wing.

John Bennett, head of Sierra Club Canada, called the audits "a war against the [environmental] sector . . . We have an important role to play in our society and we want to play that role," said Bennett. "But we need a governing system that actually welcomes public dialogue instead of discouraging it." Ross McMillan, CEO of Tides Canada, told CBC news he blamed the audits on Ethical Oil. People working for the pro-oilsands group had said publicly that its lawyers had filed complaints to the Canada Revenue Agency about Tides Canada, The David Suzuki Foundation and Environmental Defence.[26]

Why would the government go after environmental organizations, especially those that oppose oil pipelines? To thwart terrorism, of course. At least that's what Finance Minister Jim Flaherty argued when he brought down the 2014 budget. And, in the same breath, he said the taxman, not the Harper government, decides who will be audited. "We don't choose who is audited by the CRA [Canada Revenue Agency]. That's up to the CRA," Flaherty said. "We *do* give policy direction, and one of the policy directions is that charities are not to be permitted to accept money from terrorist organizations in Canada." Flaherty was asked about the audit of environmental groups, but he stuck to the terrorism talking points.

"Charities are not to be permitted to accept money from sources that are illegal. We also have FINTRAC [the agency that's supposed to fight money laundering and other criminal cash transfers], which reports to parliament through me and it tracks transactions from around the world . . . I think if Canadians give money to charity they expect it to be for charitable uses and not other uses," Flaherty said. In another speech, he warned: "If I were an environmental charity using charitable money, tax-receipted money, for political purposes, I would be cautious." And he told reporters: "The concern though remains the same, that there are some terrorist organizations, there are some organized crime organizations that launder money through charities and that make donations to charities and that's not the purpose of charitable donations in Canada, so we are being increasingly strict on the subject."[27]

New Democrat Murray Rankin said the audits are politically motivated.

> *These environmental groups have gone through super audits—not the usual routine CRA audits, the most rigorous auditing by the CRA. This is the "A team" that comes into town from Ottawa, sent to rattle the cages. They [the CRA] haven't found anything yet, but they have cost these groups an incredible amount of money in audit fees—which takes the spending away from what the groups are supposed to do, which is environmental education and advocacy. This a serious allegation—to use the state tax system against government opponents. But the dots are starting to connect, especially combined with the BC Civil Liberties Association's allegations against CSIS and the RCMP.[28]*

Soon afterwards, environmentalists got their hands on a copy of a government strategy document that calls First Nations, environmentalists, the media and competing industry groups "enemies." The document, with interesting frankness, describes the supposedly neutral National Energy Board as an "ally," along with oil and gas companies, industry associations, the government of Alberta and several Canadian government departments including Natural Resources Canada, the Aboriginal and Northern Affairs Department, Environment Canada and the Privy Council Office. The strategy plan was written in 2011. It describes how European politicians, "especially from the ruling and influential parties" should be targeted by government-paid lobbyists. The

221

Europeans would be pressured to oppose climate-change policies that would require Canadian oilsands operations to reduce greenhouse gas emissions. "While Europe is not an important market for oilsands-derived products, Europe legislation/regulation, such as the EU Fuel Quality Directive, has the potential to impact the industry globally," said the document, which was obtained by Climate Action Network Canada.[29]

Sometimes, the Tories are able to convince opposition MPs to support their censorship and Harper's attacks on environmentalists. For example, Green Party leader Elizabeth May was the only MP to vote against second-reading approval of a bill that makes it nearly impossible for environmentalists to photograph the annual Atlantic coast seal hunt. In May 2014, MPs voted 258 to 1 to extend a security cordon around the killing zones to 1.6 kilometres from the previous 900 metres. "It's an issue that has been deliberately polarized," May said. "It puts virtually every MP in the House of Commons on the wrong side of the majority of public opinion across Canada." Conservative MP Greg Kerr, who sponsored Bill C-555, admitted the law targets critics of the hunt who would "disrupt the industry." The law allows the RCMP to arrest everyone but sealers or federally licensed "observers" within the hunt area. Observer permits only cost $25, but the Department of Fisheries has refused licences to news photographers, animal rights protesters and the European Union environment commissioner. "For decades now there have been many radical groups that have wanted to disrupt the seal hunt," Kerr, MP for West Nova, Nova Scotia, said in the House of Commons. "Any person failing to respect the condition of the licence can indeed be fined or arrested."[30]

Censorship can be as blatant as banning photographers from the seal hunt with a law passed in open Parliament or as subtle as a few well-placed phone calls. Reporters who have broken stories about the Harper Tories have been subjected to the full force of the conservative media and blogosphere. In addition, perhaps even more damaging, their bosses often get veiled threats from the prime minister's operatives. Those kinds of complaints, which can be career-killers, used to be fairly common in small-town media and more rare in the national press, but now they're common everywhere.

In October 2012, Jill Winzoski, a reporter at the *Selkirk Record* in Manitoba, was fired because one of the owners of the *Record* and Winzoski's editor got an email from Tory MP James Bezan complaining about her "biased" reporting. "This MP has complained about my articles for a while now, pulling his advertising from the *Record* and other local papers over news stories or letters to the editor that were critical of the federal government. I was instructed about six months ago to refrain from any articles about the federal government, and complied—albeit with some degree of disgust—in the interest of keeping my job," Winzoski told columnist Michael Harris, who took up her case. Her real crime seems to have been signing a petition against the proposed takeover of the Nexen oil company by the state-owned China National Oil Company, a policy issue that was extremely unlikely to make the pages of the *Selkirk Record*.[31]

Stephen Maher and Glen McGregor, the reporters who broke the robocalls voter suppression story (McGregor also had the scoop on Senator Mike Duffy's housing claims), got the full Harper Machine gears. On Sun News Network, Ezra Levant came very close to saying Maher had once been kicked out of a conservative conference for being drunk. (In fact, he had mistakenly gone to a private party in a downtown Ottawa club that had been rented for the evening). Brian Lilley said on the Sun News Network show *Byline* that McGregor had worked as a DJ at a downtown Ottawa strip club (a job McGregor did have in university) and told his viewers that McGregor's mother, who had recently died of cancer, had worked for the New Democrats. Both reporters have been subjected to ugly personal attacks by members of the Blogging Tories.

Some Hill reporters say they've been targeted by calls to their bosses, but few are willing to go into detail out of fear of getting into hot water with their employers and stirring up more trouble with the Tories. The calls—and reporters in the Parliamentary Press Gallery say they are common—are often made by low-level media relations flacks who, years ago, would never have poked their heads up. One or two of these calls, if made to relatively brave news executives, won't cause many problems. But a steady stream of them can be corrosive to a journalist's reputation and career. Eventually, it becomes easier to just transfer the reporter to another beat.

That kind of pressure results in self-censorship, the most effective kind of news control. The science of self-censorship has been known for years: World War II press censors relied on it to keep journalists in line. In Canada, reporters, many of whom are neither particularly bright nor heroic, learn fast that the safe course is also the easiest and the least stressful. Reporters who go years without complaints about their accuracy or bias are the kind of people who are promoted into news media management, making it even easier for flacks and politicians to turn off the information taps.

CHAPTER 9

House of Clowns:
Making a Joke out of Parliament

They're a contemptible lot, and you'll agree that I had my full share of the
qualities necessary to political life. I could lie and dissemble with the best,
give short change with a hearty clap on the shoulder, slip out from under long
before the blow fell, talk toady and turn tail as fast as a Yankee fakir selling
patent pills. Mark you, I've never been given to interfering in other folks
affairs if I could help, so I suppose that would have disqualified me.
But for a while, I did think of bribing my way into a seat.
—HARRY FLASHMAN, THE FICTIONAL NINETEENTH-CENTURY HEROIC
VILLAIN CREATED BY GEORGE MacDONALD FRASER[1]

Canadians elect just 308 people to oversee a government that spends about $250 billion a year, owes more than $600 billion, employs more than 250,000 people, sets the level of much of our taxation, passes dozens of laws and hundreds of regulations each year, can take us into war, decides which people can come into the country, and makes rules about the hit songs played on radio stations. If those people can't think and speak for themselves, we have no representation at all.

Garth Turner is a former business editor of the *Toronto Sun,* author of a string of financial advice books and a successful investor in his own right. He was Progressive Conservative MP from the swing riding of Halton, west of Toronto, from 1988 to 1993 and revenue minister in Kim Campbell's cabinet. He was re-elected to the House of Commons and fired from Harper's Conservative caucus in 2006.

Turner has a stubborn pigheadedness, which is great when he's on your side, not so much fun when he leaves the team.[2] Turner got along well enough during his five-year stretch on the Hill during Brian Mulroney's second term. By the time he got back to Ottawa, the Internet had come along, and Turner had built up a large online following for his rather pessimistic blog on real estate and personal finance. Now Turner was able to use those skills to communicate directly with his constituents and everyone else who wanted to know what was on his mind. His use of the Internet as an always-open microphone and his belief that the voters of Halton elected *him*, not just anyone in a Tory-blue suit, to Parliament, ensured a nasty collision with Stephen Harper, who seems to have believed neither.[3]

The blog, augmented with video podcasts, was a big hit with journalists and news junkies. And it often made news itself, partly for its content, partly for the fact that it existed at all. Other Tories, like Monte Solberg, were also skilled bloggers, but Solberg ended up in the cabinet, where solidarity was expected. Turner was never welcomed into Harper's inner sanctum, so he did not feel bound by cabinet confidentiality. Years after his political career imploded, Turner wrote a book called *Sheeple: Caucus Confidential in Stephen Harper's Ottawa*. In it, he tells the story of his seemingly oft-miserable life as, first, a Tory MP, then as an Independent, and finally, after a flirtation with the Green Party, a Liberal before losing his seat to Lisa Raitt in 2008.

His months in Canada's New Government began with a nasty caucus meeting just after the 2006 election, with Tory hit man John Baird opening the session with a question: "Mr. Chairman, who is Garth Turner? The media may love him, but he's hurting this party and this government by opening his mouth. Who does he think he is? Who is Garth Turner to tell us what we should be doing here?" Not long afterwards, Harper called Turner into his office in the Centre Block and put the suburban Toronto MP in his place.

"My bottom was barely in the chair when Harper let it fly," Turner later wrote.

I am very disappointed with you, he said. It got worse quickly, and the tone was unmistakable. Stephen Harper was condescending, belittling and menacing. Here was a man with whom I had exchanged perhaps 200 words in the last year, talking to a newly elected MP, a member of his own caucus, who had just succeeded in taking a riding from the Liberals after more than a decade—a riding that was a beachhead into the constituency-rich GTA—and he spoke to me as if I were a petulant, useless, idiot child. His voice was without a single shred of respect. No acknowledging I'd been in this office before, or in the Cabinet room down the hall, or had run to be leader of a legacy party. It was as if conservativism [sic] had started with the election of Stephen Harper as leader and led directly to this moment. Prior to that, he may have believed politicians bobbed like rudderless vessels on a sea of public opinion, blown helplessly by the winds of media know-it-alls. And he alone was out to change that.

The prime minister was angry that Turner had criticized Harper and Vancouver MP David Emerson, who was poached from the Liberals days after the 2006 election and put into the Tory cabinet.

Turner was against floor-crossing and thought the cabinet gambit was a very bad way to launch Canada's New Government.

> *How, I asked, could you have been critical of what Belinda Stronach did, and now turn around and cause this to happen? Harper glared. He pointed out to me that he had not voted for legislation in the last Parliament that would have banned floor-crossing (although half his caucus did) . . . He was done with that. We moved on to me. It was not going well. Harper said he felt he could not trust me. "To put it charitably, you were independent during the campaign." The penny was dropping now . . . He turned to look squarely at me and said, "I don't need a media star in my caucus."* [4]

In the end, Harper taught Turner a lesson. Constituents simply would not be allowed access through the Internet to view official Ottawa from the inside. They were not to know how the political sausage was made. Turner found the result frustrating and sad,[5] especially after Harper kicked him out of the Tory caucus, leaving him with virtually no chance of being re-elected. "For individual politicians, a web-based society brings demands for an unachievable level of accountability and openness, wherein every position, belief, public vote, personal action, and past statement becomes the standard against which one is judged. No wonder no other federal elected official in the country followed my lead. No wonder it destroyed me."[6]

MANY MPs ARRIVE in Ottawa believing they are the voice of their 100,000 or so constituents back home. Like Turner, they're soon disabused of that notion. In fact, they are expected to be full-time public relations people for their parties, not legislators. If they are very lucky, they have a shot at a cabinet spot or might be elected Speaker of the House. Otherwise, they are supposed to trudge back to their ridings every weekend and show up at as many store openings and fiftieth-anniversary parties as possible. Even senior ministers are stuck with this work, and, for members living far from Ottawa, life as an MP ends up a blur of airport terminals and highways, and brief glimpses of their families and friends. No wonder about half of first-term MPs get divorced. To survive, and to keep alive any ambition, they must get along with their colleagues and with people in their party who have some power. For Tory MPs elected since 2006, that means avoiding any negative attention from Harper's Prime Minister's Office.

But these people are elected to be members of Parliament, not publicly paid glad-handers for their political parties. As MPs, their first priority should be making good laws and keeping a close watch on public spending. In fact, very few MPs consider attending the House of Commons to be an important part of their job. They may show up for an hour for Question Period, but they leave as soon as the show's over. They'll be assigned a few hours of "House duty" each month by their political party. From time to time, backbenchers are handed talking points for speeches on a bill that's being debated. Some MPs find interesting work on committees. But, for many, Ottawa is a lonely, unfriendly town where smart MPs find themselves without meaningful challenges.

Part of the problem lies with the media. Almost no debates of Parliament are covered, and only a few committee meetings get any media attention. Canada's newspapers used to give the House of Commons gavel-to-gavel coverage. That brought out party leaders and cabinet ministers to debates. The House of Commons often sat well into the night. And during World War II, there were even Saturday morning sessions. So even if a Churchill or Disraeli emerged from the backbenches of any of the parties these days, no one would know.

Until TV arrived, parliamentary debates were important and good debaters were rewarded with fame. But television replaced meaningful debate with sound bites. And news companies, including The Canadian Press national news service (which was originally established and heavily subsidized by the federal government to *ensure* Parliament was covered), simply stopped showing up. So did MPs, who saw no real need to stand in a near-empty chamber and literally talk to the walls. Often, the House of Commons doesn't even have quorum. A handful of MPs will sit in the chamber and debate among themselves. Transcripts of these debates may show up in the "householders," the flyers that MPs mail out to constituents, but most of those go straight into recycling bins.

It may be naive of the Garth Turners of the political world to believe they really are much more than publicly paid employees of their parties. It's necessary for our political system to have parties, and, despite what Canadians may say about partisanship, the people rely on these parties to bring forward candidates and to raise and debate issues. If we wanted a Parliament full of Independents, we would probably start voting for them. People do offer themselves as Independents and pledge to focus their attention solely on the needs of their constituents. They usually end up with a few dozen votes. In the few instances when Independents are elected, people vote for them because of one local issue, or because a popular MP has split with their own (unpopular) party and decided to go it alone, as Nova Scotia's former Conservative MP Bill Casey did.

To have a serious chance of being elected, a candidate has to make a deal with a party: support the platform and the leader, and, in return, get the benefit of the party's fundraising, national advertising, and team of political professionals and volunteers. For whatever it's worth, candidates also get to ride the leader's coattails. Many Canadians vote for leaders and parties, not local candidates, which explains why so many MPs are non-entities. But many good, hard-working people are also elected in all parties, and they are faced with a tough, sometimes soul-sucking, juggling act.

Since the 1850s, Canadian prime ministers have been very powerful. In many ways, our system is descended from the old colonial governments, with a council advising a royal governor holding strong executive powers. Legislators sat only as advisers and props (and, if on the government's side, distributors of the patronage that was so important to keeping the system working). A few private members—powerful MPs, some belonging to parties, some sitting as Independents, some having power over a handful of other MPs—did challenge the executive in the early post-Confederation years and brought the government down during the Pacific Scandal, when Sir John A. Macdonald was caught taking bribes from the backers of the Canadian Pacific Railway. But through most of the country's history, the cabinet and prime minister have been able to dominate MPs.

Still, in theory, MPs have quite a lot of power. The House of Commons "clearly occupies a central place in the country's political life," respected political scientist Donald Savoie recently wrote.

As R. MacGregor Dawson once observed, the House of Commons "can speak, as no body in the democracy can pretend to speak for the people . . . It serves as the people's forum and the highest political tribunal." It is the country's great debating chamber and the only national institution with direct political ties to all communities. It enables communities to organize themselves behind a political voice, and, once elected, that voice has a right to be heard in

Ottawa, however unwelcome it might be to other communities and other voices. In Canada, communities are free to elect even people dedicated to breaking up the country."[7]

Parliamentary privilege, the rights that give MPs the freedom to speak their minds without risk of lawsuits or prison, and to scrutinize government spending, was a hard-earned thing. Parliament is still, in theory, a court with serious powers, although, unlike legislators in Tudor and Stuart England, members of Canada's Parliament never got to use bills of attainder to commit political murder of their opponents. The House of Commons has the power to jail people. It hasn't sent anyone to the cells since 1913, although Privacy Commissioner George Radwanski came close to being tried at the bar of the House of Commons in 2003 for his expenses.[8] But, in reality, the agenda of the House of Commons, and the words spoken by many of its members, are created in the offices of the party leaders.

THE PRIME MINISTER has tremendous power to reward loyalty. All of the hiring in the Prime Minister's Office is at his discretion. The top jobs in the civil service and Crown corporations are also his to give, as are positions on immigration tribunals, federal commissions, boards of directors and federal courts. He appoints ambassadors and consuls. The Governor General, provincial lieutenant-governors and senators owe their jobs to him. In the House of Commons, about seventy government MPs hold some position of power or influence because of the good will of the prime minister. If they're lucky, they're members of cabinet, with the prestige and perks that come with heading, at least as figureheads, a federal department.

Cabinet ministers get some time with the prime minister, have communications and political staffers, access to some of the tools of patronage, use of the government's small fleet of business jets, better pay, and a chance to develop a higher public profile that may make them safer at election time. If they are very shrewd and discreet, they can quietly build the organization for a serious shot at the party leadership. Opposition MPs have slightly more independence, are expected to know more about policy issues, but have little real power in the political system, especially during a majority Parliament.[9]

But, for people on either side of the House, actually debating new laws in Parliament is just an afterthought to the public relations work of the permanent election campaign. All MPs spend much more time as full-time candidates than as lawmakers. They work very hard to be elected to a job that few of them actually put much time into: being active members of a legislative body.

May 13, 2014, was a typical afternoon in the House of Commons. I went into the chamber to see what was happening. MPs were debating the third reading of the so-called Fair Elections Act, the last task of the lower house before the bill went to the Senate. The Harper team had imposed closure to tightly limit the amount of time that MPs were given to debate the bill. Most of the heavy scrutiny of the law had taken place in a parliamentary committee. So, as MPs gave the bill its last few hours of debate before a parliamentary vote that was already a foregone conclusion, just twenty-two MPs were in the chamber. One MP, Joe Comartin, an NDP workhorse from Windsor, Ontario, was in the Speaker's chair. There was one member of the cabinet, one journalist, twenty people in the public galleries, and 286 empty seats. Two NDP MPs were talking to each other, three were reading, and the rest were typing on iPads, BlackBerrys or laptops. Joe Preston, a Conservative backbencher, was talking about the delights of speaking to kids in schools, which was, to him, one of the best parts of his job.

Compare that to the British Parliament, where MPs still have some real clout. They have the power to overthrow unpopular and overbearing party leaders, including prime ministers, and they use it. In August 2013, Britain's Conservative government introduced a non-binding motion asking for the House of Commons' support of military action against Syria for that country's use of chemical weapons against civilians in rebel-held areas. The motion was defeated 285 to 272. Prime Minister David Cameron said he respected the will of Parliament. It was clear that the people of Britain did not want military action, so there would be no attack by the United Kingdom against Syrian government forces. What's the possibility of that happening in modern Canada? Slim to none. MPs would debate using talking points and vote on straight party lines, if they were consulted at all.[10]

That's one reason why few important MPs actually spend their days in Parliament. Stephen Harper, during his years as opposition leader and while he's been prime minister, has never engaged in a debate on a law, no matter how important it might be. Only Elizabeth May, the leader of the Green Party (which is not actually a legal entity in the House of Commons because it does not have twelve MPs), shows up regularly to debate bills.

"I do believe it's the job to be in Parliament," May said.

I was elected as a member of Parliament. Other than being on a House committee—and I'm not allowed to be on one until the Green Party elects at least twelve MPs—my job is to represent my constituents, my job is to be in the House of Commons. That's what I was elected to do. My constituents expect that of me. I also believe participating in debates is important. Parliament is an import-

234

ant place. The fact that it's almost universally denigrated is a bad sign for democracy. I believe in Parliament, I love Parliament, I work in Parliament, and I want to elevate the tone of Parliament. That's why I'm there all the time.

The growth—and it's a trend over time—in the power of political parties is such that when MPs are elected they open a book to find out what the rules of Parliament are, they take all their instruction from the leaders' offices, and the leaders' offices hand out a duty roster. If it's not your time to be on House duty, you think you shouldn't be in the House of Commons. There's no reason why you shouldn't be. The place is empty most of the time. That's why I have more interventions on the record, in Hansard, than anyone else. I'm there all the time, and the reason why I'm there all the time is that these bills are the job of Parliament and my only way to probe the bills, to ask questions, to make points, to suggest ways to actually improve the bills, is to actually ask questions. Since Harper uses closure on every bill, the speaking roster rarely comes around to me, so that I can give a full speech. So my only opportunity to speak on these bills is in "questions and comments," and that's why I'm there all the time.[11]

Justin Trudeau saw things differently. In an attempt to head off the kind of savaging that Jack Layton gave Liberal leader Michael Ignatieff over his poor House of Commons attendance record during the 2011 leaders' debate, Trudeau's party sent out an email claiming the House of Commons simply wasn't worth bothering with. The email, posted on the Internet in the spring on 2014, claimed Trudeau went to 520 events in 105 cities in his first 387 days as leader. "So when Thomas Mulcair asks 5 questions in the House & gets the usual Conservative non-answers . . . But Justin Trudeau speaks to 600 university students about their future, which leader engages more Canadians?" the email asked in text embedded in its very hip graphics.[12]

EVEN IF TORY MPs wanted to risk the Garth Turner treatment, or if the Liberals and NDP did try to make Parliament the real focal point of debate on Canadian issues, they'd be up against an administration that has effectively crippled the House of Commons by limiting debate. Closure motions, which set limits on the amount of time MPs get to debate new laws, are imposed on almost every important piece of legislation. The Harper government limited debate on the Supporting Vulnerable Seniors and Strengthening Canada's Economy Act, the Safe Streets and Communities Act, the bill to ratify a free trade deal with Panama, the legislation to kill the long-gun registry, a new law that is supposed to enhance the accountability of the RCMP, the Safe Drinking Water for First Nations Act, the Not Criminally Responsible Reform Act (which makes it tougher for mentally ill offenders to get out of high-security institutions), the new Copyright Act (which strengthens the hand of big entertainment companies), a law regulating shared property rights of married people on First Nations lands, the First Nations Elections Act, the First Nations Financial Transparency Act, Fair Elections Act, Protecting Canada's Immigration System Act, Expansion and Conservation of Canada's National Parks Act, Canadian Museum of History Act, Tackling Contraband Tobacco Act, and various budgets.[13]

This makes for some very sloppy law-making. For instance, in the gigantic 2013 budget omnibus bill, which was rammed through Parliament by the Tories, the Canadian government "accidentally" doubled the corporate income tax on credit unions, on top of another tax increase on credit union profits. Opposition politicians and credit union executives never saw the tax increases coming, and no MP or senator, on either the government or opposition side, spotted the increases as the budget bill was rushed into law. There were no pre-budget consultations, no heads-up, not even a press release. Months after the budget was passed, accountants hired by Credit Union Central discovered the mistake. "It was pointed out this was a drafting error," said Gary Rogers, vice-president of financial policy at Credit Union Central. "We contacted the Department of Finance and were assured they will fix this retroactively." In fact, the extra tax was never collected.

"The mistake in the budget would drive credit unions right out of business," Ralph Goodale, a Saskatchewan Liberal MP and former finance minister in Paul Martin's Liberal government, said. "Instead of being taxed at the same rate as banks, they would have been more heavily taxed than banks." So who was the villain? Within the credit union movement, some people eyed their old sparring buddies in the chartered banks with some suspicion, but Goodale said his Bay Street sources told him the banks didn't lobby for the tax hike. They were just as surprised as credit union managers when it turned up in the budget. And it wasn't the only "drafting mistake" in that budget. Another Finance Department "error" would have doubled the tax on Brazilian cane sugar to $30 million and likely would have forced the closure of at least one of the country's three sugar refineries. That one was fixed before the refineries went broke.[14]

Governments had fair warning that omnibus bills are a bad idea. In 1994, a young Stephen Harper had warned Jean Chrétien:

> I would argue that the subject matter of the bill is so diverse that a single vote on the content would put members in conflict with their own principles . . . Second, in the interest of democracy I ask: How can members represent their constituents on these various areas

237

*when they are forced to vote in a bloc on such legislation and on
such concerns? We can agree with some of the measures but oppose
others. How do we express our views and the views of our constituents when the matters are so diverse? Dividing the bill into several
components would allow members to represent views of their constituents on each of the different components in the bill.*[15]

MPs on all side of the House are subject to the whips, the title of
the people who are in charge of making sure their party's MPs show
up to vote and that they follow the party line. Bruce Hyer, the NDP
member for Thunder Bay–Superior North, refused to be whipped
into voting with his party on the long-gun registry and found himself being disciplined by the NDP's leaders. He decided to sit as an
Independent and became the central character in a documentary
called *Whipped*, made by Mount Royal University journalism professor Sean Holman. Both Hyer and Holman believe MPs are just
puppets of their party leadership, and Canadians are ill served by a
House of Commons that is filled with MPs who are gagged. (Hyer
went on to join the Green Party).

Some MPs try to make a meaningful contribution to the governing of the country by introducing private member's bills. These
bills are rarely passed, and few of them even get serious debate, but
sometimes they do get through Parliament. They're either adopted
by the government and become one of its own laws, or they're so
sensible that there's no real excuse not to pass them on the spot.
Mostly, though, they're a way to stimulate debate on issues that are
important to government backbenchers and to opposition MPs.

Edmonton Tory MP Brent Rathgeber thought he had a winner.
He introduced a bill to force the Harper government to disclose the
salary of senior bureaucrats and employees of government-owned
corporations like VIA Rail, Canada Post and the CBC, creating a

so-called sunshine list, which already exists in several provinces and municipalities.

The proposed law was approved in principle by the House of Commons, but the government used its majority to change the wording of the bill so that the salaries of only a few public servants would be disclosed (though the CBC salaries would have been published). In June 2013, Rathgeber learned to his surprise and horror that, despite its talk about financial accountability, the Harper team actually opposes sunshine lists. Rathgeber asked that his bill be killed instead of ruined, and, when the leaders of his party refused, he quit the Conservative caucus. Speaker Andrew Scheer, himself a Tory MP, called Rathgeber's request to kill his own piece of legislation "an unprecedented situation."

The Alberta Tory backbench MP said: "I'm only doing what I need to do for myself and for my constituents. I don't think that I can continue to represent them when I am told how to vote, told what to speak. I support the government generally but I don't support it unequivocally," he said. "That created problems for me."[16]

The move shocked old-time Reformers and many Tory backbenchers. "I really believe—and it was an unwritten rule when I was in those positions—you don't amend a private member's bill at committee without the support of the sponsor. To me, that's sacrosanct. And to me, you look at what happened with Brent Rathgeber and his private member's bill, I thought that was tragic, to be honest," former Tory House whip Jay Hill told *The Globe and Mail* after speaking at the 2014 Manning Centre conservative conference in Ottawa.[17]

Rathgeber got some support from his normally gun-shy colleagues. Saskatoon MP Maurice Vellacott gave notice of a motion that he hoped would stop the government from muzzling backbenchers by blocking their private member's bills and motions.

"That kind of muzzling is a blight on democracy," the Tory MP wrote in a statement sent to Hill reporters. He called the committee's decisions "arbitrary," "capricious" and open to political interference.[18] Vellacott's motion didn't pass.

PARLIAMENT'S FIRST and most basic job is to make sure Canadians' tax money is used efficiently. Good governments provide the information that people need to determine whether public funds are well spent. Even Augustus Caesar, who wrote the financial books of the Roman Empire in his own hand, published accurate *ratione imperii*, "accounts of the empire," and had them publicly posted.[19] The House of Commons was created in the Middle Ages to set tax rates, collect the money and ensure that the government—back then, the king and his court—did not waste cash. MPs voted for "supply," the tax levy. They still do. And they were expected to paw through the government's accounts, looking for ways to save money. Governments are much bigger now, but unless MPs do this job, empire-builders and spendthrifts will burn through public funds. Conservatives may want less government, progressives may want more, but no one benefits from waste and corruption.

People have worried for years that Parliament is losing control of spending. In his 1976 annual report, legendary auditor general J.J. Macdonell warned: "I am deeply concerned that Parliament— and indeed the Government—has lost, or is close to losing, effective control of the public purse . . . financial management and control in the Government of Canada is grossly inadequate. Furthermore, it is likely to remain so until the Government takes strong, appropriate and effective measures to rectify this critically serious situation." A year before, he said "the present state of the financial management and control systems of departments and agencies of the Government of Canada is significantly below acceptable standards of quality and effectiveness."[20]

There were quite a few reasons. Government managers believed there would always be more money. They would not be held personally accountable for waste or for overspending. And, according to Macdonell, a lot of managers simply didn't know how to manage. He recommended the government appoint a "chief financial officer of the government, preferably with the title of Comptroller General of Canada, with deputy minister status and a direct reporting relationship to the President of the Treasury Board."[21] People who cared about public affairs were shocked by the auditor general's blunt warning. Pierre Trudeau, the prime minister at the time, appointed a commission to look at how Parliament controlled the public purse, to find ways to make the bureaucracy more efficient.

The 1979 Lambert Commission, the product of Macdonell's warning, was just one of several big examinations of government spending and the management systems of the public service. None of them was particularly effective. For many years and through Liberal and Tory governments, money management systems have come and gone, and spending has tended to grow along with the public service. (In fairness, the population and economy have also grown, but usually at slower rates). Government, and government spending, has become much more complex and is now mind-numbingly complicated. Even if the members of the House of Commons want to put in the time and energy to try to develop some kind of serious understanding of how Ottawa spends, it would be a life's work.

Government accounting and financial reporting practices don't make life easier for MPs. "If these evaluations, as it is claimed, were designed to assist Parliament to hold the government to account, they have failed where it matters the most—in helping those [they are] intended to help—MPs," respected political scientist Donald Savoie wrote a few years ago. "Most of the mountain of information that the government sends to Parliament every year is simply ignored. A former secretary to the Treasury Board suggests that even ministers no longer understand the process." Therefore, MPs, according to Savoie's Treasury Board source, "cannot properly interpret results without detailed information on staffing, budgets, geographical location of spending patterns—information they no longer receive . . . Thirty-five years ago, the estimates process held valuable advantages to MPs. The information was accessible and easy to grasp, given its focus on input costs." Now, it's not. In simple terms, according to Savoie and former parliamentary budget officer Kevin Page, only a handful of people have any idea how Ottawa spends your money, and none of those experts are elected by the people.[22]

Savoie says the annual spending estimates, which the government publishes once a year, are cloaked in mystery. Public servants simply can't or won't help our elected representatives understand what's going on. They are "the engine of a fragile process which has been so impossibly burdensome that Ministers and parliament alike have effectively given up. The answer that a government MP gave to my question—'Do you believe that civil servants speak power to truth when they appear before your committee?'—is telling: 'They speak volumes, not necessarily truth.'" So, over the years, the public relations aspect of the MPs' job has come to replace the historic task of members of Parliament, going back to the Middle Ages: to determine whether the people's money is well spent and ensure that taxpayers get value for their money.[23]

Page warned in 2011: "There is a genuine concern that Parliament is losing control of its fiduciary responsibilities of approving financial authorities of public monies as afforded in the

Constitution."²⁴ In an interview, Page said Macdonell's fears have come true. Parliament, he says, has lost control over the public purse. Even worse, few people seem to understand or care about the danger that the loss of elected oversight over government spending poses to both democracy and to our institutions. Secret, out-of-control spending breeds waste, incompetence and corruption. The present spending control system, he said, is utterly broken and no one is trying hard to fix it.²⁵

But the clock was never reversed. CTV bureau chief Bob Fife, speaking to about a hundred people at the Manning Conference in February 2014, said it appears no one, especially in Parliament, has a grip on the way Ottawa spends:

> It used to be many years ago, when a budget came down, the very next day the spending estimates would be introduced. There was a lock-up for the spending estimates. That's because the budget and the spending estimates matched each other, so you knew exactly what the government was spending the very next day. You could comb through that and have a real understanding of how the budget was allocated and how the budget was spent. Those days are gone. That doesn't happen anymore. In fact, it often happens that the spending estimates are tabled before the budget. The only way we have any idea how our money is spent is once a year we get a look at the public accounts, which is an end-of-the-year book which tells you how money was spent. That's the only way we have any idea. And Parliament is supposed to play the role of being able to question how money is being spent, and that's simply not happening.²⁶

MPs can't rely on government data to determine if Harper's economic plan, whatever it might be, actually works. The Tories cut spending on what bureaucrats in Jason Kenney's Employment

243

Ministry call Learning and Labour Market Information—the gathering, analyzing and sharing of employment and labour data—to $66.9 million in 2013–2014. That was a big drop from $80.8 million in the previous fiscal year and $84.9 million in 2011–2012. Presumably the cuts also made it more difficult for Kenney to have a grip on the jobs situation across Canada at a time when the country was trying to recover from the 2008 downturn.[27]

PARLIAMENT IS, in theory, the country's greatest kennel of watchdogs. It's the only democratic institution that has a chance of making sure the country is run efficiently and fairly and can protect Canadians from political hacks and runaway bureaucracy. Embedded within the parliamentary system and the bureaucracy itself are several institutions and officers who have stood up to Harper and his operatives and have paid the price. They've been publicly and privately attacked, delegitimized, and, in many cases, fired.

Just how good are these federal watchdogs that frighten the Harper government? Sometimes, not very. Months before the Senate expense scandal blew up, Auditor General Michael Ferguson looked at how senators claim expenses and decided the "honour system" that the Senate used wasn't so bad.

Then there was Christiane Ouimet, whom the government gave $500,000 in return for her resignation in 2010. Ouimet was in charge of protecting whistle-blowers. And even though she received 228 complaints from civil servants alleging wrongdoing or reprisals, she dismissed every one of the complaints as unfounded. Not even the Harper government could believe that all of those whistle-blowers could be wrong. Then news broke that her office was a snake pit where staff lived in fear of their own managers, who were always on the hunt for—wait for it—whistle-blowers who might spill Ouimet's secrets.

Jennifer Stoddart, when she was privacy commissioner, lifted talking points from Veterans Affairs Canada and used them in her 2012 annual report. The boilerplate said Veterans Affairs, which had been accused of passing around a critic's medical file, took privacy seriously. She—and the department—went so far to say that Veterans Affairs fosters a "culture of privacy." Despite this defence of Veterans Affairs, she was seen as an advocate of privacy, especially for Internet users whose data was mined by Google and Facebook. When Stoddart was replaced in 2014 by public service lawyer Daniel Therrien, who had worked for a decade for the Public Safety, Defence and Immigration departments, opposition MPs and privacy experts were worried.

Therrien was chosen for the role by Treasury Board president Tony Clement. But critics said Therrien was deeply involved with the same parts of the bureaucracy that were prying into people's private and cyber lives. "He's an inside man in the bureaucracy so we want to make sure he's a strong independent voice," NDP critic Mathieu Ravignat said. "We have concerns about that, but ultimately Mr. Therrien has to prove that he can do the job and that he understands the issues." Ann Cavoukian, Ontario's respected privacy commissioner, suggested the Harper government should have found a candidate with expertise in information technology rather than in administrative law.[28] People outside government were more harsh.[29] Two dozen academics, privacy advocates and groups, including the Canadian Civil Liberties Association, signed a letter to Harper in late May saying Therrien is "accustomed to approaching privacy issues from a wholly opposite perspective" and called the choice "indefensible."[30]

Ethics commissioner Mary Dawson insisted she wasn't a watchdog at all. In an interview with Postmedia News, she said she sees public office-holders as honest and trustworthy. If they've broken any rules, "they've done it not maliciously or anything; they just have done it because they sort of forgot."[31]

In one of his most spectacular failures, Harper chose Arthur Porter to chair the civilian board that oversees the operations of CSIS. As a member of the Security Intelligence Review Committee, Porter was told some of the country's most sensitive secrets. Three years later, he resigned after the *National Post* ran a series of stories showing his connections to international arms dealers and to the president of the country of his birth, Sierra Leone. In 2013, Porter was arrested in Panama on a Canadian warrant for his supposed role in a massive money laundering and kickback scheme. At the time of writing, Porter was lodged in a Panamanian jail, fighting extradition. If he dies there, the flag on the Peace Tower will fly at half-mast, as Porter is still a member of the Queen's Privy Council for Canada.[32]

Thought police in the Conservative ranks wanted even more power to curb publicly paid troublemakers and those with suspect loyalties. In 2014, just as Parliament was recovering from the brawling debate over Harper's so-called Fair Elections Act, Tory backbencher Mark Adler introduced a private member's bill that would have further defanged Parliament's watchdogs. If that bill had become law, parliamentary officers, including the auditor general, the privacy, information and ethics commissioners, and the parliamentary budget officer, would have been forced to disclose any partisan political work activities that they had ever been involved with. MPs and senators who fretted about the loyalty of their staff would have been able to have them investigated to see if they had ever actively supported any political party.

The watchdogs who take their job seriously have been getting the full Harper treatment: attacks by cabinet ministers and Tory backbench MPs, character assassinations by Tory strategists and assaults from Harper's media cheerleaders. David Christopherson, an NDP MP, said, with good reason, "The government still sees the Chief Electoral Officer as an opponent. Canadians see the Officers of Parliament as their friends."[33]

Joe Clark, who served as prime minister in 1978–1980, opposed Harper's rise. He fought the 2003 shotgun marriage of the Canadian Alliance and the Progressive Conservatives. Clark's fears have been realized. He's watched as Harper has attacked parliamentary institutions, clipped the wings of MPs and broken his promise to fix the Senate. Harper and his people, according to Clark, show disdain for the "principle of an independent electoral commission. They've done it with regard to first ministers' conferences, which were an informal but I think very important institution. I think there's a pattern here that is quite a cause for concern because not only is it coming from the highest authorities of the government, it seems to be accepted by other members of the government and other members of their caucus, which is alarming."

Outside of government, Harper has gone after non-governmental organizations, killed the National Round Table on the Environment, and wrecked the International Centre for Human Rights and Democratic Development. "Institutions have statutory lives of their own, but they depend upon legitimacy, and if public opinion and the legitimacy of our most basic institutions is gradually narrowed by whatever source, that's a danger for democracy," Clark told *Toronto Star* reporter Tonda MacCharles. "And when the source is the prime minister himself, I find that quite alarming."[34]

On March 25, 2013, Parliamentary Budget Officer Kevin Page turned out the lights in his office for the last time. His public service career was over, though he would soon land on his feet with a research and teaching chair at the University of Ottawa. For five years, he had been a spending watchdog who believed his job was to explain to Canadians how their government used their money. In his last major report, which he released just a few days before he left Parliament Hill, Page reported a $1.5 billion shortfall in the Harper government's budget to replace two old navy ships. Earlier, he had worked out the real price of F-35 stealth fighter planes and showed they, too, would cost more than the Harper government had told Canadians. He was able to show that the government fudged its estimates of future federal deficits and criticized the sloppy management of federal infrastructure money spent during the 2008 recession. There were other embarrassments, including some that hit at the core of Harper's warrior nation and unsafe streets messages: figures from Page's office showed the true cost of Harper's law-and-order agenda and the war in Afghanistan were much higher than the Tories claimed. Page had to start from scratch to calculate the amount of money spent on the Afghan war, after Harper's government refused to hand over its figures.

THE PARLIAMENTARY BUDGET OFFICE was a good initiative, and Harper deserves credit for creating it. The very idea of it, though, was bound to cause trouble. For one thing, Harper said the office was created to "ensure truth in budgeting," which economists and accountants at the Department of Finance could hardly have seen as a show of confidence in their integrity.[35] The Parliamentary Budget Office, whose ancestry can be traced to the somewhat effective Congressional Budget Office in Washington and similar policy-costing shops in other developed countries, was a creature of the 2006 Accountability Act. In those early days of Canada's New Government, the prime minister may well have believed

Canadians would be better governed if MPs had some kind of help analyzing public spending. The office-holder was supposed to be an independent officer of the Library of Parliament, and be objective, independent and non-partisan. The officer's job was to determine whether government plans and expenditure estimates are realistic, unlike the auditor general, who looks to ensure that the government got value for money that was already spent.

Page, a former senior public servant, was chosen after the Library of Parliament hired a headhunting firm to seek good candidates. Page didn't want the job. His friends warned him that it would be the end of his career in the public service. Others in the top echelon of the public service wondered if he'd be forever tarnished as some sort of prime ministerial lapdog, since he would be hired by Harper and serve "at pleasure" of the government. Page's name was chosen by Harper and his advisers from a shortlist drawn up by the headhunters and vetted by retired senior public servants.[36] He earned between $139,000 and $164,000 and ran a department with a staff of fourteen supported by a budget of just under $43 million. Throughout his term, Page said his office was far too small to be able to do its job. He had scrounged the best staff he could find from other departments and had made his case to politicians, but extra money never came.

Supposedly, the parliamentary budget officer was expected to help MPs understand the intricacies of government spending, but the job quickly morphed into fact-checking the figures issued by the Finance Department and other federal agencies. As the years went by, the facts exposed by the officer interfered with Harper's information control fetish and the government's propaganda campaigns. Page became a media star, since he actually gave out solid, useful information and spoke plainly about the funny numbers floated out by the Tories. So Harper and his team decided to smother the baby they had created.

Tories criticized Page harshly for his report of government spending in the first six months of the 2012–2013 fiscal year. The Harper government said it would save money by cutting administration costs, but, Page found, most of the savings had come from chopping front-line services to Canadians. Page also angered Harper and his foot soldiers by saying the Tories fudged the numbers to make it look like the old age pension system was financially unsustainable.

"Their big problem was they had created this office, then had cloaked themselves in secrecy," Page said. "People saw value in our work. We had a small group of people putting out good quality products, while the government was coming out with half-page press releases and numbers that simply weren't believable. Maybe they wanted us to be a lapdog. Whatever happened, they felt that we challenged their reputation as good fiscal managers."[37]

There was another serious problem: timing. The Tories had been elected when the economy was on a roll. Harper inherited solid budget surpluses from Paul Martin's Liberals. The federal debt to gross domestic product ratio was tumbling as Ottawa paid down years of accumulated deficits. Money saved on interest on the national debt could be used to cut taxes or create new programs. Having someone to explain government finances seemed like a good idea when the numbers made the government look like great managers. Senior financial advisers in the government warned Harper not to get too cocky, though, since Canada would soon have to come to terms with the pension and health care demands of the baby boom generation. Then, by late 2008, Canada, along with the rest of the world, was in a recession. The big plans of the new government for balanced budgets, tax cuts and—after the Harper government finally admitted there was a financial crisis—stimulus spending, simply did not add up.

It was Page's job to break the bad news. He did it publicly, believing his office was of no real use unless it shared its findings with all Canadians. Then Finance Minister Jim Flaherty called Page "unbelievable, unreliable and incredible." In Flaherty and Harper's world, Page was out of control, far overstepping his boundaries while offering support and succour to the opposition and the media.

Flaherty said the parliamentary budget officer "would kind of work like the Congressional Budget Office in the United States—to report to the elected people in the House of Commons about how the government was doing its budgeting. So, sort of being a sounding board, a testing board. He's kind of gone off that course." And he didn't deserve more staff or a bigger budget. Page had "not yet" provided value for money.

Treasury Board president Tony Clement, known by many Canadians for his enthusiasm for expensive gazebo construction in his Muskoka riding during the 2010 G8 summit, accused Page of having "his definitions wrong" and being "ill-informed" on government spending issues. Other Conservative MPs accused Page of becoming part of the opposition parties' research departments. They claimed to worry that material that Page found for them could be handed out to opposition MPs and to the media. But NDP finance critic Peggy Nash argued that "the parliamentary budget officer has been invaluable at helping Canadians see what the real costs are when you think of things like the F-35, the war in Afghanistan. Every time he has raised concerns that are in the best interests of Canadians he has been attacked by the government." Nash introduced a private member's bill to make the Parliamentary Budget Office independent of the government, but it was killed by the Tory majority.[38]

Fred DeLorey, an in-house Conservative strategist, made the Harper government's position crystal clear in a column he wrote in the *Hill Times* newspaper: "What is very unfortunate is that the current Parliamentary Budget Officer, Kevin Page, clearly overstated his role and his mandate." And Harper himself, after refusing to extend Page's contract or reappoint him, said he wanted a budget office that was "non-partisan and credible." Really, what he seems to have wanted was, at most, someone who could brief backbench Tory MPs so they'd have some idea what they were voting for when they passed the annual spending estimates, and otherwise keep his or her mouth firmly shut.

"The instinct of this government was to attack. I never took it personally," says Page, who now holds the Jean-Luc Pepin Research Chair at the University of Ottawa and, among other work, helps countries set up effective legislative budget offices. "I never lost any sleep over it."[39]

AFTER PAGE LEFT THE HILL, things did not improve for the Parliamentary Budget Office. Sonia L'Heureux, who temporarily held Page's job until Jean-Denis Fréchette was hired as the full-time replacement, issued a press release describing how government departments and agencies tried to thwart her from getting the information she needed to do her job. She wanted information for an analysis of the 2013 federal budget because a parliamentarian had asked her for it. "The first deadline for providing it came and went, and the majority of departments and agencies did not comply with the totality of my request," she said. L'Heureux complained to the Speaker of the Senate and the Speaker of the House of Commons. Still, she said, "I have yet to be provided with all the information that I need to undertake the requested analysis. If and when I am provided with it, I look forward to performing the analysis and, thereby, discharging my legislative mandate."[40]

But if Page drew Harper's contempt, it was nowhere near as strong as the prime minister's determination to hobble Elections Canada, the agency that makes sure the country's elections are clean and fair. Harper has always had a special place in his heart for Elections Canada. Before becoming prime minister, Harper was best known as the plaintiff in *Harper v. Canada*, a lawsuit he filed in June 2000 on behalf of the National Citizens Coalition to allow pressure groups and other third parties to buy political advertising during election campaigns. Its investigation of the "in and out" scandal had dogged the government and Tory campaign strategists through the minority years. Then came the robocalls scandal.

After Elections Canada started investigating reports that Tory operatives made misleading phone calls to try to trick and confuse people identified as opposition party supporters during the 2011 campaign, Marc Mayrand, the chief electoral officer, was attacked for his supposed bias. Elections Canada staff were accused of leaking information to reporters Glen McGregor and Stephen Maher, who said there was no evidence it came from the agency. (For details on the robocalls scandal and other vote suppression schemes, see Chapter 12.) In 2014, the Tories rammed through their Fair Elections Act, which muzzled Mayrand, hampered his ability to investigate election rigging, and, in its early drafts, would have even stopped him from running the normal ad campaign to encourage people to vote.

Pierre Poilievre, the minister of state for democratic reform, told a Senate committee that Mayrand was dangerous. "He wants more power, a bigger budget and less accountability." He also said "the referee shouldn't be wearing a team jersey," a hockey analogy that must have generated a few chuckles when it was crafted in the Prime Minister's Office. Soon afterwards, retired auditor general Sheila Fraser defended Mayrand's integrity and impartiality and blasted Poilievre for insulting an officer of Parliament. "We [officers of Parliament] don't take these jobs to win popularity contests. We do our work with objectivity. This serves none of us well. It undermines the credibility of these institutions and at the end of the day, if this was to continue, we will all pay because no one will have faith in government, in chief electoral officers or our democratic system."[41] Fraser, one of the most respected auditor generals in recent history, was quickly attacked by Clement, who called her a "self-proclaimed expert" on election rules.

"The whole episode illustrates the complexity of the man," Harper's former mentor Tom Flanagan said during the controversy over the so-called Fair Elections Act. Flanagan suggested payback had been coming for a long time, at least since the years when Harper was president of the National Citizens Coalition. "So, the initial version of the bill really did seem to be aimed at Elections Canada, taking away powers, clipping what it can do and, along the way, putting in some features that would appear to help the Conservatives at the expense of other parties. So you might say that bill, the original bill, may have expressed the vindictive side of the prime minister, you know, pay-back time."[42]

Through the years, the government has also tried to ruin the career of Pat Stogran, who was appointed veterans ombudsman by Harper, but was tossed aside when he became a loud critic of the way vets were being treated. Linda Keen, head of the Canadian Nuclear Safety Commission, was blamed for her "lack of leadership" when she decided the aged nuclear reactor at Chalk River, Ontario, had become too decrepit to produce medical isotopes. Harper accused her of being partisan, reminding Canadians that Keen was a "Liberal appointee."

Paul Kennedy, head of the RCMP Public Complaints Commission, lost his job in 2009 after saying police brass made it impossible for him to do his work. Kennedy, a former lawyer for the government and CSIS, kept asking the government for more independence and greater powers to do his job. Instead, he ended up on the street.[43] Peter Tinsley, the head of the Military Complaints Commission, lost his job after he asked too many questions about what happened to Afghans arrested by Canadian troops in Kandahar.

Prime ministers are no longer, as they once claimed to be, the "first among equals." Now, policy decisions are made in the Prime Minister's Office. Spending priorities are set there, too. And with so little real authority, why should ministers take responsibility for the failings of their department? Ministerial responsibility—the idea that ministers are held accountable by the people, through Parliament, for the policies and actions of their departments—is the basis of our democracy. It's eroding fast. And, since Canada is an incredibly complex country with a huge and intrusive federal government, powerful and important provincial governments that need attention, and some status in world affairs, a prime minister can only get to a few issues at a time. Much of the business of the state is left to his courtiers, the people he appoints to staff his own office and to hold the senior political and administrative roles in each department.

In a situation like this, government can easily come to be reactive, with the prime minister's attention bouncing from one political issue to another. A prime minister hit with, say, a series of political scandals while juggling a recession or an economic downturn ends up with very little time to do much governing. That explains why Harper feels the need for control. There is a more simple solution, and one that's a lot more democratic: let ministers and Parliament govern the country. Canadian prime ministers should start acting as though they believe democracy works.[44]

CHAPTER 10

The Secret Government

"This is the most open and transparent
government in Canadian history."
—JOHN BAIRD[1]

If John Baird, a man known for his sense of humour, is right when he says the Harper government set the Canadian record for openness, it's still damnation by faint praise. Canada's governments have always been stingy with facts. Information is power. And Canadians, as a deferential lot, have always been willing to let the government sit on its voluminous files, as long as they, themselves, did not have an axe to grind with Ottawa, one of the provinces or their community government. In the United States, even with the clampdowns after 9/11 and the paranoia of the Obama administration, it's been much easier to get information from their governments than it is in Canada. One of the big differences is that government information in the States is seen by Americans as the property of the people. Here, in a country where, through most of its history, the people have been subjects, information has always belonged to a government over which the people felt little ownership.

And now, under Harper, information is seen as something dangerous that must be contained, or stored like nuclear waste. Those who seek it are treated with fear and contempt, even when the material that they want is in no way embarrassing to the government.

In theory, all people should have a right to see government information, as long as the material is not dangerous to the state and doesn't undermine the privacy of individuals. How else can voters make informed choices and citizens deal, with some measure of equality, with governments?

The Access to Information Act was passed by Pierre Trudeau's government in 1982. That was just a little over a year before Trudeau retired and sixteen years after Lyndon Johnson had signed the U.S. Freedom of Information Act into law. Through the 1970s, according to Ken Rubin, one of the country's leading experts on the topic, the Trudeau government "was the centre for evasion and secrecy" and was "married to the Official Secrets Act."[2] That law was used against reporters, including Peter Worthington and Bob MacDonald of the *Toronto Sun* in the 1970s, when they exposed wrongdoing in the RCMP. Even after the freedom of information law was passed, bureaucrats and elected cabinet ministers were allowed to hang on to all kinds of information, stall and charge very high research and copying fees. In many ways, it codified the secrecy in official Ottawa, with the *Ottawa Citizen* saying the new law, "with its exemptions and with its spirit undermined, could have the reverse effect to what the public thought was intended. Instead of loosening government information . . . [it] may have merely codified the ways in which information can be suppressed."[3] Not many Canadians use the system: in a busy year, perhaps forty thousand people file information requests. Journalists, researchers, political parties, lobbyists and academics make up the bulk of users.

No government really likes freedom of information laws. They exist to provide some kind of structure. Back in the 1970s, reporters and curious citizens could write to a government department or show up at the front counter of a town hall and ask to see documents created on the public's dime. Sometimes, they wanted to know what the government had on them. Other times, a person might want to know who owned a particular piece of property so they could make the owner an offer to buy it. At all three levels, most governments had no set policy on who could see what.

Freedom of information laws were supposed to be a way to set out a legal process for people to ask for public documents. And, if the bureaucracy turned them down, there were supposed to be ways for people to appeal. In theory, documents that weren't controversial—that had always been available—would still be easy to get. More controversial stuff would have to go through a vetting and, maybe, an appeals system. But, instead, Access to Information has become a shield that allows public servants and politicians to delay or deny all documents, making the appeal process the punishment.

A new bureaucracy was created, both to handle the applications and to staff the appeal process. The federal government created the job of information commissioner to advocate for openness and to point out situations where bureaucrats and politicians had thwarted curious members of the public, of whom journalists made up a part. The Chrétien Liberals were notorious for keeping secrets. Retired journalist John Grace, who served as information commissioner under Jean Chrétien, banged his head against the Liddle Guy's regime, observing in his final report in 1998 that freedom of information had turned out to be anything but:

> *If some of its architect's fine hopes were unrealistic and unrealized, the fault lies not in the stars, not in the law: It must be placed at the feet of governments and public servants who have chosen to whine about the rigors of access rather than embrace its goals; chosen not to trust the public with information which*

taxes have paid for. The insult is equal only to the intellectual arrogance of it all. The commitment, by word and deed, to the principle of accountability through transparency has been too often faltering and weak-kneed.

Former MP John Reid, Grace's successor as commissioner, made it clear that he wasn't going to be pushed around. He warned early in his mandate that he had "zero tolerance" for bureaucrats who were late handing over documents. He would use the full power of his office against them. But two years later, he was forced to concede that his powers caused little fear among public servants: "A full counter-attack [is] in progress" by the "stubborn persistence of a culture of secrecy in Ottawa" that "distorts the thinking of the citizenry, giving rise to unfounded conspiracy theories and an unnecessary high level of mistrust of government," he said in one of his annual reports. This "love of secrecy is so deeply entrenched that extraordinary steps are taken by public servants to maintain it even in the face of a legislated right of access."

He described how the act had changed the way the government operates: "The attitude has truly become: 'Why write it when you can speak it? Why speak it when you can nod? Why nod when you can wink?'" The opposition Tories had lots of fun using this stuff against the Chrétien and Martin Liberals. They did not want the system to be used on them.

In 2006, right after it took power, Harper's government set up a separate computer database and Internet server to protect ministers' documents from Access to Information applications. Responses to requests for information are put through the Centre. Frequent requesters, especially those asking for sensitive information, are profiled. Requests from journalists and opposition parties are usually stalled, sometimes by political staffers in ministers' offices.[4]

From the beginning, the workings of the system created by the information law have been under attack by the staffs of prime ministers and by bureaucrats. Some of the kind of meddling done by Harper went on during Jean Chrétien's term—and long before that. Chrétien imposed his will on Communication Canada, which was responsible for administering access requests. The department showed its obedience to Chrétien's Prime Minister's Office by trying to thwart people who asked for information on the crooked federal sponsorship advertising system in Quebec.

Under Harper, the Privy Council Office replaced Communications Canada as the vetting centre for access requests. Cabinet ministers' offices meddle, too. In many cases, a request for information is a red flag to message spinners in the Harper government that previously ignored material is valuable or dangerous, and they get to work to try to make sure it's kept under wraps. In February 2009, Information Commissioner Robert Marleau filed a report to Parliament saying the Conservatives are "addicted" to secrecy. Marleau, the former clerk of the House of Commons, found "deficiencies" in information management, poor consultation, lousy training and poor executive leadership. Time limits were routinely extended. People requesting information were threatened with hefty fees for "preparation time" that bureaucrats claimed they needed to find and organize public documents. "The President of the Treasury Board, as the designated minister under the Act, must provide the political leadership to change a transparency adverse culture," Marleau reported.[5]

He found that bureaucrats put "amber lighting" on selected information requests—ones that came from journalists, parliamentarians and immigration lawyers. The Canadian Newspaper

Association found that "more than one in four of all requests designated for special handling comes from media requesters, even though fewer than one in six requests overall come from the media. In fact, media requests are about twice as likely to get the tougher treatment as requests overall."[6]

The next information commissioner of Canada found three Conservative staffers were involved in "systemic interference" with Access to Information requests. Suzanne Legault, the commissioner, wanted to bring in the RCMP, but the Public Works Department, which was the target of the Tory interference, said no. The staffers worked as political aides to the minister of public works and tried to prevent information from the department from being released. But Public Works officials said it would be a waste of time to call in the RCMP, since, in at least one similar case, they had done the same kind of investigation and the police would not lay charges. In fact, the RCMP is notoriously, perhaps deliberately, inept when it comes to investigating anything with political overtones.

"Through the investigation that is the subject of this report, I found a pattern of improper involvement by a small group of ministerial staff members at [Public Works] in responding to requests under the Access to Information Act," Legault wrote in her 2014 annual report. "These staffers inserted themselves in various ways into a process that was designed to be carried out in an objective manner by public servants. Consequently, the rights conferred under the Act were compromised." The Access to Information and Protection of Privacy Act prohibits people to "direct, propose, counsel or cause any person" to conceal a government record, with a maximum penalty of $10,000 and two years in jail. No one has yet been convicted under the section.[7]

Sometimes, the whole thing becomes completely ridiculous. In September 2011, a very important person visited Ottawa. He was met at the airport by someone. But, under the privacy rules in the Access to Information law, government documents showing the identity of the visitor and just about everything to do with his trip are officially not available to the public. There's nothing particularly sinister about the trip itself. British Prime Minister David Cameron was the visitor. He was met at the Ottawa airport by Defence Minister Peter MacKay. The visit was a goodwill call. But the law protects Cameron's privacy to the point that almost every detail of his trip was censored out of material released by the Privy Council Office. And those censored documents were released after bureaucrats gave the people who applied for the material a two-year run-around.

When the papers were finally released, most of Cameron's agenda was blacked out, even though the British prime minister was safely and securely back in London. The rule used to protect Cameron's privacy—even though the British prime minister had never asked for the censorship—can be overridden by another part of the law that allows bureaucrats more flexibility when dealing with the records of public figures. But rather than just hand over the very mundane documents, Harper's office, again, chose to make life difficult for people trying to see public information.

In 2012, in recognition of his skills as a hoarder of information, Harper won the Canadian Association of Journalists' Cone of Silence Award. It's not much of a prize, since it recognizes the most secretive government, department or publicly funded agency in Canada. "This was the overwhelming choice—while we received a few other worthy nominations, no single one outnumbered the Harper government in volume or depth," CAJ president Hugo Rodrigues said in presenting the award at the association's 2012 convention. "The death grip on information has long frustrated journalists in this country, but it may now be reaching a point where the public at large is not only empathetic, but shares it." It wasn't just journalists who felt that way. A 2012 report by the Halifax-based Centre for Law and Democracy ranked Canada 55th out of 93 developed countries for the weakness of our information laws.[8]

Information commissioners appointed under the Access to Information Act have complained for years about foot-dragging in the bureaucracy and a culture of secrecy in Ottawa. In 2010, Marleau warned of "inappropriate use of time extensions and the increase in time-consuming consultations among institutions."[9] The following year, Legault reported:

> Over the past decade, there has been a steady decline in two import-
> ant measures of access to government information. In terms of time-
> liness, slightly more than half of all access requests made to federal
> institutions are now completed within the 30-day limit set by the
> Access to Information Act. In terms of disclosure, fewer than one-fifth
> of all requests currently result in all information being released. Far
> from reaching the presumption of disclosure inherent in the Access
> to Information Act, the exercise of discretion in determining which
> information to disclose has been skewed toward greater protection
> of information. For example, the percentage of exemptions claimed
> for national security has increased threefold since 2002–2003.[10]

By 2013, departments were no less secretive. And, with budget cuts, they could now plead poverty as an excuse for foot-dragging. "One organization was so understaffed it could not acknowledge access requests until months after receiving them, and even then could not say when it would be able to provide a response," Legault said in her annual report. "Another took an extension of more than three years for responding to an access request. Others failed to live up to commitment dates my office had negotiated for providing records to requesters on files that were already considerably overdue. Still others did not retrieve and analyze records before telling requesters they could not have access to them. A common refrain was that budgetary restraint is having a direct and adverse impact on the service institutions provide requesters."

Departments and agencies were being merged and reorganized, and no one was in charge of handling old information requests. Complaints in 2012–2013 were up by 9 per cent over the previous year and were rising month by month. Legault warned there are "unmistakable signs of significant deterioration" in the federal Access to Information system, a gentle way of saying the wheels have pretty much fallen off. "What is required is leadership, most notably on the part of the government and the individual institutions that respond to access requests. Ministers and officials at the highest levels must regularly and vigorously promote the intent and spirit of the Access to Information Act, to foster a culture of openness in their organizations and to communicate the importance of meeting their obligations under the law."[11]

Legault said fewer requests were being answered within thirty days in 2011–2012 than in the previous year, and about 15 per cent of them were answered late. Treasury Board secretary Tony Clement went to bat for the government, saying in a press release that "there has never been a time when Canadians have had so much access to government information." Legault disputed that, countering: "I think that there's lots of work to be done in order to be considered a transparent government."[12]

SOME FORMER TORY staffers realize how bad the system has become. Guy Giorno used to be Harper's chief of staff. Now, he's one of the Conservative Party's lawyers and a partner with the Ottawa office of the law firm Fasken Martineau DuMoulin LLP. Giorno often uses the Access to Information system, and he's changed his tune about information control. Giorno told a Canadian Bar Association seminar in 2013 about being jerked around when he tried to get information out of the Mounties. The RCMP refused to acknowledge it had even received his information request. They wouldn't give the application a file number that Giorno could use to check back on his request. When Giorno appealed his case to the information commissioner, her office said she couldn't do anything unless Giorno could give her a file number. "This is actually outrageous. I'm all for giving the commissioner additional jurisdiction to issue orders but this idea that an institution would be able to set the limits on jurisdiction—is that a resource issue? Is that a training issue?" Giorno asked his fellow lawyers.

Giorno, in his new private sector career, also wants more access to cabinet ministers' documents, especially after the Privy Council Office told the information commissioner not to show them to him. Harper's government argues that the salaries of ministers' staff, the titles and duties of ministers' employees and a lot of other information about ministers' offices should be exempt from the Access to Information law. Giorno wants the information commissioner to be given the power to issue legally enforceable orders.

"It's got to be fixed . . . This is absolutely outrageous now," Giorno said. "All sorts of information that nobody would ever think should be withheld from the public is simply inaccessible. It is indefensible that sort of basic material when it refers to a minister's office should not be released." When a reporter asked why he believed government officials were trying to hide information, he said: "Because I worked for ten years in government."[13]

Reporters who try to cover national affairs are up against approximately 3,200 media relations staffers in the Ottawa bureaucracy, along with the communications staff of lobby firms, business associations and non-governmental organizations. These people often have a vested interest in killing stories and undermining the credibility of journalists. So when journalists have to deal with political staffers and bureaucrats who strive to please the Harper team, it becomes very tough for reporters to do their jobs. A few reporters have become experts on Access to Information. Others have hired professional information ferrets like Ken Rubin to dig out data. And, in extreme cases (such as The Canadian Press's long campaign to see the police files on Tommy Douglas), journalists have gone to court.

There's even secrecy about the rules of secrecy. In December 2013, The Canadian Press asked for a background briefing with an official from Library and Archives Canada to learn about the laws and regulations concerning the saving and deleting of government emails. People in the provincial Ontario Liberal Party had recently been criticized by the province's privacy commissioner over the destruction of emails about the controversial decision to cancel the building of gas-powered electricity generating plants in Mississauga and Oakville. The leaders of Dalton McGuinty's government had made that decision during the 2011 provincial election campaign.

Reporters wanted to know about the federal rules when they read a police document suggesting all of lawyer Benjamin Perrin's emails had been destroyed after he resigned from Harper's office. Perrin had possibly been in the loop when Prime Minister's Office officials discussed the prospect of chief of staff Nigel Wright repaying Mike Duffy's controversial housing expense claims. A few hours after receiving The Canadian Press's request, Library and Archives Canada had found an expert on its staff who could brief the news agency's reporters to ensure they got their story right. A media relations officer wrote to the expert: "Since you are a pro at doing interviews and understand the [Library and Archives] Act like no other

. . . well, let's just say yours was the first name to come up. Pending approval from [the Privy Council Office, the director general] has given her OK that you be the one to have this informal chat."

But there would be no chat. After kicking the idea around among thirty-two bureaucrats, the Privy Council Office and the Department of Canadian Heritage nixed the plan to let the expert share his expertise. Rather than make sure the major print news service in this country knew what it was talking about, Library and Archives Canada was leaned on to tell The Canadian Press that the expert was "out of town." (In the end, it turned out Perrin's emails were, like those of the Ontario Liberal plotters, "frozen" and were not lost forever, and they were turned over to the police officers investigating the Wright-Duffy payment.)[14]

The Harper plumbers have also tried to plug leaks from the Department of National Defence. Military officers are notorious gripers and chatterboxes. Lt.-Gen. Marquis Hainse said the loose talk was killing the army's credibility. "It is hurting the army, it is counter-productive, and it needs to stop," he wrote. "I intend to pursue disciplinary action against any member of the army who is found complicit in the unauthorized release of information."[15]

That memo, too, was leaked after an internal fight. The Conservatives created a new system that requires all media requests of "regional and national" importance—including those dealing with the Canadian Forces—to be cleared in advance through the Centre. Retired Gen. Lewis MacKenzie, who served with distinction as head of the Canadian peacekeeping mission in the Balkans in the 1990s and ran unsuccessfully for the House of Commons as a Conservative candidate, said the new information control system would hurt, not help, the reputation of the Canadian Forces. The government itself was likely to see trouble from it, too: "These things never seem to accomplish the goal, which is to control the flow of information . . .

I can only say from a personal perspective that if I was in the public affairs branch, I'd be quite disappointed. Certainly at a most critical moment, when we are fighting a war, they're doing a good job, from the CDS [Chief of the Defence Staff Rick Hillier] on down."

Ottawa Citizen military analyst David Pugliese believed Harper's office and senior executives in other government departments thought the Canadian Forces were getting too much positive media coverage—something that was usually not seen as a problem at the military's downtown headquarters beside the Rideau Canal. Even worse, the military's public affairs officers were not answerable to the prime minister's media handlers. Most departments had already been hamstrung by the Prime Minister's Office so that press communications had been limited to short email answers to reporter's questions (if there was any response at all). The Department of National Defence was the last major part of the government to operate its own independent media relations shop.

Pugliese wrote that the last time the Canadian Forces had clamped down, during the 1993 Somalia affair, military officials were severely limited in what they could say to defend the military against charges that it had covered up the murder of a Somali teenager by members of the Airborne regiment. Critics were able to pound the military while its media relations staff was prevented from answering charge after charge. It was one of the worst public relations disasters that the military faced in modern times. Under Harper, the military dreaded another Somalia-style black eye.[16]

In early 2014, journalists found one unlikely hero in the Department of National Defence. Doug Drever, a civilian employee in the military's public affairs division, had started his public service career in media relations under Prime Minister Brian Mulroney. In February 2014, he defied his bosses and insisted the military release the embarrassing email that was sent to soldiers by Lt.-Gen. Marquis

Hainse, warning soldiers to keep quiet. Drever had been told to tell the media to try to get the email through Access to Information. He told his superiors to find someone else to do it. "Gotta stand for something once in a while," Drever said in an email.

Within a few minutes, Drever's bosses found someone to do their dirty work. Drever didn't let the matter drop. "This approach is wrong," Drever wrote to colleagues in an exchange released later under the Access to Information law. "It is in violation of the spirit of the Access to Information Act and in deference to the Hon. Ged Baldwin, father of access to information in this country, I won't do it." (Baldwin was a nine-term Progressive Conservative MP from Peace River, Alberta, who earned an Order of Canada for a decades-long campaign to make government more transparent.)[17]

IT'S HARD TO BELIEVE a change of government would make much of a difference. Already, MPs in all the parties with official standing in the House of Commons[18] have tried to gag the staffers who work in their offices. In 2014, members of an all-party House of Commons committee tried to force Parliament Hill employees to sign an agreement with lifetime secrecy rules similar to the ones imposed on the public servants.

When staff of the House of Commons and the people who work in MPs' offices began to mutiny over the proposed gag law, the Tory-dominated Board of Internal Economy, which handles most House of Commons employment issues, quietly backed down. The blanket lifetime ban on disclosure was replaced by a general confidentiality agreement that still contains "indefinite protection" for personal information like constituency files, along with data protected by secrecy laws and parliamentary privilege. Political information about the "employee's employer" is confidential for five years. After that, staffers can talk to journalists, academic researchers or their friends and family.[19]

While you can't find out much about *them*, the people who run this country's government can learn an awful lot about *you*. Spies creep the Facebook pages and Twitter feeds of hundreds of thousands of Canadians. They monitor political blogs, not just to track the ranting of basement-dwellers but also to collect data on the often bizarre people who post comments underneath blog entries.

Political parties don't have to worry much about anyone's privacy. Colin Bennett, who teaches political science at the University of Victoria, told the Canadian Bar Association's national convention in 2013: "Essentially, you have a bit of a wild west here in my view and I don't think it is a situation that can be allowed to continue . . . There is no legal obligation for them to keep that information secure, no legal obligation for them to train employees, no legal obligation for them to give access . . . Political parties are not covered under PIPEDA [Personal Information Protection and Electronic Documents Act] or the Privacy Act." Only B.C. has privacy laws that are broad enough to cover the activities of political parties.

The Conservative Party developed the Constituent Information Management System (CIMS) database, which is one of their most important campaign tools. Bennett said the system has been collecting information about voters for about a dozen years. The database is a foundation for the Conservative's election campaigns. It tracks supporters, identifies potential fundraisers, tracks emerging issues—and identifies enemies.

"Everybody in the CIMS database has a number, from minus 15 to plus 15. If you're plus 15, you're on the right of the political spectrum. If you are minus 15 you are on the left of the political spectrum. You are a pinko, leftie, environmentalist, academic probably," Bennett told the lawyers.[20]

Treasury Board president Tony Clement defended a $3 million government program to pay for round-the-clock surveillance of social media. The Department of Public Works hired people to monitor Facebook, Twitter, YouTube videos and other sites. They also watch for "top influencers" on blogs and chat rooms.[21]

"That is the whole point of social media, to engage in a dialogue with citizens," Clement told the House of Commons. "That means better public policies in the end," said Clement. "My handle is @TonyClementCPC, if anyone wants notes. It is not a state secret."[22] In the House of Commons, he told Charmaine Borg, one of the young Quebec NDP MPs elected in 2011, that she "is not a rookie when it comes to social media, so she would know anything posted on Facebook or Twitter is public information. In fact, most people are on Facebook or Twitter to be read, to be seen, to be part of the dialogue. We want to be there too."[23]

In the name of protecting Canadians from cyberbullies and child pornographers, the Harper government brought in Bill C-13 in 2013. But critics say this cybercrime bill is a full-on assault on anything resembling online privacy rights. Ontario Privacy Commissioner Ann Cavoukian said the bill is overkill. "The time for dressing up overreaching surveillance powers in the sheep-like clothing of sanctimony about the serious harms caused by child pornography and cyberbullying is long past," Cavoukian said in a letter to the House of Commons committee that studied the bill.[24] The Tories invoked the names of Rehtaeh Parsons and Amanda Todd, two teenagers who had been driven to suicide by cyberstalkers and bullies. Critics of the bill, which allows the federal government to expand its cybersnooping, included Amanda Todd's mother, Carol, who told a parliamentary committee:

While I applaud the efforts of all of you in crafting the extortion, revenge, porn, and cyberbullying sections of Bill C-13, I am con-

271

cerned about some of the other unrelated provisions that have been added to the bill in the name of Amanda, Rehtaeh, and all of the children lost to cyberbullying attacks. I don't want to see our children victimized again by losing privacy rights. I am troubled by some of these provisions condoning the sharing of the privacy information of Canadians without proper legal process. We are Canadians with strong civil rights and values. A warrant should be required before any Canadian's personal information is turned over to anyone, including government authorities. We should also be holding our telecommunication companies and Internet providers responsible for mishandling our private and personal information. We should not have to choose between our privacy and our safety. We should not have to sacrifice our children's privacy rights to make them safe from cyberbullying, sextortion and revenge pornography.[25]

But you don't have to be in a database or on the Internet to be watched. The National Capital Commission, which has Foreign Affairs Minister John Baird as its political figurehead, spied on Occupy Ottawa protesters. It collected photographs of people, took down licence plate numbers, clipped newspaper stories, taped newscasts and recorded Facebook posts. In all, more than a thousand pages of staff memos were written by NCC staff about protesters who camped in one of its parks near Parliament Hill. No one was charged at the Occupy camp, which opened on October 15, 2011, with a speech by Brigitte DePape, a former Senate page who embarrassed the Tories by holding up a "STOP HARPER" sign during a speech from the throne. It lasted until frigid winter weather caused the last of the occupiers to decamp.

"Some of the crowds are anti-police," minutes of a November 2, 2011, Ottawa City Hall conference between federal and city staff noted. "Any time there is a camera in the park, protestors are accusing." The federal spies sniffed the air for marijuana smoke and checked out a woman who brought baskets of home-cooked food for the protesters. "She delivered 4–5 large baskets of fresh food as a donation. [Said] she was not working for any organization. She baked the food with her husband," the snoops noted.[26]

New Democrat MP Dan Harris, a former information technology consultant from Scarborough, Ontario, told Parliament the surveillance was a problematic use of resources and disturbing in scope. "Keeping lists on who their friends are and who isn't—that's what this is all about," Harris said in an interview with *Blacklock's Reporter*. "We're on the verge of Big Brother territory here. The more they monitor what Canadians are saying and doing online, the more that information could potentially be abused. This is taxpayers' money that is being used to determine whether someone is popular or not," Harris said. "Without strict rules and procedures as to what information will be gathered and what it's going to be used for, the sky's the limit."

In Parliament, Harris attacked the government: "Canadians posting on social media do not expect to be monitored by their government. They imagine that perhaps the Conservatives might have better things to do than follow their tweets and Facebook posts. Social media monitoring is a problematic use of government resources. We know the Conservatives like to keep lists, so thanks to the new Twitter monitoring program, how many more Canadians are going to wind up on the Conservatives' enemies list?"[27]

Outside the House of Commons, his party leader picked up on the issue. "These numbers are incredible. The very fact they put up a wall around the privacy commissioner shows that they were trying to hide this, trying to mask what they were up to," NDP leader Thomas Mulcair told Parliament Hill reporters the day the numbers were released. "Since they've arrived, the Conservatives have shown a scornful lack of respect for rules regarding the rights of the public to have access to information on the government, and they've shown the same scornful disrespect for people's privacy, their personal lives, their confidential information."

The privacy commissioner said, "This information can be sensitive in nature in that it can be used to determine a person's leanings, with whom they associate, and where they travel, among other things. What's more, each of these pieces of information can be used to uncover further information about an individual."[28]

When Liberal leader Justin Trudeau's handlers sent out an email to supporters announcing the birth of his son at the end of February 2013, well-wishers weren't asked for teddy bears, formula or flowers for the mom. Instead, the Liberals asked for email addresses and postal codes to feed into their database as they scrambled to catch up to the Tory organization. And when the Aga Khan visited Toronto at about the same time, the Conservatives offered, at stephenharper.ca, the prime minister's personal political website, "exclusive access" to the Ismaili Muslim leader in return for those precious postal codes and email addresses.[29]

Enforcement of Canada's fairly tame Personal Information Protection and Electronic Documents Act, passed in 2000, is so weak that privacy commissioner Jennifer Stoddart asked the government to give her some kind of power to charge and fine companies that break the law. Corporations aren't required to disclose data breaches like the massive Target Stores credit card information heist of 2013. Harper's government answered Stoddart's criticism with Bill C-12, but it died in Parliament after a wave of criticism that police would be able to get information about people from the Internet and businesses without the inconvenience of a warrant, and those whose files ended up in the hands of the cops would never know the electronic search had happened.

Information about dissent in Canada gets analyzed by the Government Operations Centre, a section of the Privy Council Office, which is Harper's personal ministry. Its job is to coordinate strategy against threats to the "national interest." In June 2014, it effectively turned the entire federal public service into spies when it sent out a memo to all federal departments saying: "The Government Operations Centre is seeking your assistance in compiling a comprehensive listing of all known demonstrations which will occur either in your geographic area or that may touch on your mandate. We will compile this information and make this information available to our partners unless, of course, this information is not to be shared and not available on open sources." Liberal public safety critic Wayne Easter warned, "Demonstrations, as long as they are peaceful, are part of a healthy democracy. These are the kinds of tactics you see in a police state." The NDP's Paul Dewar said, "This government is turning into Big Brother. This is clearly out of bounds from what GOC [Government Operations Centre] is supposed to do."[30]

Michael Zehaf-Bibeau's rampage on Parliament Hill on October 22, 2014, showed that this intelligent system is not perfect. Almost immediately, a debate began over whether the attack was truly politically motivated or if it was the work of one troubled man. The evidence points strongly to the latter, putting the attack into the same class of crime as shootings at Dawson College, Concordia University and École Polytechnique, along with Denis Lortie's attack on the Quebec National Assembly in 1984 and Robert Crawford's shooting rampage at the Alberta legislature in 1988. Large public buildings and powerful people are magnets for angry and delusional people. The President of the United States gets, on average, thirty death threats a day, and the Secret Service files on the people who have made those threats—a massive amount of data going back to 1865—are an important research tool for forensic psychiatrists.

Still, Harper quickly labelled Zehaf-Bibeau's assault a "terrorist attack" on "our soil." Very quickly, trial balloons were floated. Conservative media and blog sites began discussing possible new laws that would regulate hate speech—something the right in Canada was obviously prepared to flip-flop on if they were doing the prosecuting rather than the hating. Even more intrusive powers to spy on Canadians without warrants and search their online property were discussed. But nowhere in Harper's words, nor in the actions of the government, was the issue of the thousands of untreated, impoverished, mentally ill people on the streets of the country's cities. While Tories talked about Islamic terrorism, police looked for the source of Zehaf-Bibeau's gun by questioning addicts and mentally ill people living in Ottawa's homeless shelters. They didn't go to mosques.

A few days after 9/11, Jean Chrétien did go to Ottawa's largest mosque to make sure it was plain to Canadians that the government and the people of the country harboured no ill-will against Muslims. While Canada would go after actual terrorists, the Muslim community was a welcome part of Canada, Chrétien said. But after Zehaf-Bibeau—a convert whose aggressive talk got him banned from a Vancouver mosque—attacked Parliament Hill, the government was mute when it came to reassuring people. There would be no mosque trip by Stephen Harper, and the far-right fringe, both in mainstream media and on the Internet, would feel free to Muslim-bash to its heart's content.

MEANWHILE, the Harper government paid more for a new spy agency headquarters in Ottawa than has ever been spent on a government office building in this country. Even adjusting for inflation, the new headquarters of the mysterious Communications Security

Establishment Canada cost more than the buildings on Parliament Hill. Over the past few years, people shopping at the strip mall at Blair and Ogilvie roads in the east end of Ottawa wondered what was going to be inside that big white building, the size of a domed stadium, that rose in the woods just across the road.

Was it a zoo? Another museum? Will it be a new National Library full of cool books and art? No. In fact, the building is the headquarters of the agency that intercepts phone calls and Internet communication for the federal government. It cost at least $1.2 billion, a third higher than the original price tag of $880 million. So, in a way, it's only fitting that it resembles, at least in outward design, the Velodrome at the 1976 Montreal Olympics.

The 72,000-square-metre building is a public-private partnership with Plenary Group Canada, an Australian company that specializes in contracting for the construction of government buildings. In effect, it's a ninety-storey building turned on its side. Some of its ultra-perks, like a grand fireplace, were cut from the design, but it's still being called a spy palace. The headquarters was supposed to be finished by the end of 2014. The building is entirely open concept, with plenty of natural light. Outside, the woodlot will be landscaped with gardens, nature tails and duck ponds. It's right next door to the Canadian Security Intelligence Service headquarters. CSIS looks for threats inside Canada. Right now, its focus is on terrorism, but it also tries to catch foreigners who steal Canadian technological and industrial secrets. It has also spied on labour unions, First Nations, university student activists, domestic communists and many other people.

CSEC is supposed to look for foreign spies and terrorists. It reports to the minister of defence, Rob Nicholson, while CSIS is, at least on paper, under the control of Public Safety Minister Steven Blaney. The new CSEC makes the corner the country's ground zero of domestic and foreign spying and the focal point of the fantasy life of hundreds of paranoiacs. More than 1,700 staff, many of them stellar mathematicians, work for CSEC, which spends over $300 million a year. And they have a lot to do. CSEC goes through more data in a day than all of the combined transactions of Canada's banks. It works closely with the National Security Agency, the United States' signals interception network. The NSA is unfathomably vast, with spy satellites, a huge ground-based interception system, and an army of code-breakers based in Fort George Meade, Virginia, just outside Washington. It's had its own troubles recently, with former employee Eric Snowden leaking thousands of embarrassing documents.

Snowden gave the Canadian Broadcasting Corporation data that showed CSEC spied on Canadians who used Wi-Fi hot spots at airports in this country. The NSA, like CSEC, breaks codes and taps phones, but it also engaged in cyberwarfare. Its most famous success was getting the Stuxnet worm into Iran's nuclear research computer in 2009, probably by having a spy leave a flash drive in the parking lot of the Iranian lab and letting a curious employee do the rest.[31] In fact, CSEC likes the NSA so much that it bought office equipment, including used encrypted telephones and fax machines, from the NSA, presumably trusting that the Americans had no taps on the phones or faxes.[32]

At CSEC, secrets are everything. A recruitment video on the CSEC website asks prospective agents, "Can you keep a secret?" Because, the agency says, being a math genius isn't enough. You can't go around blabbing about your work. In fact, for years, governments denied that CSEC existed and hid its budget in the money set aside for the Canadian Forces. Civil libertarians are worried about the Harper spy fetish. In February 2014, forty-five civil liberties and social justice organizations launched a campaign to try to convince MPs to oppose paying billions toward Canada's online spying apparatus, part of an international campaign to curb cyber-spying. That's not what CSEC is supposed to be for. Signals intelligence—snoops and code-breakers, in real-speak—are supposed to grab enemy communications and decipher them.[33]

CSEC has had its successes, though, of course, it rarely talks about them. But in 2010, John Adams, the Rhodes Scholar who headed the agency, told an interviewer: "If you were to ask the Canadian Forces if there is anyone that has saved Canadian lives in Afghanistan, they would point to us." Canada routinely shares its spy data with other members of the Five Eyes group: Britain, the United States, New Zealand and Australia. In that world, you have to pay to play. In the early 2000s, according to WikiLeaks documents, then Prime Minister Paul Martin worried the Americans would cut us out of Five Eyes because we refused to send troops to Iraq and were not spending enough on agencies like CSEC.

The mailing address of CSEC is Box 1984, Station B, Ottawa.

The problem is, Canadians don't know what the agency does or whether it's been let loose on us. In 2014, the budget of CSEC almost doubled leading up to the opening of its new headquarters. The spy agency got $829 million in 2014–2015, up from about $444 million the previous year. That included a one-time payment of $300 million for work on the new headquarters, and $100 million for maintenance.[34] CSEC has had a 32 per cent increase in its staff since 2006, according to payroll records.

CSEC has barred MPs from its new Ottawa headquarters. In a report to Parliament, interim privacy commissioner Chantal Bernier noted, "The right to privacy is fundamental in Canada. It is central to personal integrity. There are not sufficient official forums for the national security agencies to inform Canadians about how they operate, and how they protect privacy within their operations." She wanted cabinet to clarify the roles of the country's spy agencies and fix what she called an "accountability gap." Bernier said, "To correspond to the reality of intelligence gathering, which is multi-faceted, we should have the proper coordination of oversight for national security agencies' activities."[35]

So far, the agency is showing some frightening signs that it believes its work trumps Canadians' rights, including those of its own employees. The CSEC investigated what it called "serious breaches" of its values and ethics code after a whistle-blower in the agency told executives there was some kind of problem (which the agency would not explain). CSEC reassured the public that it was not the victims of the wrongdoing, or that there was some sort of corruption connected to the construction of its new building. After the agency investigated itself, it found it had problems. But it would not tell members of Parliament what had happened when its ethics were seriously breached, though CSEC said it was improving its training and management and financial systems.[36]

CSEC has the ability to listen to anything that's carried over wires and airwaves. Bell Canada owns a database of cellphone and Internet users' private information the government often uses to collect information on Canadians. The federal government pays Bell for the information, and neither the government nor the telephone company inform people when the government dips into that pool of data. Word of the existence of the databank came out in early 2014 when the Competition Bureau released documents to Parliament showing it had used the Bell Canada Law Enforcement Database about twenty times between April 2012 and March 2013.

That was minimal compared to the Canada Border Services Agency, which said it used telecom customer data almost nineteen thousand times in 2013. That information may have come from Bell, but it's possible most or all of the big telecommunications companies run similar databases. The border cops got a deal on the information, paying telephone and cellphone companies just three dollars for each data request. University of Ottawa law professor Michael Geist said it appears Bell—and possibly other telecoms—grants the government fairly open access to the files it keeps on its subscribers. "I realize technically they are allowed to do this under the law as long as this is part of an investigation," Geist told reporter Paul McLeod of the Halifax *Chronicle Herald*. "But the notion that there is no real review of the legitimacy of the [data requests] and whether or not it's appropriate to provide the information strikes me as simply wrong."[37]

Three of the country's big telecommunications firms admitted they gave authorities information about more than 785,000 customers in 2010. There are over thirty major telecommunications and Internet providers in the country.[38]

The Harper government came up with Bill C-30, the Lawful Access Act, in 2012, which makes it legal for government spies to monitor the digital activities of Canadians in real time. The law is aimed at cybercrime, but it allowed the government to force Internet service providers to hand over, without a warrant, information on any web surfing that's done by Canadians. The bill was replaced with another law that makes the handover "voluntary," but, since most Internet providers are owned by big cable and telecommunications companies that are regulated by the federal government, they really don't have a lot of choice. Whether you've been watching Islamist videos or engaging in cybersex, chances are you've been spotted, tagged and downloaded.

ENEMIES OF THE STATE take all kinds of forms. Recently, Canada's spies turned their attention on people protesting the disappearance of bees. The Global Operations Centre, a little-known spy group run by the prime minister's staff, watched the Bee Die In, held the same day as the speech from the throne in October 2013. Agents took notes as people dressed as bees and flowers pretended to die on the front lawn of the Parliament Building, hoping to draw attention to the worldwide loss of pollinators. It was one of five protests that day that the operations centre spied on. The information on the dead bee people was shared with U.S. intelligence agents. The other protests were a First Nations Day of Action, an Idle No More protest in Ottawa, and two shale gas protests in New Brunswick.[39]

And, of course, there are the government's own employees, who, by the nature of their work, have the data and the expertise to do serious damage to the Harper government. In March 2014, the federal cabinet imposed a lifelong gag order on bureaucrats and lawyers working in sensitive government departments. Most of the gagged public servants work, or have worked, in the Department of Justice and the Privy Council Office. They face up to fourteen years in prison if they ever talk about their work.

"The practical implication of this is that it puts a terrific chill on the possibility of drawing on practitioner expertise, particularly the retired practitioners, to contribute to any kind of debate on intelligence and security matters in Canada if people followed the letter of the law," Wesley Wark, a University of Ottawa professor and one of Canada's leading experts in national security and espionage, told a *Toronto Star* reporter. He said Canada needs "those voices more than ever" since 9/11 and the revelations of out-of-control spying, wiretapping and computer hacking revealed by Snowden and other whistle-blowers.

"Special operational information," which can never be shared with the public, is loosely defined in this federal law as the identity of persons or groups approached as confidential sources by police or security agencies, Canada's plans for military operations, the country's methods for collecting intelligence, the target of any investigation, or the identity of spies. But it also includes "information or intelligence similar in nature" to those categories received by or relating to any foreign entity, such as the NSA.

"The security and intelligence community has certain operational requirements that need to be respected," a government notice of the new rules said. "[This] order enables the Government of Canada to provide additional assurances to its international partners and allies that special operational information shared with Canada will be protected." This suggests the regulation was made at least partly because of Canada's intelligence commitments to the United States and other allies, especially in the wake of the 2013 sentencing of Sub-Lt. Jeffrey Paul Delisle, a former naval officer based in Halifax, and Ottawa, for selling state secrets to the Russians. He was given a twenty-year sentence.[40]

The government tabled documents in the House of Commons showing that in its first six years in office it made at least forty-four requests to website-hosting companies to take down content from the Internet and to wipe the material from Google's search engine. Almost all of those requests were made between 2010 and 2012. The Department of National Defence made the largest number of these demands. Some seemed reasonable. The government asked Facebook to take a federal logo off of a page set up by supporters of a federal prisoner. It also tried to protect information about people who were applying for refugee status. Those files normally weren't available to web surfers, but smart users of Google could extract them. Some other requests seemed more political. For example, Environment Canada demanded the removal of two Netelligent parody websites that spoofed the department's own site. "I think what we are seeing is that the departments are becoming increasingly politicized," New Democrat MP Charlie Angus said. "They are being run by the 20-some-year-olds who are the political shock troops of the prime minister."[41]

Plumbers, ratfuckers, whatever they're called in Ottawa these days, they're always on the hunt for people who spill the government's secrets or show signs of disloyalty. The Tories were big friends of whistle-blowers when the Liberals were in power. Now they're treated as enemies of the state. Whistle-blowing has become so commonplace that there's now an organization, FAIR, that gives aid and comfort to those who come forward from the ranks of the public service and from corporate offices to expose corruption and stupidity.

Still, some whistle-blowers fight on. In 2012, Department of Justice lawyer Edgar Schmidt challenged his own department in Federal Court. He had been a whistle-blower who revealed details about the guidelines used by federal lawyers to draft legislation. Schmidt, who had been writing parliamentary bills for a decade, said lawyers in the Justice Ministry knew some of these bills violated the Charter of Rights, but the government did not warn Parliament. Schmidt took his worries to the top lawyers and executives in his department. Unsatisfied with their responses, he filed a court case.

As soon as Schmidt came forward, he was suspended without pay. The government argued that Schmidt violated solicitor-client privilege. The suspended lawyer said in court, "It's my position that solicitor-client privilege is never available to protect illegal instructions."

"The day after the filing of this statement, bang: 'You're suspended," Federal Court judge Simon Noël noted after each side made its case in Schmidt's wrongful dismissal lawsuit. The judge said the federal government had stripped sixty-year-old Schmidt of his income and, probably more importantly for a lawyer, his good reputation. "It's unbelievable," Noël told the government's lawyer. "Your client has done everything it can to kill this thing. The court doesn't like that . . . We see that in different countries and we don't like it . . . Canada is still a democracy."[43]

The Harper government would soon show how it felt about courts that get in the way of its plans.

CHAPTER 11

Baffle Them with Bullshit

Bullshit baffles brains.
—HAROLD BALLARD, FORMER OWNER OF
THE TORONTO MAPLE LEAFS[1]

Propaganda is scary stuff. It conjures up images of mind control, of Joseph Goebbels and Adolf Hitler, Lenin and Stalin, of Mao and *The Manchurian Candidate*. We fear it the same way we fear rats: because, like their plague-carrying fleas, propaganda kills. The British unleashed one of the great propaganda campaigns of history to get the Americans to join the Allied side in World War I, then bragged about it in the decade after that war. The backlash that resulted in the United States went a long way to keeping the Americans out World War II, until the Japanese attacked Pearl Harbor. Propaganda helped depose Mussolini. The British spread a very effective rumour that, when the going got tough, Mussolini would abscond with Italy's gold and foreign currency reserves. That's one of the reasons Mussolini was overthrown and the Italians sued for peace as soon as Allied troops landed on the Italian mainland.

After World War II, Canadians were leery about government propaganda. The Liberals under William Lyon Mackenzie King were terrified of the monster that they had created in the fight to beat

Hitler. King feared a "Canadian Goebbels" and fired John Grierson, the head of the country's propaganda department, partly because he thought Grierson was a communist. (Grierson was replaced by Davidson Dunton, a brilliant journalist who later co-chaired the Royal Commission on Bilingualism and Biculturalism and, at various times, headed the CBC and Carleton University).

The suspicion among the people and in the corridors of government that propaganda is the tool of totalitarian states, not liberal democracies like Canada, persisted long after the war. The Glassco Commission, which examined ways of modernizing the bureaucracy, was headed by J. Grant Glassco, a banker. In its 1962 report, the commission warned that government advertising had gone far past telling people the business hours of post offices and museums. Government promotion of its actions was "debatable," Glassco and his fellow committee members agreed. When governments went into publicizing the "newsworthiness" of their actions, they crossed the line. "There is no fixed line between exposition and argument, between publicity and propaganda." The role of government advertising was to be strictly factual and "to inform rather than to persuade." The Glassco Commission came to a conclusion that, in today's Ottawa, could be part heresy, part naïveté. The "ultimate decision on what is news and how it should be presented must be left to the media." A distinction had to be drawn between "material which genuinely informs and that which is calculated only to impress; the latter has no place in the information activities of government."[2]

In closed societies like North Korea and China, state control over information—modern and historical—makes it easy for the government to shape not only what people know, but also the way they think. Educating children in schools where blind obedience to the state is knocked into them and where they are fed a steady diet

286

of lies and half-truth ensures everyone grows up to do exactly what's expected. The overcurious and the skeptical learn quickly to keep their mouths shut or risk the unpleasant consequences.

In Western societies, propaganda is much more subtle and nuanced. Kids in our schools are trained to think critically and to see themselves as citizens with some obligations—at least, to vote. People might argue about the quality of education in our schools and the ideological bent of teachers, from grade schools to university, but we wouldn't have this debate at all if we weren't brought up in the belief that we have the right to have these conversations. In our society, personal knowledge is a sort of soup that everyone wants to add to. We get propaganda in government and corporate ads, from the Internet, from media. What is an election campaign except great waves of propaganda washing over the electorate? And why wouldn't people apply the same kind of skepticism to election promises that they'd apply to any other obvious propaganda, especially if they had previously voted for political parties that ignored the promises they had made?

The Harper government would love to be masters of propaganda. For example, they could rewrite history, marginalize science, convince people that environmentalists are fools and screwballs, dupe voters into believing the Liberals are nothing but reckless spenders while Conservatives are sound fiscal managers—modern deficit numbers be damned—and, most important, win re-election.

Sometimes, there is subtlety to Tory messaging and propaganda. For example, as Richard Nimijean notes in a recent article, Harper's promotion of Arctic sovereignty, and patriotism in general, is closely linked to the Tories' promotion of the military, especially big-ticket procurement of hardware like the F-35 stealth fighter planes.[3] His constant verbal attacks on Vladimir Putin and the Russians in 2014 over their takeover of the Crimea and parts of eastern Ukraine make much more sense when you consider that many voters in Western Canada have Ukrainian ancestry.

In the last few decades, an entire media manipulation industry has been created in Canada, with links between political parties, government departments, pollsters, lobbyists, ad agencies and, sometimes, academics. The lobbying industry has grown into a monster, and the Tories are not fully to blame. Jean Chrétien's Ottawa was a lobbyist's heaven. Sometimes, the government and its friends even share the same lobbyists. When the many problems plaguing the F-35 fighter plane became known to the public, mainly through the work of congressional committees in Washington, the builders of the plane, Lockheed Martin, as well as the Department of National Defence, the Ministry of Public Works and Government Services, and Industry Canada all used the same public relations firm, Thornley Fallis, to calm the public's fears. The three federal departments paid the company $700,000 between 2007 and 2012, mainly to say "no comment."[4]

THE TORIES STARTED their time in government with a rebranding. They would be "Canada's New Government" in everything that was sent out in the first twenty months of Harper's premiership, when the Tories had just a minority government. It was inscribed in every item that went out in print and over the airwaves. Every public servant was required to use those words to describe the federal government in anything that was released to the public. On September 5, 2005, Andrew Okulitch received an email from senior managers at Natural Resources Canada saying everyone who worked there had to use "Canada's New Government," with all of the words capitalized. Dr. Okulitch, a scientist under contract to the Geological Survey of Canada, answered that email with an undiplomatic rejection of the request, and, very quickly, found himself jobless (or at least officeless, since he was an emeritus scientist, meaning he worked without pay in a space provided by the government). Within an hour, he had this reply from Dr. Irwin Itzkovich, a special adviser to the deputy minister of natural resources: "Given your strong though misdirected views of the role and authority of the Government as elected by the people, and your duty to reflect their decisions, I accept that you are immediately removing yourself from the Emeritus Program. I wish you every success in your future." Cassie Doyle, the deputy minister of the department, called Okulitch at his home on Saltspring Island, B.C., to confirm the bad news. Within two weeks—after Okulitch's firing hit the media—the scientist got another call saying he could come back to work.[5]

In 2009, "Canada's New Government" morphed into the "Harper Government." During his years in power, the federal government, staffed by almost 200,000 public servants who are expected to be professional and non-partisan, has, at least in its self-description, belonged to the Tories and to Stephen Harper, rather than to the people of Canada.

Simplicity, whether it's slogans like "Canada's New Government," oversized blue cheques for bridges and roads handed out at staged photo ops, or short attack ads on TV and radio between elections, is important to getting the Harper message out. Dumbing things down has become an important part of their strategy. That's why talking points are so important in Harper's Ottawa. The message, whatever it is, must be crafted in the most simple language and terms and be implanted directly into the various media, whether those media are real or government-controlled: "It is hard to escape the conclusion that, at the federal level at least, a government hopelessly enamored with 'talking points' as the anodyne response to every question really isn't interested in talking at all, in the hope that government will neither be talked to nor talked about. This poses its own risk for the future," Christopher Waddell, the chair of Carleton University's journalism school, said in a recent article.[6]

The sloganeering that generated "Canada's New Government" gave us a slew of new laws with catchy titles: the Federal Accountability Act; Tackling Violent Crime Act; Cracking Down on Tobacco Marketing Aimed at Youth Act; Fairness for the Self-Employed Act; Truth in Sentencing Act; Balanced Refugee Reform Act; Celebrating Canada's Seniors Act; Eliminating Entitlements for Prisoners Act; Fairness for Military Families (Employment Insurance) Act; Protecting Victims from Sex Offenders Act; Tackling Auto Theft and Property Crime Act; Fair and Efficient Criminal Trials Act; Keeping Canada's Economy and Jobs Growing Act; Protecting Canadians by Ending Sentence Discounts for Multiple Murders Act; Standing up for Victims of White Collar Crime Act; Citizen's Arrest and Self-defence Act; Helping Families in Need Act; Jobs, Growth and Long-term Prosperity Act; Safe Food for Canadians Act; Safe Streets and Communities Act; Safer Witnesses Act; Not Criminally Responsible Reform Act; Protection of Communities and Exploited Persons Act (banning street prostitution); and Fair Elections Act.

Harper went to Edmonton in May 2014 for a photo op with his wife, Laureen, Tory MPs and police dog trainer Matt Williamson to announce the Justice for Animals in Service Act (Quanto's Law) in honour of Quanto, an Edmonton police service dog that was stabbed to death by Paul Joseph Vukmanich in October 2013. The dog-slayer was high on drugs and running from the police, who let Quanto loose. Under Quanto's Law, anyone who kills a police or military dog, or a dog used by a person with disabilities, will serve at least six months in jail and could be imprisoned for four years. But there was already a law against animal cruelty that protected Quanto and other police dogs, and the man who had killed Quanto was jailed for eighteen months for his crime (and eight months from fleeing from police).[7]

Harper's government didn't invent the use of cute phrases for naming laws. It started in the United States during Newt Gingrich's term as Speaker of the House of Representatives and was mimicked in Ontario by Mike Harris's Progressive Conservative government, which passed gems like the Fewer Municipal Politicians Act.

In the months before Harper won power, he got a lot of mileage criticizing the vast amount of money that the governing Liberals had spent on advertising (real ads, not just the fake billings in the sponsorship kickback scheme). Once elected, Harper started to spend liberally to get the Tory message out. For example, the government paid more than $200,000 to buy a full-page ad on the inside back page of the April 14, 2014, issue of *The New Yorker* magazine. The ad showed what looks like a lovely, clean river in Canada's wilderness. It not designed, however, to tempt *The New Yorker*'s affluent readers to visit Canada, though the tourism business certainly could use the boost. Instead, it was a pitch for the Keystone XL oil pipeline.

Globe and Mail columnist Eric Reguly called the ad's text "slick pieces of propaganda—misleading without being outright lies." The word "Keystone" didn't appear in the ad at all. And there were a lot of false comparisons. Reguly noticed the government's claim that Canada and United States have the same greenhouse gas emissions targets, which is true, but that's no big deal, since neither country is now a signatory to the Kyoto accord. And just because Canada has a target to reduce greenhouse gas emissions by 17 per cent between 2005 and 2020, that doesn't mean we'll actually meet it. In fact, Canada probably won't. And there's no penalty for failure. The ad talks a lot about Canada's stringent "regulatory environment," but don't confuse those words with "environmental regulations" because the regulations the ad talks about cover everything from construction boots to water pollution standards. The ad skirts around the fact that, unless there is some radical technological change to the way oil is extracted from the Athabaska sands, greenhouse gas emissions will rise as the oilsands development increases production. And expanding the oilsands production is the point of building Keystone.[8]

For years, Canadians were bombarded with ads for Canada's Economic Action Plan, the infrastructure program that the Harper government created—under duress from the opposition parties, after first denying there was a problem with the economy—after the 2008 financial meltdown. From 2009 to 2014, the government spent more than $100 million on the Economic Action Plan ads, expanding the use of the phrase over the years to cover almost all of its spending. From then on, the government sent out a confusing message: Canada had escaped the worst of the global downturn, and the government was spending billions on infrastructure to bring the country back to prosperity. The ads used the Tory party's blue colours and election-style imagery.

That's nothing new to Canadian government advertising—the Ontario Progressive Conservatives probably won the prize for that in their 1980s recession ads with the tagline "Life is Good Ontario. Preserve it. Conserve it"—but they were enough to stimulate David McGuinty. The Liberal MP from Ottawa (and brother of former Ontario premier Dalton McGuinty) introduced a private member's bill to ban ads that use the same colours and imagery as a political party. His brother had brought in a similar law that required Ontario government advertising to be vetted by the provincial auditor general. "He's taking public dollars and he's using public infrastructure—IT services, computers, cameras, office space—and he's running a political action campaign ad every Thursday night involving Mr. Harper and this is all about trying to shore up his support," David McGuinty told *Globe and Mail* reporter Bill Curry. "When he takes Canadian taxpayers' money to do this kind of thing, he's cheating."[9]

In the 2013–2014 fiscal year, Harper's team even spent $2.5 million to promote a job-creation grant called "Better Jobs" that didn't even exist. The government spent $3.1 million to explain its cuts to old age security.[10] Another $8.2 million went for ads designed to convince Canadians that the extraction of the country's natural resources is the key to the country's economic future.[11]

And the self-promotion of the Economic Action Plan advertising campaign is just part of what Harper's government spends on government ads. Overall, they had spent $69 million during the 2012–2013 fiscal year. There's been a big drop since 2009–2010, when the Tories only had a minority government. Then, cash was cascading out the door to Canada's ad agencies; the government spent $136 million that year. Most of that money was spent on television ads,[12] particularly on ads on sports shows.

THE THIRTY-SECOND Canada Action Plan TV spots ran in the fall of 2012 and from February to April of 2013. They showed happy tradespeople building a plane, a car and a ship. A silken-voiced narrator talked about federal money for apprenticeship grants, student loans and technology research. A poll done in the winter of 2013 showed some outright hostility to the ads, with people saying they were "propaganda" and a "waste of money." A survey taken a few months later found the ads didn't do what they claimed to do: tell people how to get more information about the government's recession-fighting programs. There was a solid way to see if the ads were effective ways of getting this information out. All of them told viewers to visit actionplan.gc.ca, a website created in 2009, to learn more about Canada's Economic Action Plan. A survey of 2,003 adult Canadians completed in April 2013, not long after the new federal budget was tabled, found just three people in the survey sample who actually visited the website. (The poll, which cost $29,000, was said to have a margin of error at plus or minus 2.2 percentage points, 19 times out of 20.)

The Harris/Decima poll, one of nine surveys commissioned by the federal Finance Department since 2009, showed only 6 per cent of those who said they recalled the TV ads reported being stimulated to do anything as a result. That compared to 25 per cent of the people who had remembered seeing TV ads in 2009, and went on to check out Ottawa's home renovation program. (This program had been wound down by the time the 2013 survey was taken.) The government was forced by its own laws to run the survey to test whether the ads were effective. The results were embarrassing: the TV ads flashed a toll-free phone number, 1-800-O-Canada, that offered more information. Not one of the 2,003 people polled had bothered to call it. A spokesperson for the Finance Department, Jack Aubry (who, in a previous career had covered the Senate for the Canwest chain), claimed that the various ad campaigns raised public awareness of Canada's Economic Action Plan. Some 62 per cent of Canadians knew about it, up from just 20 per cent in 2009. He also said visits to the action plan website had risen to 12,000 a day from 2,300.[13]

So, if, as polls suggested and critics said, the ads were so useless, why bother with them? Canadian Press reporter Dean Beeby dug around to find out. He learned that, since 2006, Library and Archives Canada has operated a website where "final reports of all public opinion research for which a contract was awarded" are posted within about six months of their creation. If, however, the government did its own, in-house surveys, the results would not be posted online. And those internal surveys found that the ads did, indeed, pay off. Maybe people weren't thronging to websites or overwhelming the operators at 1-800-O-Canada, but they did make people feel better about the government. Of the people surveyed, 42 per cent of the people who had *not* seen the ads approved of the overall performance of the government. But that number jumped a full five percentage points, to 47 per cent, of people who had seen the ads. So maybe people weren't stimulated to learn more about the government's recession-fighting, but a hefty percentage of them—the kind of numbers that could make a serious difference in a federal election—got a tingle inside for the Tories.[14]

In an editorial, *The Globe and Mail* said the ads were a waste of money, other than to the Conservatives. Rather than tell people something useful, like, say, where to get an application form for a home renovation grant, the ads were full of pretty pictures, soft music and smooth, empty talk. "It is nothing novel to see a government pump its own tires, or project an aura of progress in a tough economy," the newspaper said. "But the polished and cheery ads— which have cost at least $113-million since 2009 and have become fixtures on television—are often replete with broad allusions to 'better infrastructure to make us more competitive' or 'more efficient government to keep taxes low.' No wonder most people tune them out . . . Where public dollars are paying for air time, ads should make clear what is on offer, and spare Canadians the rosy platitudes about prosperity."[15]

The government has spent millions on ads pushing oil pipelines and delegitimizing critics of exploitation of the oilsands. They've also had lots of free publicity and support from Canada's oil and gas sector and from pressure groups like Ethical Oil. These campaigns all tried to mask the Harper government's dismal record on the environment. At the same time that Harper's government put out a five-page press release boasting about a new conservation program to protect national parks and connect Canadians to nature, the federal cabinet allowed the expansion of truck routes through the Northwest Territories' Nááts'ihch'oh National Park Reserve near the Yukon border to move 25,000 tons of ore a day from a zinc mine owned by Chinese investors. Harper announced the creation of the park reserve on his August 2012 northern tour, saying it would protect the watershed of the South Nahanni River, along with the habitat of grizzly bears and caribou. Environmental groups, however, said the boundaries of the park had been drawn to set aside large swaths of pristine land for mining leases.

As EYES SHIFT from TVs and newspapers to computer screens, so have Tory propaganda campaigns. The Conservatives literally applied a blue tint to the Government of Canada's websites in the run-up to the 2015 election. The government's website name was changed from gc.ca into canada.ca (canada.com had been snapped up by Izzy Asper's Canwest media company and is now used by Postmedia). Along with the new tint of the pages, the government's website was rejigged to make it easy to find information that most people might need. The redesign also made it much more difficult for policy wonks and journalists to find information on how the government operates and the ways it spends its money. The new pages carry government boilerplate about its achievements. There's lots of talk about the Economic Action Plan and, in the early spring of 2014, Environment Canada's local weather page carried blurbs for the Prime Minister's Volunteer Awards and the Korea free trade agreement. The Tories defended the new blue look with talking points saying blue was easy on the eyes and had tested well with focus groups.[16]

Someone in the bureaucracy leaked Harper's "web presence renewal strategy" in the spring of 2013. The strategy was initiated by Harper himself, who wrote a letter to Treasury Board president and Muskoka gazebo builder Tony Clement telling him to make it so. The plan calls for a big cut to the number of government websites. Material considered "unpopular" will be stripped from the sites that survive. And, of course, the Centre will carefully supervise the posting of all information on government websites and on social media. Ministry websites will be replaced with sites reflecting "user needs," providing simple information on services but not a lot of facts. Things that aren't all that popular and receive few hits, like hard-to-read science reports, won't make the cut, except, maybe, on difficult-to-find archive pages. All of these changes were supposed to be made by the spring of 2014.[17]

The Harper government has spent hundreds of thousands of dollars on sponsored tweets. Most of that money was spent by Harper's Privy Council Office. Between 2012 and 2014, the entire federal government spent $456,324. Veterans Affairs spent $103,694 on promoted tweets during fiscal 2013–2014 year, mostly to remind people about Remembrance Day. News of the department's Twitter spending incited fury among vets, who took to Parliament Hill to protest. Veterans Affairs spent an extra $4 million that winter, leading Liberal critic Frank Valeriote to say to Julian Fantino, the minister in charge of veterans affairs, "I'm wondering how you can justify for us your department spending more on advertising—a $4 million increase in advertising—and less on the actual programs themselves." A few minutes after that confrontation, Jenny Migneault, the spouse of a veteran suffering from PTSD, shouted at the minister "Mr. Fantino, I'm just a vet's spouse. You're forgetting us, once more. We're nothing to you."[18]

Canadian Heritage spent $20,000 on tweets that year. The

CBC wrote cheques to Twitter for $77,291 to pay for promoted tweets and a promoted account on Twitter in 2013–2014. Business Development Bank of Canada spent $167,189 on tweets between 2012 and 2014, while the Canadian Institutes of Health Research spent $10,172 and Public Safety Canada spent $51,000. The Department of National Defence and the Canadian Forces spent $10,000 on promoted tweets in 2013–2014 as part of the "priority occupations" marketing campaign to showcase the Forces "as an employer of choice."[19]

But the best propaganda is always free. And the very best looks like journalism and commentary from public-spirited citizens who just happen to support everything the government says or does.

In 2006, the Tories came up with an innovation. They would forge links with the right-wing blogosphere, something that had already been done years before in the United States where the extreme Right of the Republican Party had mouthpieces like Free Republic and, before about 2007, *Little Green Footballs*. In 2005, Adam Daifallah met Tom Flanagan at a Civitas meeting and told him about the Blogging Tories, a group of conservative bloggers who had set up a system of linking to each other, knowing such a group would have influence greater than the sum of its parts.

Flanagan recruited Stephen Taylor, who operated as Conservative Party of Canada Pundit (and later went on to take Harper's old job as head of National Citizens Coalition), to coordinate the blog network. Taylor's blog, stephentaylor.ca, was among the most popular in Canada (along with *Small Dead Animals* and Steve Janke's *Angry in the Great White North*) and had no serious Liberal challengers. Tory campaign leader Doug Finley put some of his staff to work monitoring the blogs and getting out stories that, as Flanagan later wrote, "were not quite ready for the mainstream media."[20]

In fact, the Tories have used blogs to float trial balloons of some of their more controversial ideas. They also use the bloggers to handle "low-road" attacks on political opponents, media critics, non-governmental organizations, environmentalists, First Nations leaders and anyone else who gets in the way. The Tory bloggers can say anything they like while giving Harper and his government arm's-length deniability. Sometimes, the bloggers are threatened with lawsuits by people hit with smears, and, in at least one case, involving Ottawa lawyer Richard Warman and the owners of *Free Dominion*, they've been saddled with serious damages and costs.

Still, the bloggers can undermine the credibility of their targets. It was conservative bloggers who led the attack on Attawapiskat Chief Theresa Spence when she went on a hunger strike in Ottawa in late 2012 to early 2013 that was heavily publicized in the mainstream media. Conservative bloggers have been able to push the reach of Sun News by posting links to its website and by featuring its videos. Some conservative bloggers have also hyped Harper's *24 Seven* video posts. And they've launched some very nasty personal attacks against journalists.

Commenters on these blogs can post material that's even nastier than the blog posts themselves, although the court's decision in Warman's case against *Free Dominion* has probably curbed the worst of it. (The libels in that case were, for the most part, in comments posted about Warman by anonymous writers.) These "ordinary Canadians" can seem to have far more credibility than actors in government ads. They seem especially real when they're voices coming over the radio. Harper's operatives prepared questions for grassroots supporters who called into open-line shows, some of which, like *The Lowell Green Show* in Ottawa, are among the highest-rated programs on local radio. All people who were willing to shill for the Tories needed to do was go to the party website and type in their postal code. They would get a list of talk shows and advice on what to say on given topics.[21]

For those who like to see who's talking—especially when it's the prime minister—the Harper team has developed a strategy of making sure the image of the leader is carefully crafted and easily accessible. And they need their man to look good. Harper has hired, at public expense, a manager of visual communications and a manager of new media and marketing. He also has an image consultant who picks out his clothes, styles his hair and does his makeup.[22]

IN MAY 2009, Governor General Michaëlle Jean made a well-publicized tour of the Canadian Arctic. At one Inuit village, the local people served up a feast of northern delicacies including raw seal heart. Most people would be squeamish, but Jean not only ate the seal heart but also even seemed to enjoy it. (The author, having eaten seal meat with far less pleasure, gives Her Excellency a tip of the hat.) Four months later, Harper and several of his cabinet ministers did their own tour. And, again, seal was on the menu (seal meat this time, not heart). Jean had eaten her seal with newspaper photographers and videographers in tow, but Harper's handlers barred all media. The Prime Minister's Office distributed a photograph showing Harper and the ministers holding toothpicks. No reporters or photographers actually watched them eat the seal. No one could really be sure they did it, or if they (like the author) found seal to taste wretched to the untrained palate. The Canadian Press wire service filed an official complaint, and, a few months later, the Canadian Association of Journalists expressed its concern in a letter to Harper: "It's getting tougher to find an independent eye recording history, a witness seeing things how they really happened—not how politicians wish they'd happened."[23]

The Tories had already learned the hard way that pictures can be politically lethal. There's always the old story of Robert Stanfield, then Progressive Conservative leader, who playfully played catch with reporters in 1974 while cameras clicked. Stanfield was an intelligent and athletic man, and he caught and threw the football well, but the one picture that made the front page of newspapers was the shot of Stanfield fumbling the ball, with devastating consequences to a campaign that the Tories had been winning. There were the Harper in dude-ranch clothes shot from the Calgary Stampede and the Harper man-boobs shot that inspired Harper to never be photographed without a suit jacket. And, at the height of the KAIROS scandal, the Bev Oda as Roy Orbison shot, taken while the minister in charge of CIDA was having a smoke outside the Parliament Building.

The Tories began serious planning of their photo handout strategy after the 2004 election when party strategists realized visuals appeal to swing voters who don't spend much time following politics and make up their minds about candidates based on the way they present themselves. Tory strategists, according to a party expert quoted anonymously by political scientist Alex Marland, became "obsessed" with the details of "photo backdrops, stage positioning, colors schemes and the leader's clothing." They picked out business suits that hid Harper's waistline (which has fluctuated though the prime minister's political career). They chose backdrops of Parliament, especially the big wooden doors in the foyer of the House of Commons. Canadian flags were brought into places where they're normally not seen to generate a bit of national pride and to remind people that Harper leads the country.

There is a split between larger media, which rarely, if ever, uses Tory handouts (although in 2014 the *Toronto Star* did use a Liberal handout photograph on its front page of Justin Trudeau having coffee with Adam Vaughn before Vaughn announced he was running for the Liberals in a by-election to replace outgoing MP Olivia Chow). Some editors of small newspapers told Marland that they used the pictures because they are free, and they cannot afford pictures from Ottawa that come from news services that charge for pictures.[24] In general, Marland found, Canadian media were more likely than their colleagues in Britain and the United States to use handouts (even though photographs and videos issued by heads of governments in larger countries tend to be better than the material made by the Harper Prime Minister's Office). It will be interesting to see whether, as large media companies continue to face tough times, they will be more tempted by the free images.

But even if they aren't, Marland notes in his study of the issue, the images still have some effect. Editors who see them, even for a moment, are part of the target audience. After seeing hundreds or thousands of the free photographs cross their desk or screen, the image of Harper in the minds of photo editors may be shaped by this propaganda. They may buy into the framing of Harper as a serious leader in a suit who plays guitar and piano and likes kittens. Eventually, they may expect their own photographers to deliver pictures of Harper that resemble the visual image that Harper's team ties to create.

The photographs are also used on government web pages. Tory operatives make sure that government websites have plenty of pictures of the prime minister. One former government communications staffer tells a story of being called late at night by senior staff in the Prime Minister's Office and ordered to remove pictures of hungry Haitian children on a Department of Foreign Affairs web page and replace them with photographs of Harper.

Internet video is likely the next frontier. Badly staged photo ops, like those of *24 Seven* and Sun TV's fake swearing-in of new Canadians (using employees of the citizenship ministry) don't get much traction with the public: they're obviously fake and they're not quite bad enough to be funny. So far, only true believers and a few reporters spend much time watching the stuff. But, once they get better at it, the Tories hope to use their video propaganda campaign to link up with more potential donors and campaign foot soldiers.

Anyone who wanted to watch a live-stream video of the Aga Khan's speech to Parliament had to fill out an online form that asked for their email address. Days before the respected religious leader addressed the House of Commons and a rally at Massey Hall in Toronto in March 2014, thousands of people received an email from Employment Minister Jason Kenney—who had done so much to build the party's ethnic support when he was immigration minister—telling them that the Aga Khan's speech would be broadcast on the Conservative-owned website stephenharper.ca.

A few days after the speech, everyone who had signed up to watch the Aga Khan got an email from the Conservatives asking the primarily Ismaili Muslim viewers for a donation. Immigration Minister Chris Alexander reminded the Aga Khan followers and fans that the speech was "a truly meaningful and unforgettable occasion." Then came the pitch, which asked the email recipients to go back to the website to watch a Tory campaign-style video showing Harper and the Aga Khan talking together. "I encourage you to watch it and be moved by the important words of two great world leaders, Please feel free to share this opportunity with your friends and family, as well."[25]

Those people can expect to hear back from the Harper team, who will want their donations, their vote, and a spot on the lawn for a sign. Propaganda and information-gathering is an essential part of modern retail politics. So is poisoning the wells of your enemies and, if need be, making sure their supporters stay away from the polls.

CHAPTER 12

Attack, Attack, Attack!

*No aspect of responsible government is more fundamental
than having the trust of citizens. Canadians' faith in the institutions
and practices of government has been eroded. This new government
trusts in the Canadian people, and its goal is that Canadians will once
again trust in their government. It is time for accountability.*
—Speech from the Throne, 2006

Harper's critics say he has eagerly adopted the Alberta provincial
tradition of attacking enemies with torches and pitchforks. The
Wild Rose province does have quite a history: the tradition builds
on the foundation laid by Bible Bill Aberhart, a schoolteacher
and amateur preacher who went into politics during the Great
Depression. He became convinced that a quack economic theory—
based on inflation and fiat currency—could solve Alberta's and
Canada's economic problems. Social Credit offered free money,
printed by the provinces, as a sort of dividend that would stimulate the economy. As a theory, it was harmless enough and might
have even done some good, but in practice, it was illegal. Only
the national government can print money. Aberhart's government
went after Ottawa and the big eastern banks, along with Toronto-
and Montreal-based corporations, framing them as the enemies

of Albertans. They were "rats, sons of Satan, liars, fornicators," according to the premier.

Aberhart was years ahead of his time in his dealings with the media. His government passed a law forcing the province's papers to print government press releases and giving the government wide censorship powers. This law was needed, he said, because the media was "the mouthpiece of financiers" that printed "their spurious articles" from their "mad dog operations" to promote "privilege, lawlessness and gangsterdom." The Supreme Court and the Judicial Committee of Britain's Privy Council threw out that law, and Alberta weeklies and dailies collectively became the only Canadian newspaper to win a Pulitzer Prize for political writing.[1]

Alberta has, through much of its history, been dominated by conservative parties. Some, like Peter Lougheed's 1970s government—which launched the current Alberta Progressive Conservative dynasty—have imitated the middle-of-the-road managerial system that worked so well for Liberal and Tory politicians in Ontario, at both the federal and provincial levels. However, Alberta politicians have tended to latch on to the more aggressive tendencies of the American right. The confrontational styles of Newt Gingrich and the Tea Partiers are now embedded in Alberta conservatism as it sidesteps from the centrist politics of the Progressive Conservatives to the populism and corporatism of the Wildrose movement.

Harper adopted the Alberta way of politics with the enthusiasm of a convert. He had started off as an Ontario kid who admired Pierre Trudeau, but, by the 1990s, became convinced, as had Aberhart, that Eastern Canada was out to pluck the West. Had Harper never been elected prime minister, he might have been remembered as an advocate for a "firewall" around Alberta, and for spouting off about the Maritimes' supposed "culture of defeat."

Alberta's us-and-them political culture is well suited to people who don't like other people. Harper's mentor, Tom Flanagan, a far more personable man than his most famous student, says Harper has a "Nixonian" view of politics. Harper "believes in playing politics right up to the edge of the rules, which inevitably means some team members will step across ethical or legal lines in their desire to win for the Boss."[2]

Alberta-style politics does not fit the rest of Canada. To tailor the approach to the political cultures of British Columbia and Eastern Canada, neo-conservatives had to use U.S.-style think tanks, political action groups and grant-giving foundations to put some intellectual clothes on it. And once they led the way, left-wing Canadians copied the template, so now the country is awash in people professing economic, environmental and social justice expertise working for important-sounding organizations that are often no more than shells.

Tasha Kheiriddin and Adam Daifallah, two bright and personable neo-conservative easterners who helped redefine Canadian conservatism in the early years of this century, were loud proponents of the think tank system that has existed in the States since the 1960s. The think tanks don't just do research of varying levels of quality and objectivity, they also provide stables of quotable "experts" to the media. Some of these experts become pundits in their own right. They, through their access to the media and the cachet that's given to their expertise, can change the language of politics, and, in doing so, the way people think. Kheiriddin, a lawyer, gave them some suggestions: "For the Liberal terms 'medicare' and 'public health care', substitute 'state health care monopoly'; for the Liberal 'social services,' substitute 'government programs'; for the Liberal 'investing tax dollars,' substitute 'spending taxpayers' money'; for the Liberal 'budget surplus,' substitute 'amount Canadians were over-taxed.'"[3]

The Fraser Institute has arisen as one of the country's most successful think tanks, and its research—often of inconsistent quality, and almost always agenda-driven—is used without much questioning by most of the Canadian media. The Fraser Institute has copied Florida businessman Dallas Hostetler's Tax Freedom Day and picked up many other American crusades. At the same time, it has attacked the Canadian medicare system for its wait times, with the suggestion that a mixed or, even better, private health care system would be more effective. The Fraser Institute has also pressured the provinces to return to back-to-basics education, using headline-grabbing school rankings.

When Canwest bought the former Southam papers (large dailies in Montreal, Hamilton, Windsor, Calgary, Edmonton and Vancouver, among others) from Conrad Black in 2000, Izzy Asper, the company's president, was a member of the board of the Fraser Institute. Fraser Institute alumni working in the media include Fazil Mihlar at the *Vancouver Sun*; Danielle Smith, a columnist at the *Calgary Herald* before becoming leader of the right-wing provincial Wildrose Party in Alberta; and John Robson at Sun Media and CFRA radio in Ottawa. Other conservative organizations, such as the Donner Foundation, have worked to remake the Canadian political landscape and change the way Canadians see their own country. The Donner Foundation spent $2 million a year from its $200 million endowment to start and support right-wing think tanks.[4] It also covers the cost of one of the country's richest non-fiction book prizes.

The oil industry and the Harper government set up and paid for the Canadian School of Energy and Environment at the University of Calgary and a think tank called the Energy Policy Institute of Canada. The emphasis of the University of Calgary school was much more on energy than on environment. And the industry/government choice of manager and founder of the two bodies was interesting. Bruce Carson was a disbarred Ontario lawyer who had served two short stretches in provincial jails for fraud. He had also been bankrupt and, for some time, had been living with a young Ottawa woman who'd previously made her living as an escort and now ran a business selling clean water technology to Aboriginal reserves. Carson was a former senior policy adviser to Harper who had somehow cleared the security checks that are normally done on senior staffers. After he left government in 2009 to start and run the Calgary think tanks, Carson was a frequent visitor to Ottawa. It was there, in 2012, that he was charged with influence peddling and illegal lobbying on behalf of his girlfriend's water treatment technology business.[5] Two years later, he was charged again, this time with illegal lobbying and influence peddling on behalf of the oil and gas industry.[6]

Much of the lobbying and shilling is done on behalf of the oil industry. And in the oilsands, one of the largest foreign investors is the conglomerate owned by the Koch brothers, who are big financers of opponents of scientists who believe the climate is being changed by carbon dioxide emissions from fossil fuels. In Canada, the oil lobby is headed by the Canadian Association of Petroleum Producers, which has paid for pro-oilsands advertising campaigns and has hired mainstream journalists like Peter Mansbridge and Rex Murphy, at hefty speaking fees, to address its conventions and conferences.

But the biggest group of petroleum lobbyists sits on the government side of the House of Commons. A strong case can be made that Canadian oil is more ethical, at least from a human rights point of view. That argument, though, is used to push away legitimate environmental fears. As we have seen, the Harper government has effectively gutted environmental assessment of pipeline and other oil infrastructure projects. It has turned the intelligence agencies of Canada against environmentalists and First Nations that have gotten in the way, and has hammered its enemies in conservative media like Sun News and on the often vicious Tory blogs.

PETRO-STATES have one thing in common: they're undemocratic. The fast, vast profits from oil seem to have a corrupting influence on countries that rely on them. In Canada, we're seeing that corrosion in Alberta, where political discussion is limited to right and centre right, the media is weak, and all political and media leaders circle the wagons when outsiders like Neil Young and Bishop Desmond Tutu say the oilsands are an ecologic disaster.

Taken to the extreme, the Harper government has built a system of attack ads and personal slurs in Parliament against anyone who threatens the regime and its backers in Alberta. The boundary between personal and political lives has been broken down, and anyone is fair game to be insulted, humiliated or branded a thief or a traitor, no matter how much they love the country and how hard they have worked to serve it.

This system exists to crush anyone who emerges as a threat to the neo-conservative vision of Canada. It has been used to destroy Paul Martin, Stéphane Dion and Michael Ignatieff, and has been turned loose on Justin Trudeau. In 2013, retired Canadian Gen. Andrew Leslie, who went to work for the federal Liberals, felt its sting for billing the government to move him into a new home in Ottawa. Leslie had used a perk that's offered to all military personnel. Members of the Canadian Forces are allowed the full cost of one last household move. Usually, the move gets soldiers, sailors and air force members out of isolated places like Cold Lake, Alberta, and Gagetown, New Brunswick. It was seen by Forces personnel as a sort of bonus and thanks to military families for years of putting up with frequent moves.

Leslie lived in Ottawa when he retired. His children had grown up and moved out, and he wanted to downsize. So he took advantage of the benefit, using it to cover the cost of selling his old house in Ottawa and moving a few blocks to a home that suited his needs. Legally, he was solid. Politically, it left him in the crosshairs of members of a government that had never, until that point, gone after soldiers who had asked for their moves to be paid. Tory Defence Minister Rob Nicholson was just settling into the job when he launched his attack on Leslie, who had suddenly morphed from a respected general to a Liberal political hack in Torytalk.

"Expense claims for Liberal Defence Advisor Andrew Leslie's in-city move appear grossly excessive. As such, I will be asking the Department of National Defence to examine how an in-city move could possibly total over $72,000. In the meantime, it is important for Andrew Leslie to explain why he believes this is a reasonable expense for hard working Canadians to absorb," Nicholson said in a statement. "This is a matter of judgment and the responsible use of taxpayer dollars."

Leslie fired back: "I knew when I signed on to be an advisor to Justin Trudeau that I would be subject to partisan attacks and scrutiny very different than other retired soldiers. I can take it. I have been shot at by real bullets. What is disappointing is that this particular attack may raise questions over a military retirement benefit and I do not think veterans deserve to have another measure called into question."

Generals can usually stand up to this kind of smear. It's more difficult for ordinary people who are targeted for joining a cause and speaking out against Tory government policies. Conservatives tried to crush Native activist Cindy Blackstock. She was the executive director of the First Nations Child and Family Caring Society, hardly the sort of thing most governments would find particularly threatening. Blackstock was surprised and perplexed when she was told that officials would cancel a 2009 Parliament Hill meeting on Aboriginal child welfare if she was in the room. Ontario First Nations chiefs wanted her at the meeting because she is an expert in child advocacy. Blackstock filed a request under the Privacy Act and received 2,500 pages telling her what the Harper government knew about, and thought about, her.

Bureaucrats in the Justice and Aboriginal Affairs departments knew a lot about her professional and personal life. They had been following her Facebook and Twitter accounts. And they seemed to have a fine time using that information to mock her in emails that circulated among publicly paid officials. "Our girl's on a roll," one bureaucrat wrote in an email. Another talked about "our dearest friend Cindy Blackstock . . ."

Nothing about Blackstock, a member of the Gitksan First Nation in British Columbia, seemed too insignificant for officials in the two departments. They even passed around and commented on recipes Blackstock had posted on Facebook. Ten public servants shared an email about Blackstock's appearance at a public event that included the smarmy comment: "Day One opened with the Cindy Blackstock show, a tour de force that seems to fire up a ready-to-be impressed audience . . . after this clever argument she rattled through some general statistics (or gave the impression of doing so) and was whisked away to the airport."

Twice, federal bureaucrats applied for and received Blackstock's Indian status information. They made a copy of a post on her Facebook page written by a twelve-year-old Aboriginal child and commented among each other about an event Blackstock went to in the Australian desert. Digging through the stack of emails, Blackstock found that 189 senior officials from the Justice and Aboriginal Affairs ministries gathered information about her and shared comments about her life. She told the *Toronto Star* she was "shocked by the level of sarcasm and the nasty tone about me by people I've never met. These are officials employed by the government acting in the context of their official duties," she said.

"It was so negative and deeply personal—and nobody ever appeared to ask if it was appropriate." Blackstock believes she hit the Harper government's radar when her child advocacy organization and the Assembly of First Nations filed a complaint with the Canadian Human Rights Tribunal in 2007. The group argues Aboriginal children across Canada get less money for education and social programs than non-Native kids.[7]

In 2012, she amended the Human Rights complaint to include the information about the government's stalking and mocking, saying she would donate any penalty payment to charity. And the Aboriginal Peoples Television Network promised to broadcast any Human Rights Tribunal hearings that may be held to adjudicate Blackstock's complaint. The government's decision to harass a critic who advocated for more federal money for Aboriginal schools seems petty and mean. The way it carried out its invasion of privacy and shared her personal information in juvenile emails can hardly be considered a great moment in reconciliation between the Government of Canada and the First Nations.[8]

BLACKSTOCK IS NOT ALONE. The Harper government also tracks many other Canadians' social media comments on sites like Facebook and Twitter, YouTube, chat rooms, message boards and blogs in both English and French. The Public Works Department pays for round-the-clock, "real-time analysis of social media content," with the ability to "target key influencers found in blog commentary and social conversations," and includes analysis of the "sentiment or tone of posts," according to contract bid documents released in the fall of 2013 by the government.[9] The government tracks the posts of top influencers at blogs and chat rooms and the comments sections of online publications. Public Works Canada also has an Electronic Media Monitoring Program that tracks mainstream broadcasters and print media for other government departments.

But the really big guns are saved for institutions, because the only way the Harper regime will make lasting changes to this country is by destroying the reputations of organizations, agencies and government departments that act on behalf of Canadians. In 2008, Ezra Levant was brutally frank with his blog readers when he told them to "denormalize human rights commissions in the court of public opinion." Levant was complaining about the hate speech laws enforced by provincial and federal human rights commissions, saying that investigations and hearings into complaints against him, *Maclean's* magazine and author Mark Steyn were punishment-by-process and attacks on free speech.

It was clear Levant wanted the commissions gone for good. He hoped the publicity from his fight with the Alberta Human Rights Commission and his defence of a libel suit filed by former Canadian Human Rights Commission lawyer Richard Warman would "ensure that the excesses of the commissions are in the news every day for years, showing them to be the un-Canadian institutions they have become."[10]

This type of recasting of institutions into villains has been fairly successful. Conservatives across Canada accept the idea that somehow human rights commissions are out of control and should be abolished, despite the fact that the cases against Levant and Steyn were thrown out by provincial human rights commissions, and the federal body refused to investigate the complaints at all. It would have been interesting to see Levant's reaction if he had *lost*.[11]

Hate speech complaints make up a minuscule number of cases dealt with by the federal and provincial human rights commissions. Most of their work involves people who have been hurt by discrimination based on colour, religion, gender, disability or country of origin, but it would be hard to convince Canadians that, say, nannies from the Philippines should no longer have government protection. Better to cast a lawyer or a magazine as victims, and Muslim activists as bullies, in league with rogue bureaucrats to muzzle Canadian conservatives.

In this bizarre world of attack politics and delegitimization of opponents, enemies lurk everywhere. Before the 2013 cabinet shuffle, Erica Furtado, one of the prime minister's advisers responsible for issues management, sent a memo to political staffers in ministers' offices telling them to make lists of troublesome bureaucrats and "enemy" stakeholders. The checklist of ten items included "bureaucrats that can't take no (or yes) for an answer," and "friend and enemy stakeholders." The lists were put into the binders that were distributed to new ministers and members of cabinet who changed jobs.

Someone in a minister's office leaked a Prime Minister's Office order to make the lists, which were essentially a blacklist of public servants and stakeholders, sending it out to several Parliament Hill reporters. When staffers in one minister's office objected to the exercise, they were labelled "politically unreliable" and cut off from further communications on the matter, one of the "unreliable" staff told Global TV news reporters. The network's source said the stakeholder enemies included environmental groups, non-profits, and civic and industry associations who didn't agree with the Conservative agenda. Staffers were also supposed to come up with an enemies list of reporters, but the PMO decided to drop the idea, much to the chagrin of reporters who hoped to be on it.

"I think it's a little bit of paranoia at play," said Megan Leslie, deputy leader of the NDP. "But really it is about control. It's about making sure there is an absolute strangle-hold on these ministers, that they are not developing their own relationships, that they're not working with groups or individuals that the government sees as enemies."[12]

During the scandal over Bev Oda's supposed doctoring of a government document to cut off aid to KAIROS, the religious group that opposed some aspects of Harper's foreign policy, interim Liberal leader Bob Rae accused Harper of using unqualified young "jihadis" in his office to enforce the prime minister's will throughout the federal government. The prime minister's spinners turned the tables and accused Rae of being soft on terrorism and callous to the suffering of its victims. Rae stuck to his guns.

"If the 25-year-old jihadis in the prime minister's office can't control it, it doesn't happen," Rae explained. "That's the pathology that affects everything that moves in this government. It's a pathology. It's terrible. This is a disease, this excess of control. This is a bunch. It's a culture of people who are ideologically attuned in one area, who are fanatically loyal to what the prime minister is trying to do, and who are given responsibility far above their abilities." Harper's spokesperson Dimitri Soudas called Rae's remarks "extreme comments that are insulting to victims of terrorism and jihadism."[13]

EAGER STAFFERS exist in many governments, and they are always willing to do the bidding of this prime minister, just as some were willing to attack people who got in the way of Jean Chrétien.[14] Young, bright, ambitious people are drawn to Parliament Hill, and many of them will do whatever it takes to stay there and move up the political food chain.

When Justin Trudeau held an open-air news conference near the Centennial Flame on the lawn of Parliament Hill in June 2013, just as the Senate expense scandal revelations were leading the news, Conservative Party interns and young staffers working in the Prime Minister's Office, pretending to be ordinary tourists and voters, gathered around the Liberal leader to disrupt the event. The PMO gathered the interns and gave them protest signs quoting Conservative attack ad slogans, after getting a tip-off on Twitter that Trudeau would hold the news conference, where he announced several policies that would, he said, increase transparency in the House of Commons. The young Conservatives stood behind Trudeau as he read a statement on live TV. They left when the RCMP reminded them that they had no permit to protest or picket and told them how to apply for one. After reporters and Liberal researchers were able to identify six of the protesters as Tory interns, Jenni Byrne, the Conservative Party's director of political operations (she would become deputy chief of staff in the fall of 2013), instructed the young people not to speak to the media.[15]

And it was likely a summer intern in Justice Minister Peter MacKay's office who posed as a Liberal at a rural riding association meeting in May 2014 and taped Liberal MP John McKay talking about a potential Justin Trudeau "bozo eruption." The Liberals had gathered to hear McKay talk about water quality, but an eager young man pulled McKay aside and chatted him up about Trudeau's recent remarks about sex-selective abortions. McKay thought he was talking privately, but a recording of the conversation was handed over to CTV News.[16]

These jihadis have real power. In 2008, the limousine of Paul Dubois, Canada's ambassador to Germany, was navigating the streets of Berlin, on its way to the radio studios of a big public broadcaster, when Dubois got a text message from Ottawa. The career diplomat, who had been in the German capital for four years, was en route to do a media interview about Canada's relatively strong economy and its vibrant society. But the text, from the Prime Minister's Office, told him to cancel the interview. There was no explanation. "Hell, we're doing this interview," Dubois later told the *Toronto Star*'s Rick Westhead. "It's ridiculous. Most ambassadors cave in and just say no to speaking invitations now. It's insulting to have to check your speeches with some 23-year-old kid in the Prime Minister's Office. As a result, fewer people around the world know about Canada and Canadian values. Public engagement is so important."[17]

Dubois was able to talk, but a report by the Canadian Defence and Foreign Affairs Institute said Canadian diplomats are being forced by the activists in the Harper government to let the social media revolution roll past them. They can't use Twitter or Facebook to explain what they do for Canadians.

The practice of international diplomacy is undergoing a revolution. As activists, private and public organizations, political leaders and mass publics embrace Twitter, Facebook and other forms of social media, foreign ministries have come under increasing pressure to update their operating methods. Many countries, including the U.S. and Britain, are now encouraging their diplomats to use social media as a regular part of their job—not simply as a virtual "listening post" to monitor political discussions, nor merely as a megaphone for broadcasting press releases, but as a forum for participating directly in these discussions. Foreign ministries that fail to adapt to the social media revolution will lose influence over time: they will forgo opportunities to shape public discussions that are increasingly channeled through social media, to correct errors of fact or interpretation in real-time, and to build networks of interlocutors and followers.

317

Canada is lagging far behind the U.S. and Britain in digital diplomacy. Aside from a few recent experiments, the Department of Foreign Affairs and International Trade (DFAIT) has largely sat on the sidelines of this revolution. DFAIT operates few social media channels and these channels tend to have few followers, compared to our two closest allies. Further, the Conservative government's centralized control of public communications makes it virtually impossible for Canadian diplomats to engage in real-time substantive exchanges, which is the currency of the medium. Unless DFAIT joins its American and British counterparts in embracing new channels and methods of diplomacy, Canada's voice will progressively fade in international affairs.[18]

When reality isn't good enough, Harper's jihadis have not been too proud to engage in fakery. Just days before the May 2011 election, a senior strategist offered Sun News a bombshell. And there was just enough truth in the back story to make it believable. Michael Ignatieff was a Harvard professor when the Iraq war was launched in 2003, and he had publicly supported the Bush administration's reasons for invading Iraq. Five years later, when no weapons of mass destruction were found, Ignatieff joined the large number of politicians and intellectuals who said they had been duped. Harper, as leader of the official Opposition, had in fact also supported the invasion of Iraq, and demanded the Chrétien government back the American coalition. He even took that message to the United States.

Sun News's vice-president, Kory Teneycke, was contacted by Patrick Muttart, the former deputy chief of staff to Harper. Muttart claimed to have damning information showing that Michael Ignatieff was a key player in the Bush administration's planning of the invasion of Iraq. He had "proof" that the Liberal leader had worked at a U.S. forward military base in Kuwait helping State Department officials and American military officers plan the air and ground attack strategy for the invasion. Muttart also offered the biggest prize of all: a picture of Ignatieff in combat fatigues, brandishing an assault rifle, and posing with American soldiers, supposedly taken at Christmas 2002.

The man in the image looked like Ignatieff, but it was a low-resolution shot, and Teneycke needed a better-quality picture for the newspapers. He also wanted proof that the picture was taken when the Tory source said: December 2002. Finally, Teneycke received the higher-resolution picture. It had, indeed, been taken in December 2002, but it was also obvious that the man in the picture was not Ignatieff. Teneycke killed the use of the photograph, rather than go with an obvious error. Still, Sun News ran two stories. One, by Brian Lilley, repeated Muttart's claim that Ignatieff had been very active in planning the Iraq war. The other, written by Sun's owner, Pierre Karl Péladeau, was about Tory dirty tricks, including the bogus picture. In that opinion piece, Péladeau explained what happened:

> Bad information is an occupational hazard in this business, and fortunately our in-house protocols prevented the unthinkable. But it is the ultimate source of this material that is profoundly troubling to me, my colleagues and, I think, should be of concern to all Canadians. It is my belief that this planted information was intended to first and foremost seriously damage Michael Ignatieff's campaign but in the process to damage the integrity and credibility of Sun Media and, more pointedly, that of our new television operation, Sun News.[19]

The rest of the media picked up on the second story, and Muttart was dropped from the campaign.

In June 2013, PMO communications officer Erica Meekes sent the *Barrie Advance* newspaper details of a 2007 speaking engagement that had netted Justin Trudeau a $10,000 fee, but left Georgian College with a $4,118 shortfall. Trudeau had given the talk at the college before he was elected to the House of Commons.

The paper was told to quote a "source," rather than the Prime Minister's Office, when it used the material: "As a follow-up to the growing controversy over the weekend on Justin Trudeau charging charities for his speaking services, I have enclosed further materials that demonstrate the scope of this practice, cost on the organizations, and in many cases, poor outcomes and large deficits as a result of his speaking tour," the email stated. "As discussed, these materials are provided to you on background, and should be attributed to a 'source.'" Harper's staff gave the small newspaper invoices, a poster for the Georgian College session, and a receipt for Trudeau's stay at the Four Seasons hotel in Toronto.

Meekes, who would later become a spokesperson for Indian Affairs Minister Bernard Valcourt, wrote to the *Advance*, "To be fair, there is an in-house yoga studio at the Four Seasons!" A reporter at the Barrie newspaper called the Prime Minister's Office to ask why it had been sent the Trudeau documents; Meekes replied that it's normal for the PMO to reach out to the media. She also suggested the *Advance* call local Tory MP Patrick Brown for on-the-record comment. When the paper contacted Brown, he said Trudeau shouldn't get a free pass for Georgian College's financial loss, despite the fact that it was the college, not Trudeau, that had arranged the event. "I don't know why he wouldn't do it for free even before he was an MP. He didn't charge the Liberals to do speeches at their partisan events," said Brown. "Why charge charities and not-for-profits, especially when they are losing money, based on his professional ability to draw crowds?"[20]

In 2009, Harper suspended Communications Director Ryan Sparrow and forced him to apologize for taking on Jim Davis, the father of a Canadian soldier killed in Afghanistan. Sparrow claimed the grieving man's criticism of the government's Afghanistan policy, which he called "irresponsible," may have been politically motivated. Sparrow had sent an email to Jenna Fyfe, a CTV News producer, saying Davis was a supporter of Liberal deputy leader Michael Ignatieff during the Liberal leadership race. Campaigning in the Montreal-area town of Saint-Eustache, Harper said, "I have set a tone and expectation for this campaign and I am going to make sure that it is followed all the way to victory." Harper had previously apologized for Tory Internet ads engineered by Sparrow showing a puffin pooping on Stéphane Dion's head—Dion had said the Liberals were hard-working, like the puffin—and another that showed Dion surrounded by bullet holes. Sparrow would go on to become a conservative media dial-a-quote and a lobbyist.

JUST WEEKS AFTER the 2011 election, people employed by a Toronto-based polling company run by Nick Kouvalis started calling voters in the Montreal riding of Mount Royal. Kouvalis is a controversial figure. He worked as Toronto mayor Rob Ford's deputy campaign manager in 2010 and, later, as his chief of staff. During the 2014 Toronto mayoral campaign, he was John Tory's chief strategist. Kouvalis was paid by the Conservatives to tell Montrealers that Irwin Cotler, a former justice minister, law professor and human rights activist, was planning to quit politics very soon.

In fact, Cotler wasn't going anywhere. He was working hard to try to stop the Harper government from ramming through its tough-on-crime legislation. "The calls didn't happen accidentally, they happened at a time when I was most engaged as an MP in matters that Conservatives most cared about, for example, the crime bill," Cotler said. They were an attempt to draw him back to Montreal to protect his political base. When asked about the loaded poll meant to sway public opinion, called a push-poll, Kouvalis said, "We're in the business of getting Conservatives elected and ending Liberal careers. We're good at it."[21]

Seven complaints of professional misconduct were launched against Campaign Research Inc., the company owned by Kouvalis. "The actions of Campaign Research have likely caused the Canadian public to lose confidence in marketing research and have tarnished the image of the marketing research profession," a three-member panel of the Market Research and Intelligence Association said. They voted to censure the polling company.

Cotler rose in the House of Commons months later and asked Speaker Andy Scheer to rule that the fake polling was an attack on his ability do his job as an MP.[22] Tory House leader Peter Van Loan called the Tories' tactics freedom of speech. Cotler didn't buy it. "This defence that it is somehow a matter of free speech, that to me was one of the more absurd attempts to defend this odious practice. We have laws in this country against lying in order to protect the right to a fair trial, we have laws in this country against misleading advertising in order to protect consumers, we have laws against defamation in order to protect people's standing and reputation," Cotler said.

The Conservatives admitted they were behind the calls. They owned up to hiring Campaign Research to "identify" possible Tory supporters, but they had told the call centre to say there were "rumours" but nothing more. Scheer ruled he was "entirely sympathetic" and there was "no doubt that he had been bombarded by telephone calls, emails and faxes from concerned and confused constituents," but he didn't believe that these "reprehensible" tactics caused Cotler "great difficulty" carrying out his duties.

"I am sure that all reasonable people would agree that attempting to sow confusion in the minds of voters as to whether or not their member is about to resign is a reprehensible tactic and that the member for Mount Royal has a legitimate grievance," Scheer said. But, concluded the young Tory Speaker, "Canadians contacted this way should be more wary and judge more critically any information presented to them by unsolicited callers. After studying the precedents in these matters, I am not able on technical ground to find that a prima facie case of privilege exists in this case."

Cotler told reporters outside the House of Commons that Scheer was wrong. "I think that the judgment, his judgment today, his ruling was mistaken, both in relation to the facts, in relation to the principles, in relation to the precedents, in relation to the law on breaches of privilege," Cotler said, adding there was ample precedent for the Speaker to rule in his favour.[23]

Harper's brain trust also hired former Montreal city councilor Saulie Zajdel to work for the prime minister and made him the Tories' "shadow MP" in Cotler's riding. He was advertised as the go-to person for people in Mount Royal who needed help with problems involving the federal government. In June 2013, Zajdel was charged, along with acting mayor Michael Applebaum, with bribery, breach of trust, fraud and corruption for offences allegedly committed while Zajdel was still on the Montreal council.[24]

The Tories have also gone after their old whipping boys, the unions. One private member's bill introduced by a Tory backbencher would force unions to divulge the salaries of their staff members. But the big guns were trained on the unions that represent federal public employees. The sweeping changes to the Public Service Labour Relations Act in the 2014 budget implementation bill surprised and shocked the people who run the public sector unions. Union leaders said Tony Clement, whose Treasury Board negotiates wage deals with federal government employees, never let on that he was planning to change the bargaining rules.

Ron Cochrane, who has negotiated many deals between the government and its unions, told Kathryn May of the *Ottawa Citizen* that he had never seen such radical changes to the bargaining system. "This bill removes any semblance of fairness in collective bargaining," he said. "[Clement] has taken every caution to make sure that no matter what happens, he will win. He has stacked the deck in his favour and that is unheard of in labour relations anywhere. And it will be pretty hard to fight an employer that stacks the deck against you . . . This has become a game of cards where [unions] don't get any cards. The employer holds the deck."[25]

A GOVERNMENT CAN ATTACK its critics and even its own employees. It can hide public information and prevent elected members of the national legislature from understanding how the people's money is spent. Those things are frightening enough, but there's no greater assault on democracy than denying people their right to vote.

Conservatives in the United States pioneered vote suppression. The Canadian right has begun to mimic its American heroes, who have worked for decades to manipulate voters and voting rules to keep poor people, blacks and immigrants from voting.

Keeping opponents away from the ballot box, either through legal means or trickery, is an important part of North American right-wing strategy. Radical right strategist Paul Weyrich told fifteen thousand conservative ministers and preachers in 1980, "I don't want everyone to vote. Elections are not run by a majority of the people. They never have been from the beginning of our country and they aren't now. As a matter of fact, our leverage in the elections quite candidly goes up as the voting populace goes down."[26]

Winning elections is not just about door-knocking, advertising, and making sure your supporters get out. "Sometimes," one California Republican strategist said, "vote suppression is as important to this business as vote-getting."[27]

In Canada, robocalls are the most famous vote suppression strategy. It's unfortunate that the Canadian media did not come up with a better name for the scandal that was uncovered in the 2011 election. People get robocalls all the time, mainly from tour companies, insurance sellers and cable TV corporations. They're annoying, but they're not illegal. Vote suppression robocalls are a different thing altogether. They're designed to trick people into not voting. In Canada, callers told people that their polling station had moved to a distant location. That was one of the more simple kinds of robocalls.

In Canada and the United States, all parties use robocalls to some extent. They're mainly bought, at a very cheap rate, from call centres to advertise on behalf of candidates and attack opponents. People all over Canada got robocalls in the 2011 election campaign reminding them to vote. Barack Obama and John McCain both used robocalls in the 2008 presidential election.

In the United States, sleazy robocalling is now common in elections. Many of these calls are quite sophisticated and sometimes comical: candidates impersonating each other, calls made in the middle of the night to deliberately infuriate voters, calls with fake caller ID numbers that make them appear to come from an opponent's campaign. Vote suppression robocalls are supposed to keep people away from the polls. Mainly, they're used by Republicans, although Hillary Clinton did use them during her campaign against Barack Obama in the 2008 primaries.[28]

In 2012, voters who signed a recall petition to force a new election for governor of Wisconsin got an interesting phone call. The robocaller told them that, since they'd already made their feelings known by supporting the petition, there was no need to vote in the recall election.[29] In November 2010, more than a hundred thousand people in predominantly Democratic and African-American areas of Maryland got calls telling them not to bother voting in mid-term congressional and local elections because the Democrats were going to win anyway. A soothing voice told them to "relax."[30] (The ringleader behind the calls was convicted of vote fraud, but the more surprising fact is that the calls cost just $2,000.)

Latino voters in Los Angeles were targeted with robocalls in 2010 telling them to make sure they got out and voted on November 3. The actual election was on November 2. Voters in Louisiana, Maine and New Hampshire got phone calls telling them to vote online instead of showing up at polling stations. They were directed to websites with bogus applications for absentee ballots. Not only were the websites decoys, but they were also set up to gather information about the people who fell for the ploy.[31]

In the 2011 election, Canadians started getting vote suppression robocalls. Quite likely, robocalls sending people to the wrong polling place were just part of a plan to play fast and loose with people's right to vote. At least one polling station was in the clubhouse of a gated community. Four polls in Willowdale, Ontario, where Tory Chungsen Leung took the seat from Liberal Martha Hall Findlay by 932 votes, were placed in the Willowdale Lawn Bowling Club, even though there is a public library and civic centre two blocks away. (The Tories won three of those polls by more than 400 votes). In Mississauga East, Ontario, four polls were tucked away on the second floor of a mammoth grocery store, above a deli and sushi counter. Conservatives won three of those polls. In 2006, Liberal MP Mark Holland had swept six polls in Ajax–Pickering, Ontario, that were placed in a high school. Five years later, the Tories handily won the same polls, which were now moved to the evangelical Forest Brook Church.[32]

Then there are voter ID laws, which Canadian opposition politicians fought ferociously during the debate on Harper's Fair Elections Act. These laws have been used to make sure thousands of voters, mostly poor and minority citizens, do not vote.

In the United States, some academics have called the practice of using ID rules to monkey-wrench the system "vote caging." The practice goes back at least as far as the 2004 presidential and congressional elections. The goal is to prevent as many people as possible from voting for your opponent. Often, this form of vote suppression is artfully done.

Take, for example, the registered letter campaign that supposedly identifies people who have moved away from an electoral district but, in fact, does much more. Here's how it works: the team backing a candidate sends registered letters to a large number of people living in areas where most people vote for their opponent. Invariably, a lot of these letters are returned. Some people have moved. Some aren't home when the letter carrier comes and don't bother going to the post office to pick up the mail. Some people know that demand letters from creditors and bill collectors come as registered mail, so they won't sign for them. Sometimes, especially in poorer neighbourhoods, letter carriers don't try too hard to get registered mail into the hands of people.

The names of the people whose letters are returned are put on what are called caging lists. The candidate gives the list to the poll clerks. The people on the list will be challenged when they show up to vote, and will have to show a lot of identification and proof of residence. But here's where the real art of the thing comes into play. Not only will the people on the caging list find it difficult to vote, but so will the dozens, perhaps hundreds, of people stuck in long lineups as each person on the caging list is forced to show ID or swear an affidavit. Many of the people waiting to vote will become bored or frustrated and drift away from the line. Others will show up at their polling station, look at the crowd that's formed, and wander off. So a lot of people in the targeted area will not vote, which is the point of the exercise. To make this work, a candidate just needs to buy some stamps and know the voting patterns of a district.[33] Waits of up to ten hours at some U.S. voting stations have caused many people to simply give up and walk away.[34]

The so-called Fair Elections Act was designed to create a framework where voter ID laws would suppress the vote for the benefit of Conservatives, while hobbling the ability of Elections Canada to catch and punish illegal vote suppression. Yves Côté, the official at Elections Canada who investigates electoral fraud, said he was not consulted about the changes to the election law. He told MPs on the committee studying the bill that the Tories' plan would make fraud investigations much more difficult.[35]

Tova Wang, a Brussels-based senior fellow at Demos, a New York–based pro-democracy non-governmental organization, said the Tory plan to get rid of the vouching system was a "solution in search of a problem," because there was no evidence of widespread voter fraud in this country. "It's sort of the like they're taking the worst of the conservative playbook in the US and taking it to Canada," she said. Elections Canada's system was held up as a model to the world, she added.[36]

The Globe and Mail's Jeffrey Simpson explained voter suppression to his readers: "Various measures have been designed to discourage voting by chunks of the electorate not central to the Conservatives' targeted core and that additional 10 per cent they hope to woo. By making vouching more difficult and preventing Elections Canada from encouraging higher turnout, the Conservatives are trying to help themselves, although this is explained tortuously as a matter of 'principle.'"[37]

Former auditor general Sheila Fraser, who co-chaired an advisory board created by Chief Electoral Officer Marc Mayrand in the fall of 2013, told Canadian Press reporter Joan Bryden that the election bill was an attack on Canada's democracy. She said it will disenfranchise thousands of voters, undercut the independence of Elections Canada's electoral fraud investigators, strengthen the power of Canada's rich, established political parties and undermine Canadians' faith in the election system.

"Elections are the base of our democracy and if we do not have truly a fair electoral process and one that can be managed well by a truly independent body, it really is an attack on our democracy and we should all be concerned about that," Fraser said. "When you look at the people who may not be able to vote, when you look at the limitations that are being put on the chief electoral officer, when you see the difficulties, just the operational difficulties that are going to be created in all this, I think it's going to be very difficult to have a fair, a truly fair, election."[38]

THE COURTS ARE the last resort for people who want to challenge Harper's vision of a meaner, more militaristic Canada where individual rights are things to be subverted. No other government has gone after the courts the way Harper's has. His mouthpieces have, for years, yammered about "unelected" and "unaccountable" judges, hoping to put pressure on the judiciary to toe the line until the current generation of judges can be replaced as they retire. So far, the courts have held their ground.

When the Supreme Court ruled that Harper could not use the budget omnibus bill to change the rules for appointing Quebec judges to the Supreme Court, Chief Justice Beverley McLachlin got the full treatment from Harper and the Prime Minister's Office. After years of mutterings about "activist judges" and attacks on "unelected" members of the Supreme Court—ignoring the fact that no country elects Supreme Court judges—Harper accused McLachlin of acting unethically, which is probably the most serious allegation that can be made about any judge.

Harper claimed McLachlin tried to meddle in the appointment process that ended with Marc Nadon, a semi-retired judge of the Federal Court of Appeal, being appointed to the Supreme Court of Canada. Soon after the appointment, all of the judges on the Supreme Court agreed that Nadon did not meet the qualification requirements, and that the government could not change those rules without support from the provinces for a constitutional amendment.[39] Behind closed doors, PMO staff told a reporter that McLachlin "lobbied" against the appointment of Nadon. This, according to Harper's team, was unethical, and far below the standards set for politicians, who get into a lot of trouble when they phone judges and try to sway their decisions.

"Neither the prime minister nor the minister of justice would ever call a sitting judge on a matter that is or may be before the court," the PMO statement said. "The Chief Justice initiated the call to the Minister of Justice. After the Minister received her call he advised the Prime Minister that given the subject she wished to raise, taking a phone call from the Chief Justice would be inadvisable and inappropriate. The Prime Minister agreed and did not take her call."

Harper took it a step further later that day. "I can tell you this," said Harper, speaking in London, Ontario. "I think if people thought that the prime minister, other ministers of the government, were consulting judges before them or—even worse—consulting judges on cases that might come before them, before the judges themselves had the opportunity to hear the appropriate evidence, I think the entire opposition, entire media and entire legal community would be outraged. So I do not think that's the appropriate way to go."

Because of the nature of her job and its demand for complete discretion, McLachlin could not properly defend herself. In truth, when McLachlin called MacKay there was no nominee, let alone no looming court case. Nadon was just one of six people whose name was on a short list. The lawsuit against Nadon's appointment would come somewhat out of the blue from Rocco Galati, a Toronto-based lawyer who took up the issue on his own time and paid for his own counsel. It would be the first legal challenge of an appointment in the 139-year history of the Supreme Court. McLachlin had the right to discuss the rest of Harper's secret list of six candidates, which included one Federal Court judge warned for plagiarizing government pleadings. The list had been shown to her by the five MPs appointed to vet the prime minister's picks, and apparently that's when she decided to warn the government that a Federal Court appointee might not qualify for a Quebec seat on the Supreme Court.

In an unusual move, McLachlin fought back as much as she could. Owen Rees, the court's executive legal officer, put out a statement saying McLachlin was one of the people who was consulted during the search for a new Supreme Court judge, but she hadn't overstepped her role when she tried to alert Harper. "The chief justice did not lobby the government against the appointment of Justice Nadon," Rees wrote in an email sent to journalists. Yes, Rees said, McLachlin or people in her office flagged a potential problem to both Justice Minister Peter MacKay and the prime minister's chief of staff, Ray Novak. But, Rees added, she "did not express any views on the merits of the issue."

Rees quoted McLachlin saying: "Given the potential impact on the Court, I wished to ensure that the government was aware of the eligibility issue. At no time did I express any opinion as to the merits of the eligibility issue. It is customary for Chief Justices to be consulted during the appointment process and there is nothing inappropriate in raising a potential issue affecting a future appointment."

Academics and lawyers couldn't understand what Harper, MacKay and their apologists objected to. "There is nothing unusual about contacts between the chief justice and the minister of justice and the prime minister. Indeed, regular contact is healthy for the relationship between the branches of government and the administration of the country's top court," Adam Dodek, vice-dean of the University of Ottawa law school, told The Canadian Press. "Every minister of justice in this Conservative government and in its predecessor Liberal governments going back at least fifteen years has stated publicly that they have consulted with the chief justice of Canada about appointments to the Supreme Court of Canada. So where is the issue and where is the problem here?"[40]

Lawyers and law professors rallied to McLachlin's defence. Harper's attack was condemned by the Canadian Council of Law Deans. Fred Headon, president of the Canadian Bar Association, complained about the way Harper attacked McLachlin, and he was joined by all living former presidents of the association. The Advocates' Society sent Harper a letter saying "there is no substance" to the government's criticism of McLachlin's actions and no evidence that she either lobbied against Nadon's appointment or tried to interfere in a matter before the court.

The comments at issue here can only serve to undermine the respect and confidence of ordinary Canadians in the proper administration of justice, and we therefore urge you to make a public statement advising Canadians that the chief justice did not conduct herself inappropriately in any way. Nothing less than such a correction will repair the potential damage caused by these remarks.[41]

Instead of retracting his accusations, Harper changed his story, saying he hadn't needed to talk to the chief justice about his choice for the Quebec seat because he believed Nadon's appointment would be challenged in court. Also, he said he was ready with supportive opinions from two retired Supreme Court judges and Peter Hogg, a constitutional scholar who had advised the Governor General to accept Harper's request to prorogue Parliament in 2008, when it was obvious Harper had lost the confidence of the House of Commons.

Brent Rathgeber, a lawyer and former Conservative MP who, while in the Tory caucus, vetted two Supreme Court appointments for Harper, said Harper was trying to rewrite history. "The narrative now is, 'There was no need for me to talk to the chief justice because I was already aware of the issue, as opposed to the original narrative, which was, 'It would have been inappropriate for me to talk to the chief justice,'" Rathberger told Tonda MacCharles of the *Toronto Star*. "Now it's changed to, 'It would have been redundant and unnecessary for me to speak to the chief justice.' And I'm fairly confident the reason they changed that narrative is that they know they messed this one up, that they crossed the line and that their insinuation that the chief justice in her administrative [heads-up] acted inappropriately was beyond the pale, over the top and unacceptable by the entire legal, judicial and media communities."[42]

And he was backed by NDP leader Thomas Mulcair, who said: "I think that one of the basic responsibilities of a justice minister, the attorney general of Canada, is to protect the integrity of our courts from any attempt to intimidate them. And this is a clear intent as far as we're concerned by the government to try to force its will on that institution, the way it's done on so many others in the past. Mr. Harper doesn't accept no for an answer. The way Mr. MacKay's behaving today, you'd almost think that he was watching the playoffs and he thinks that Supreme Court judgments are a best of seven series."[43]

More than 650 lawyers and law teachers from across Canada released an open letter in early May demanding Harper retract his criticism of McLachlin. "We . . . deplore the unprecedented and baseless insinuation by the Prime Minister of Canada that the Chief Justice engaged in improper conduct," the lawyers told Harper. "Public criticism of the Chief Justice impugns the integrity of Canada's entire judiciary and undermines the independence of Canada's courts."

At the same time, seven senior law professors asked the Geneva-based International Commission of Jurists to investigate the Conservatives' "unfounded criticisms leveled at the Chief Justice," writing in a letter:

> We fear that the unprecedented statements of the Prime Minister and Minister of Justice and Attorney General, which question the integrity and judgment of the Chief Justice of Canada, may seriously undermine judicial independence in Canada. An independent judiciary is vital to the health of any democracy and a foundational tenet of Canada's constitutional order and the rule of law. Impugning the integrity of the judiciary, including through public and personal criticism of the Chief Justice, represents an attempt to subvert that judicial independence.[44]

In the end, Canadians will decide whether Stephen Harper was out of line when he attacked the country's top judge. They'll make that decision taking into account the prime minister's skills as the real chief executive officer of our country's government. Fair elections and independent courts are our last hope. There's no point having a free press, functioning Parliament, independent parliamentary watchdogs, unfettered scientists and an end to government propaganda campaigns unless we have free elections and courts that have the power to roll back tyranny. If we lose those, it's all over. They won't be coming back. There will be no us, only them.

In the spring of 2014, after the Senate scandal, the robocalls affair, the attempt to rewrite election laws, protests by veterans, Harper's attack on the Supreme Court, and a string of other scandals and assaults on democracy, one pollster found that the Prime Minister's Office is the least-trusted institution in Canada.[45] The wisdom of the people had shown through.

CHAPTER 13

A Radical Solution: Accountability

The Government are merely trustees for the public.

—Sir John A. Macdonald

American historian Richard Hofstadter, who chronicled the evolution of America's imperial presidency, once wrote: "Third parties are like bees: once they have stung, they die." The Reform Party's promises—made in Legion halls in small-town Canada a generation ago—of open government, public participation and political accountability, are now long dead. After nine years of Harper government, the old Western populist ideal of politicians who represent the people and fear their wrath is just a relic of another age. Reformers wanted to drive the money-changers from the Temple, but the government that they helped create will now break denarii into sesterces for pretty much anyone who comes along. Government is now bigger than ever. Thousands of lobbyists are welcomed into the offices of politicians and senior bureaucrats. And, most frightening, the people are being driven from the political system.

Stephen Harper ran in 2006 on a promise of accountability. The windows of Ottawa would be thrown open and fresh air would flow through the halls of power. Government would be returned to the people. The revolving door between Parliament Hill and the high-rises of the lobbyists would be closed. An independent parliament-ary budget officer would tell people what was really happening to their money. Corporate and union money would be kept out of pol-itics. Even though Harper had promised to make an Accountability Act his first order of business, but instead had appointed his Quebec campaign manager to the Senate, in the early years Canadians still had every right to believe Harper would deliver on his promises.

Canadians are still waiting. A truly accountable government provides the people with the information they need to make informed choices and to assess the quality of their representation. This government did not show any respect for the populists who laid the foundation for its rise to power. This is not a Reform Party government. It's not a conservative government. It is a government that exists to sustain itself, shill for the oil patch, make trade deals that are often not in Canada's interests, break unions and, above all else, get re-elected.

This breed of Conservatives talks a lot about tradition, yet at the same time attacks institutions that have evolved for hundreds of years. They talk about accountability, but prevent journalists, MPs and officers of Parliament from carefully examining laws. They hide scientific evidence or prevent it from being gathered. They talk a good fight about the military and try to rebrand the country as a warrior nation, but leave war veterans struggling to get medical help and to pay their bills.

Many Canadians—and people living in most other Western countries—believe governments and the economy will just move along nicely in the hands of the political and economic elites. Judging by dismal voter turnouts, plummeting memberships in political parties, and wretched media viewing and reading num-bers, democracy is, at best, on automatic pilot. History shows insti-tutions and political systems collapse when they become corrupt and decayed. They can also die from sheer lack of interest. Once these institutions are corrupted and delegitimized, the rest of society will follow. People who live in democracies had better put some sweat equity into them, or the system won't be around forever. It's chauvinism bordering on racism to believe that we are somehow special, that our system of government can survive when so many other attempts at democracy throughout the world have failed.

What's coming out of Ottawa today is not conservatism. It's something revolutionary. Conservatives normally defend the legitimacy of established government. They don't believe agents of the state should paw through the mail, whether on paper or in Internet discussion groups. They believe scientists should be able to talk to people, especially when the scientists are paid by the people, and that research brings enlightenment and prosperity. They believe in law and order, and do not attack the courts or circumvent election laws.

This book opened with the execution of Charles I. He was an ineffective, somewhat duplicitous ruler, but at least he was honest when he expressed his views on democracy. These days, every politician claims to believe in democracy, but rarely has real government of the people been so threatened. Parliament, the institution that called Charles to account and took off his head, has become a place of mock debate staged for television cameras. Its members rarely show up to scrutinize the laws that are passed by the House of Commons. Our representatives are barely more than public relations staffers of political parties.

It's time for MPs to push back. First, they can show up for debates. Second, they can demand Parliament spend the money to make committees work. That means creating committees that have, like their counterparts in Washington, at least one lawyer and one researcher permanently assigned to them full-time. For committees like Finance, a team of forensic accountants should be working full-time on budgets and estimates so that MPs can ask informed questions that will help them understand how the government taxes and spends. Committee counsel should be allowed to examine witnesses, work with committee members to subpoena witnesses, and examine draft legislation. Too often, MPs have missed opportunities to ask probing questions and to demand witnesses show up and give honest testimony.

We should expect the government, if it's serious about getting control of national spending, to spend the money to raid the accounting firms of this country for the best auditors and efficiency experts. Sometimes you have to spend money to make money. I've spent twenty years on Parliament Hill, and I'm not impressed by the general quality of public sector management. I've seen many government departments with morale so low that nothing gets done. I've also seen well-run departments and agencies. Efficiencies can be used to improve services or reduce taxes. No party should support waste simply because reform of public administration and public accounting is difficult and makes enemies.

We can't go to Parliament and watch all its debates, or analyze the workings of the vast federal bureaucracy, so we count on journalists to do that for us. Our media is being shredded by a revolution in communications that shows no sign of slowing. Many—though not all—of the surviving journalists have reacted by ignoring the dull workings of representative government and have turned inward, trying to be insiders covering politics as some kind of sport. Rarely have journalists been held in lower public esteem.

The Harper government has used the media's problems against it. It is almost impossible for journalists to get meaningful information from this government. The Harper regime operates in secrecy, showing its contempt for the news media every day. It has started to try to replace the media with its own TV network, *24 Seven*, and has provoked fights with reporters to raise campaign contributions from Tory supporters.

It has stifled research and gagged scientists as a way of killing meaningful public debate on science-based issues. Western civilization is built on the success of its science, especially discoveries that challenged the dogmas of the ruling elites. You have to reach pretty far back in Western history to find the kind of attack on science that's been waged by the Harper administration—or deep into the hills of the U.S. Bible Belt, where the Tea Party movement is waging a similar battle. Harper's team has played with history by reshaping the country's major museums and slashing the funding for the country's archives in order to change the way Canadians see their past and their country's role in the world. Relying on public ignorance to ram through government policies is a poor way to run a country.

The gags placed on public watchdogs of all sorts are frightening to anyone who believes in democracy and liberty. The concentration of power at the Centre under the control of a single leader smacks of fascism. Add to that this government's fetish for military grandeur, its contempt for democratic institutions and its attack-dog-style campaigns against its perceived enemies, including the courts, and it's plain we're on the road to a new kind of Canada, one that very few of us will enjoy.

Pollster Allan Gregg is one conservative who took the measure of the Harper regime and decided it was bad for the country. He had been one of Progressive Conservative prime minister Brian Mulroney's insiders, and he first started worrying about Harper in July 2010, when the government announced its decision to kill the mandatory long-form census. Gregg, who heads the Harris/Decima market research and polling company, uses census material in his work. In a *Toronto Star* article, Gregg said: "I knew how important these data were to policy analysts. How could a government forsake the census's valuable insights—and the chance to make good public policy—under the pretense that rights were somehow violated by asking Canadians how many bathrooms were in their home?"

Gregg looked at the nineteen thousand federal jobs scheduled to be cut in the 2012 federal budget and realized they weren't going to be across-the-board layoffs or jobs that would not be filled when people quit or retired. They were precisely targeted at "researchers, statisticians, scientists and other organizations who might use data to contradict a government which believed that evidence and rational compromise are not the tools of enlightened public policy, but barriers to the pursuit of an agenda based on ideology over reason." It was clear to Gregg that, whether in the debate to get rid of the Canadian Wheat Board or to send potheads to jail, the Harper government did not want facts to get in the way of policy. Ridding public debate of facts ensured they would not be thrown back at the government. Hiding behind walls of secrecy then ensured that, in those rare times when debate was based on reason instead of emotion, all of the ammunition would be in the government's hands, and it could choose which to use—or misuse.[1]

Gregg lashed out at Harper, saying his government is "ceasing to use evidence, facts and science as the basis to guide policy." Instead, it has retreated "into dogma, fear and partisan advantage to steer the ship of state." Gregg wrote:

Understanding the world or explaining phenomena, through superstition, dogma, and orthodoxy—instead of facts and reason—invariably leads to some very ugly and uncivilized behavior. The reason for this is fairly straightforward—namely beliefs that are rooted in superstitions, dogma and orthodoxy are not sustainable . . . sooner or later their veracity will be tested by the facts and evidence. Those who need these beliefs to sustain their interests and power therefore must enforce them at the point of a sword or remove those who might prove them to be untrue.

Like many conservatives, Gregg wonders what this is all about. Why the war on science? Why make laws based on faith instead of reason, govern guided by dogma and turn the clock back? Why the love of monarchy, the revival of the old British ranks in the military, the hype about colonial wars? Why the self-loathing about so much of Canada and its past, including its generations of service as a peacekeeper and peacemaker? Why try to recreate a class structure in which a handful of people run the country and everyone else shuts up and does what they're told, or faces the massive powers of the state to spy, investigate and lay charges?

Maybe it's a yearning for a world that's past, a world of happy, middle-class, white people living their lives free of the worries of racial and cultural diversity. Maybe it's a desire to hear the last of climate change, genetically modified crops, nanosilver, oilsands pollution and all of the other nasty things out there that have cropped up since Harper was a boy growing up in suburban Toronto in the 1960s. Harper seems to offer national pride, strong leadership in a dangerous world, simple answers to complex questions. Those who don't support the Centre are simply troublemakers and opportunists who are trying to suck the happiness from Canadians.

It's an illusion. The world is a complicated place. Its problems, at least in this country, can only be solved by people discussing and debating the country's issues, just as we always have. Democratic institutions are more effective and efficient than fascism. People who live in functioning democracies are safer, wealthier and happier than people who live in any other political system. We need to work hard to rebuild our democracy. We can start by giving the messengers a helping hand, dusting them off, and getting them back on their feet. When they're attacked, we need to stand behind them. And when people try to kill them, we need to make sure the messengers survive and thrive.

First, vote. Second, when a political party or a politician shows strong signs that they're willing to reverse antidemocratic trends, give them some money and volunteer your time. You'll find the political class has been very generous to itself when it wrote the laws about income tax deductions for political contributions. Third, show up to all-candidates' meetings at election time, and if, as is the trend these days, there are no meetings in your riding, bird-dog your local candidate on social media and demand answers to your questions. Quite simply, be a pain in the ass if you don't get the answers you need. And if you do like what you hear, join a political party and become active at the local and, if possible, national level. Our system still relies on political parties to craft policies, find candidates and raise money. If no one gets involved, all of this work will fall into the laps of professional strategists, most of whom are also lobbyists.

Support the groups that are under attack by this government. There are many ways to do that, and some are quite inexpensive. Volunteer, write letters, give social media support to the causes you like. Do you oppose the Keystone pipeline? Fine. Make your voice heard. Do you believe the North American continent should be self-sufficient in what Ezra Levant calls ethical oil? Great. Speak up. No one should be shut out of the debate on public issues.

And don't wait for a saviour. The present dysfunctional system will be very hard to fix, and the attacks on democracy won't be reversed unless whichever party forms the next government is pressured to do so. Yes, Stephen Harper has harnessed the system to suit his own agenda and personality. But public support for democratic institutions and watchdogs was crumbling before Harper was elected, and the decay won't end until politicians feel the pressure to make it stop. To make national leaders hand power back to elected representatives and to the people requires a revolution in the way politicians and the people they represent think about the running of their country. We won't get it back until we stop thinking and talking about what "they" are doing to the country and ask ourselves what "we" are doing.

Acknowledgements

This book would not exist without the help and support of my editor and publisher at HarperCollins, Patrick Crean; his wife, author Susan Swan; and my friend Janice Zawerbny, now fiction editor at the House of Anansi. Janice and Patrick saved the book when the company that had contracted for it in 2013 went out of the book business. Tilman Lewis did an amazing job of copy editing. Any mistakes are mine, though whatever embarrassment I might feel is tempered by the knowledge that Tilman caught some real whoppers that I'm very glad didn't make it into the book.

There are quite a few people in Ottawa who should be thanked. Things get tricky here. I had a lot of help, encouragement, and a few arguments with people working for Stephen Harper and in senior roles in some ministerial offices. I've also come to know and like a number of Tory senators. They may not appreciate a big shout-out, so I'm afraid I will have to thank them personally.

The same goes for friends in the bureaucracy and the military. I've been lucky to know some brilliant members of the Canadian Forces and the public service, and some of these people have helped me to put issues in focus.

There are some people whom I will thank personally: Kevin Page, Munir Sheikh, Alex Himelfarb, Pat Stogran, Katie Gibbs, Ken

Rubin, Michael Ignatieff, Michael Marzolini, Robert MacBain, and Maria Minna.

I appreciate the help of Ian McDonald and the rest of the staff of the Library of Parliament, who hunted facts, books and articles without complaint and with a very high level of dedication.

I also appreciate the help, support and ideas of colleagues and friends Tom Korski, Glen McGregor, Steve Maher (who read the manuscript and helped with details on the robocalls scandal), Jonathan Kay, Derek Finkle, Kaven Baker-Voakes, Courtney Towers, Paul MacLeod, Kathryn May, Kady O'Malley, Susan Delacourt, Paul Delahanty, E. Kaye Fulton, Tim Naumetz, Dayanti Karunaratne, Fateema Sayani, Sarah Brown, Mark Weisblott and Christopher Guly. Also Michael Osman, M.J. Sheppard, John Bell, Mike McCaffrey, Ian Harvey, Rick Donnelly, Elizabeth McLoughlin, Noah Richler, Stevie Cameron, Michael Dorland, Vince Mosco, Christopher Waddell, Sean Holman, David Hayes and especially Lawrence Martin.

And I'd love to thank my family. My wife, Marion, and I had to develop a sort of wall between her professional life as a lawyer working for the federal government and this project. That meant I didn't ask questions or draw her into the project. However, writing this book was an exhausting, stressful and sometimes depressing exercise, and she helped me through moments when I felt overwhelmed. She, along with our children, Maia, Ian and Megan, are always the rock upon which my life is built, and I am always grateful to them.

Notes

CHAPTER 1. DEMOCRACY, MESSENGERS AND THE HARPER REVOLUTION

1. Quoted in Richard Nimijean, "Domestic Brand Politics and the Modern Publicity State," in Kirsten Kozolanka (ed.), *Publicity and the Canadian State: Critical Communications Perspectives* (Toronto: University of Toronto Press, 2014), 178.

2. These ideas are discussed with some erudition in David E. Smith, *The People's House of Commons: Theories of Democracy in Contention* (Toronto: University of Toronto Press, 2007).

3. Susan Delacourt, "'Not nice' works for many leaders, but not Alison Redford," *Toronto Star*, March 22, 2014.

4. John Ibbitson, "Michael Ignatieff's timely warning on the politics of fascism," *Globe and Mail*, October 30, 2012.

5. Tom Flanagan, *Waiting for the Wave*, 2nd ed. (Montreal/Kingston: McGill-Queen's University Press, 2009), 226–227; William H. Riker, "Implications from the Disequilibrium of Majority Rule," in Peter C. Ordeshook and Kenneth A. Shepsle (eds.), *Political Equilibrium* (Boston: Kluwer-Nijhoff Publishing, 1982), 19. Flanagan also describes Riker's theories in chapter 3 of his book *Winning Power: Canadian Campaigning in the 21st Century* (Toronto/Kingston: McGill-Queen's University Press, 2014).

6. *The Canadian Monthly*, May 1873.

7. The Ignatieff quotes are from John Ibbitson, "Michael Ignatieff's timely warning on the politics of fascism," *Globe and Mail*, October 30, 2012.

8. Tim Naumetz, "Harper Tactics," *Ottawa Citizen*, March 12, 2007.

CHAPTER 2. THE PERFECT MEDIA STORM

1. Douglas Fetherling, *The Rise of the Canadian Newspaper* (Toronto: Oxford University Press, 1990), 9.

2. Ibid., 24.

3. Michael Bate, "Memories of Mike Duffy: Lawsuits and 'smear' campaigns," *Toronto Star*, February 22, 2013.

4. See Mark Bourrie, "The myth of the 'Gagged Clam': William Lyon Mackenzie King's press relations," *Global Media Journal—Canadian Edition* 3.2 (Spring 2010): 13–30; and Allan Levine, *Scrum Wars* (Toronto: Dundurn Press, 1996).

5. For a much longer examination of insider media culture in the King years, see Bourrie, "The myth of the 'Gagged Clam.'"

6. Wilfrid Eggleston quoted in Colin W. Seymour-Ure, "Parliamentary press gallery in Ottawa," unpublished M.A. thesis, Political Science, Carleton University, Ottawa, 1962.

7. Eerily, Trudeau and Tim Ralfe, the reporter who recorded the quote, died in the fall of 2000 within a few weeks of each other.

8. Don Martin, "Only the government wins as Postmedia goes dark in Ottawa," CTV.ca, February 5, 2014.

9. Floridian Sauvageau, "Advertising Looks Elsewhere," in David Taras and Christopher Waddell (eds.), *How Canadians Communicate IV: Media and Politics* (Edmonton: Athabasca University Press, 2012), 34.

10. Ibid., 36.

11. Martin P. Wattenburg, *Is Voting for Young People?* (New York: Pearson, 2012), 13.

12. Sauvageau, "Advertising Looks Elsewhere," 32–34.

13. Wattenburg, *Is Voting for Young People?*, 13.

14. Paul Delahanty, "TV Viewers Head for Exits," *Blacklock's Reporter*, April 26, 2014; Tom Korski, "CRTC Says 62% Eye Netflix," *Blacklock's Reporter*, May 27, 2014.

15. David Taras and Christopher Waddell, "The 2011 Federal Election and the Transformation of Canadian Media and Politics," in *How Canadians Communicate IV*, 74.

16. Lewis Lapham, *Gag Rule: On the Suppression of Dissent and the Stifling of Democracy* (New York: Penguin Books, 2005), 91–92.

17. Daniel Boorstin, *The Image: A Guide to Pseudo-events in America* (New York: Harper & Row, 1961), 12–13.

18. Eric Alterman, *Sound & Fury: The Making of the Punditocracy* (New York: HarperCollins, 1992 edition), 296.

19. Carl Sessions Strepp, "Why do people read newspapers?," *American Journalism Review*, December/January, 2004.

20. Alterman, *Sound & Fury*, 307.

21. Ibid., 309.

22. Boorstin, *The Image*, 12–14.

23. Jeffrey Simpson, *The Friendly Dictatorship* (Toronto: McClelland & Stewart 2001), 36, 39.

24. Andrew Mitrovica, "Who's paying for that 'expert' opinion?," *iPolitics*, March 5, 2013.

25. David Olive, "Crazy, hazy days of convergence: US experience exposes some flaws in media marriages," *National Post*, September 16, 2001.

26. Tamara Baluja, "How well are Canadian newspapers doing with paywalls, tablets?" Jsource.ca, January 24, 2014.

27. Justin Trudeau had some 360,000 Twitter followers in 2014, a number that has to be taken seriously as a political force by even the most diehard critics of social media.

28. Delacourt later wrote a book condemning the effects of retail politics and "insiderism" on Canadian politics. The book, *Shopping for Votes* (Vancouver: Douglas & McIntyre, 2013), is an interesting account of the development of the political persuasion industry. It is well worth reading by anyone who wants to know how the permanent campaign works and who the players are.

29. Taras and Waddell, "The 2011 Federal Election," 97–98.

30. Martin Wattenburg, *Is Voting for Young People?* (New York: Pearson, 2012), 155.

31. Ibid.

32. Ibid., 71.

33. Ibid.

34. Lee Shaker, "Dead newspapers and citizens' civic engagement," *Political Communication* 31:1 (January 2014), 131–148.

35. Taras and Waddell, "The 2011 Federal Election," 113.

36. See Thierry Giasson, "As (Not) Seen on TV: News Coverage of Political Marketing in Canadian Federal Elections," in Alex Marland, Thierry Giasson, and Jennifer Lees-Marshment (eds.), *Political Marketing in Canada* (Vancouver: UBC Press, 2012), ch. 11.

37. Taras and Waddell, "The 2011 Federal Election," 104.

38. Ibid., 126.

39. Ibid., 127.

40. Pew Research, *Amid Criticism, Support for Media's Watchdog Role Stands Out*, www.people-press.org, August 8, 2013. Pew surveyed about 1,400 Americans over a one-week period in July 2013.

41. "The Globe's election endorsement: Facing up to our challenges," editorial, *Globe and Mail*, April 27, 2011.

42. For an interesting analysis of the volume of media coverage of Canadian political parties in recent elections, see Blake Andrew, Patrick Fournier, and Stuart Soroka, "The Canadian Party System," in Amanda Bittner and Royce Koop (eds.), *Parties, Elections and the Future of Canadian Politics* (Vancouver: UBC Press, 2013), 161–184.

CHAPTER 3. IT PAYS TO INCREASE YOUR WORD POWER

1. E. Kaye Fulton, "Harper's message to the news media: I'm in control," *Kingston Whig-Standard*, April 20, 2006.

2. When that trouble broke, Harper was president of the National Citizens Coalition. The secretive and somewhat strange right-wing pressure group had started out by buying full-page ads in major newspapers and courted the media to get free publicity for its causes. Under the previous president, David Somerville, the coalition had sent out dozens of press releases and held fairly frequent news conferences. During Harper's four years as president, press releases were rare and were sent only to Harper's friends in the media. During those years, Harper held just one news conference. See Gerry Nicholls, *Loyal to the Core: Stephen Harper, Me and the NCC* (Jordan Station: Freedom Press, 2009), 106.

3. "Harper wins support for control of speeches: But Kenney says gays must try to have kids," *Edmonton Journal*, February 15, 2005.

4. In the summer of 2014, the retraction could be found at www.theglobeand-mail.com/news/politics/second-reading/spector-vision/editors-note/article1849177/#dashboard/follows.

5. Tim Naumetz, "Harper Tactics powerful but disturbing," *Ottawa Citizen*, March 12, 2007.

6. Lawrence Martin, *Harperland: The Politics of Control* (Toronto: Viking Canada, 2010), 41.

7. Nicholls, *Loyal to the Core*, 110.

8. Martin, *Harperland*, 21, 60.

9. Donald J. Savoie, *Whatever Happened to the Music Teacher?* (Montreal/Kingston: McGill-Queen's University Press, 2013), 213.

10. The MEP details and the black bear press release anecdote are from Lawrence Martin's *Harperland*, 58-59; the Bethune House message control anecdote is from the author's own experience with Bethune House.

11. For an interesting analysis of Obama's media relations, see Reid Cherlin, "The Presidency & the Press," *Rolling Stone*, August 2014.

12. B.J. Siekierski, "Canada up two spots in global press freedom rankings," *iPolitics*, February 13, 2014.

13. Bruce Cheadle, "Liberals too lax, Harper swings pendulum toward tight message control," Canwest News Service, March 31, 2006.

14. Don Martin, "Harper's hatred for the messenger hurts strategy," *National Post*, November 21, 2006.

15. Kate Heartfield, "The Conservative (Media) Party," *Ottawa Citizen*, November 7, 2013.

16. Andrew Coyne, "Real conservatives would have scrapped or reformed the CBC. The Tories just profit from it," *National Post*, May 30, 2014.

17. Gillian Stewart, "Behind PM's war with media," *Toronto Star*, August 20, 2009.

18. Heartfield, "The Conservative (Media) Party."

19. William Wray Carney, *In the News: The Practice of Media Relations in Canada*, 2nd ed. (Edmonton: University of Alberta Press, 2008), 153.

20. Joan Bryden, Canwest News Service, February 6, 2006.

21. Quoted in Chris Cobb, "Harper's war on the media," *Ottawa Citizen*, April 26, 2006.

22. Denise Rudnicki, "Harper must work on his relationship with the media," *Windsor Star*, March 1, 2006.

23. Bruce Cheadle, "Liberals too lax, Harper swings pendulum toward tight message control," Canwest News Service, March 31, 2006.

24. Canadian Press, April 12, 2006. The author was at this press conference and sat next to Naumetz, who was in the middle of a crowded room and did not appear to know about the press gallery "list" until after Harper called on him to ask his question.

25. Don Martin, "Harper lowers the cone of silence," *Calgary Herald*, April 13, 2006, A7.

26. Don Martin, "Harper running a one-man show," Canwest News Service, March 10, 2006.

27. Heartfield, "The Conservative (Media) Party."

28. Chris Cobb, "Stephen Harper holds all the cards in his spat with press gallery," *The Montreal Gazette*, June 5, 2006, A19.

29. Alexander Panetta, "'Paranoid' PM cuts off press gallery," *St. Catharines Standard*, May 25, 2006, A2.

30. Allan Fotheringham, "No one cares about press gallery's woes," syndicated column published in the *Whitehorse Star*, September 28, 2006.

31. Claire Hoy, "Not a pressing issue: Harper has no obligation to speak to the press gallery in Ottawa," *Sudbury Star*, September 29, 2007.

32. Marc Edge, *Asper Nation* (Vancouver: New Star Press, 2007), 238; Kady O'Malley, "How did CanWest get its scoop? By going on the PM's list," *Hill Times*, August 28, 2006.

33. Don Martin, "Harper won the battle," *Regina Leader-Post*, October 18, 2006.

34. David Akin, *On the Hill* blog, Canoe.ca, August 25, 2013.

35. Laura Ryckewaert, "Little access on foreign trips," *Hill Times*, October 29, 2012.

36. James Travers, "Harper choosing to avoid reporters' awkward questions," *Toronto Star*, May 26, 2007.

37. Canadian Press, "Harper's bodyguards accused of assaulting Palestinian cameraman," Torontostar.com, January 20, 2014.

38. Paul Wells, "Our political editor on the controversy over conference coverage," Macleans.ca, May 29, 2014.

39. The Thibault and Ivison quotes are from Bea Vongdouangchanh, "PMO picks fight,

Hill media push back, Conservatives send out letter to supporters attacking 'media elite'. Journalists say if the PMO is deliberately picking fights to rally Tory base it won't end well," *Hill Times*, September 21, 2013.

40. Josh Wingrove, "Tories decry 'new low' for media after standoff over reporters' access to Harper speech," *Globe and Mail*, October 16, 2013; Canadian Press, "Conservatives throw down gauntlet with media," October 19, 2013.

41. Laura Ryckewaert, "Hill media to push back against access control," *Hill Times*, March 17, 2014.

42. Chris Cobb, "Prime minister's office issues 'amateurish' statement questioning credibility of Postmedia reporter," *Ottawa Citizen*, January 17, 2013.

43. "Mennonite magazine warned about 'political' articles. Canada Revenue Agency's warning a 'chill on speech,' says editor," CBC.ca, November 9, 2012.

44. Stevie Cameron, *Ottawa Inside Out* (Toronto: Key Porter, 1989), 214.

45. Lawrence Martin, "Why lying in politics works," *iPolitics*, October 10, 2012.

CHAPTER 4. REPLACING THE MEDIA

1. Garth Turner, "F," www.greaterfool.ca, March 18, 2014.

2. Don Braid, "Ottawa's weaknesses infect its press gallery," *Windsor Star*, January 27, 1987.

3. Preston Manning, *The New Canada* (Toronto: Macmillan Canada, 1992), 137.

4. Canwest News, March 28, 2006.

5. Tonda MacCharles, "Government plans media centre in shoe store," *Toronto Star*, October 15, 2007.

6. Tonda MacCharles, "Government shelves media centre plan," *Toronto Star*, October 16, 2007.

7. Gillian Stewart, "Behind PM's war with media," *Toronto Star*, August 20, 2009.

8. Jim Bronskill, "Ethics czar looking into parliamentary secretary's letter to CRTC," Canadian Press, October 3, 2013.

9. Among those who'd been offered the story by the Liberals was Jonathan Kay, a senior editor at the *National Post*.

10. "Layton found in suspected bawdy house: Former cop," Sunnewsnetwork.com, April 29, 2011.

11. For an NDP insider's take on this, see Brad Lavigne, *Building the Orange Wave* (Vancouver: Douglas & McIntyre, 2013), ch. 12.

12. Steve Laduantaye, "Sun News host Ezra Levant issues rare apology for Roma 'slurs,'" *Globe and Mail*, March 18, 2013.

13. Marc Weisblott, "Stephen Harper starts producing his own journalism," Canada.com, January 9, 2014.

14. Kelly McParland, "Old Tory dogs ready their new digital tricks," *National Post*, February 12, 2014; Donovan Vincent, "PM launches new video series about

himself," *Guelph Mercury*, January 16, 2014; "Stephen Harper's '24 Seven' show has North Korean vibes," Huffington Post Canada, January 9, 2014; Jonathon Gatehouse, "Real life with Stephen Harper. Highlights—and lowlights—of the PM's reality show," *Maclean's*, January 23, 2014.

15. Glen McGregor, "Four staff work on widely-unwatched PM promo videos," *Ottawa Citizen*, March 24, 2014.

16. Kady O'Malley, "Harper's government by Twitter isn't all bad for journalists," CBC. ca, October 19, 2013.

17. Dean Beeby, "Feds put cage around government tweets," Canadian Press, February 3, 2014.

18. Tom Korski, "Feds go Facebook creeping," *Blacklock's Reporter*, December 1, 2013.

19. Bruce Cheadle and Stephanie Levitz, "Ethnic media monitoring used to track perceptions of immigration minister," Canadian Press, November 13, 2012.

20. Jeremy Nuttall, "Ethnic media had 'weird' invite process to PM press conference: journalist," *24 Hours Vancouver*, January 12, 2014.

21. Kady O'Malley, "Not all ethnic media outlets keen to pose with PM," CBC.ca, January 23, 2014.

22. "Premier invites only ethnic media to press conference," CTVnews.ca, January 24, 2014.

23. Stephen Maher, "Giving thanks for religious freedom (except for Wiccans)," Postmedia News, October 15, 2012.

24. Tom Flanagan, *Harper's Team* (Montreal/Kingston: McGill-Queen's University Press, 2009), 239.

Chapter 5. We Don't Govern by Numbers

1. Interview with Munir Sheikh, April 3, 2014.

2. Dick Field, "The Census Long-Form—a racist document—changes are needed," Canada Free Press (canadafreepress.com), July 22, 2010.

3. Steven Chase, "Ottawa was told of flaws in census plan, documents show," *Globe and Mail*, August 10, 2010.

4. Steven Chase, "Tony Clement clears the air about the census," theglobeandmail. com, July 21, 2010.

5. Paul Wells, "Stephen Harper Engages in a Little Cowardly Vandalism," Macleans. ca, July 22, 2010.

6. Steven Chase and Tavia Grant, "Statistics Canada chief falls on his sword over census," *The Globe and Mail*, July 22, 2010.

7. Karina Roman, "Tories scrap mandatory long-form census," CBC.ca, June 26, 2010.

8. Munir Sheikh, testimony to the House of Commons Standing Committee on Science and Technology, July 27, 2010.

9. "Federal government must reconsider decision to scrap the mandatory long form Census: CAUT," CNW Group, July 2, 2010.

10. "Statisticians ask feds to keep long-form census," Canadian Press, published in *Hamilton Spectator*, July 10, 2010.

11. Canadian Sociological Association blog (www.csa-scs-ca), August 9, 2010.

12. Tavia Grant, "Economists decry loss of long-form census," *Globe and Mail*, July 30, 2010.

13. David A. Green and Kevin Milligan, "The Importance of the Long Form Census to Canada," *Canadian Public Policy/Analyse de politiques* 36.3 (2010): 384–388.

14. "Health at risk if long form census cut, say experts," *Hamilton Spectator*, September 3, 1010.

15. Roger Collier, "Long-form census change worries health researchers," *Canadian Medical Association Journal* (September 12, 2010).

16. Marsha Cohen and Paul C. Hébert, editorial, *Canadian Medical Association Journal* (September 7, 2010).

17. Karen Howlett and Les Perreaux, "Premiers make a furtive bid for truce on long-form census," *Globe and Mail*, July 29, 2010.

18. Zijad Delic, "For Canadian Muslims, long-form census is 'reliable data,'" *Canadian Islamic Congress Friday Magazine* (canadianislamiccongress.com), July 27, 2010.

19. Mags Storey, "Religious groups concerned about census reform," *Christian Week* (www.christianweek.org), August 13, 2010.

20. Munir Sheikh, "Good government and Statistics Canada: The need for true independence," *Academic Matters* (May 2013).

21. "Internal survey blasts feds for missing database," Canadian Press, May 10, 2014.

22. Heather Scoffeld, "Cancellation of long-form census taking toll on Statistics Canada data," Canadian Press, October 26, 2012; Joe Friesen, "New language data gets lost in translation," *Globe and Mail*, October 27, 2012.

23. Munir Sheikh, lecture, University of Ottawa, April 3, 2014.

24. Munir Sheikh, "Canada has lost its census anchor," *Globe and Mail*, May 9, 2013.

25. "Statistics Canada comprehensively reviewing how it gathers data," Postmedia News, February 28, 2014.

26. Quoted in Sheikh, "Good government and Statistics Canada."

27. Conrad Black, "The case against being dumb on crime," *National Post*, February 19, 2011, quoted in Paula Mallea, *Fearmonger: Will Stephen Harper's Billions For His Tough-On-Crime Agenda Make Our Streets Any Safer?* (Toronto: James Lorimer and Co., 2011), 16.

28. "Tories pressing on with tough-on-crime agenda," *Hamilton Spectator*, August 6, 2012.

29. In the past fifteen years, the author, who lives in downtown Ottawa, has had his bike and car stolen (the car was returned by the thief), along with several tools, two quick-cut concrete saws and some small change and CDs. This has hardened my views on petty crime and the inability of the police to do much about it.

30. Sexual assault reporting rates are an exception. Most go unreported.

31. Edward Greenspan, "Tough on crime, weak on evidence," *United Church Observer*, June 2012.

32. Dean Beeby, "Report cites lack of confidence in courts," Canadian Press, February 18, 2014.

33. Conrad Black, "Canada's inhumane prison plan," *National Post*, May 31, 2010.

34. "Justice Canada chops research budget, tightens control over subject matter," Canadian Press, May 11, 2014.

35. Interview with Kevin Page, May 22, 2014.

36. Greenspan, "Tough on crime, weak on evidence."

37. Kelly McParland, "Tories' tough-on-crime agenda means jammed jails stuffed with minority Canadians," *National Post*, November 28, 2013.

38. "Tough on crime? Take a close look," editorial, *Peterborough Examiner*, March 14, 2015.

39. Annie Bergeron-Oliver, "Guards and nurses raise red flag over cuts to prison nursing hours," *iPolitics*, June 2, 2015.

40. Adelina Iftene and Allan Manson, "Recent crime legislation and the challenge for prison health care," *Canadian Medical Association Journal* 185.10 (July 9, 2013): 886–889.

41. Quoted in Elaine Hyshka, Janet Butler-McPhee, Richard Elliott, Evan Wood, and Thomas Kerr, "Canada moving backwards on illegal drugs," *Canadian Journal of Public Health* 103.2 (March/April 2012): 125–127.

42. "Correctional officers send loud message to Harper government that their 'Tough on Crime' agenda is putting Canadians' safety at greater risk," Canada NewsWire, September 16, 2012; Laura Stone, "'These guys have to get out': Prison guards union to campaign against Conservatives," Globalnews.ca, May 26, 2014.

43. Howard Sapers, *Annual Report of the Correctional Investigator of Canada, 2009–2010* (June 30, 2010), www.oci-bec.gc.ca.

44. For a good journalistic analysis of this issue, see Nathan Stall, "Imprisoning the mentally ill," *Canadian Medical Association Journal* 185.3 (February 19, 2013): 201–202.

45. Gary Chaimowitz, "The treatment of mental illness in correctional settings," *Canadian Journal of Psychiatry* 57.1 (January 2012): B1–B2, C1–C2.

46. Noni MacDonald, Stephen Hucker, and Paul Hébert, "The crime of mental illness," *Canadian Medical Association Journal* 182.12 (September 21, 2010): 1399.

47. "Courts to receive new powers," Canadian Press, February 9, 2013.

48. Edward Greenspan and Anthony Doob, "Harper's 'tough on crime' is all torque," *Globe and Mail*, January 16, 2013.

49. Amy Dempsey, "Law on mentally ill offenders under fire 'Not Criminally Responsible' changes ignore science and research, experts say," *Toronto Star*, April 22, 2014.

50. John Geddes, "Are we really soft on crime?," *Maclean's*, November 9, 2009.

51. Alex Himelfarb blog (afhimelfarb.wordpress.com), May 29, 2011.

52. Sean Fine, "Court hearing pits Ottawa against judges," *Globe and Mail*, January 23, 2014.

53. "Minimum sentence for drug trafficking struck down by B.C. judge," CBC.ca, February 19, 2014.

54. Geddes, "Are we really soft on crime?"

CHAPTER 6. HARPER AND HISTORY

1. Graeme Hamilton, "Young Quebecers quick to adopt nationalist vision of province's history, survey finds," *National Post*, February 18, 2014; Jocelyn Letourneau, Je me souviens? Le passé du Québec dans la conscience de sa jeunesse (Anjou, QC: EditionsFides, 2014).

2. Alan Taylor, *The Civil War of 1812: American Citizens, British Subjects, Irish Rebels, & Indian Allies* (New York: Vintage, 2011), 313–317.

3. Steven Chase and Daniel Leblanc, "'Little-known war' of 1812 a big deal for Ottawa," *Globe and Mail*, August 10, 2012.

4. Randy Boswell, "Library and Archives Canada buys War of 1812 memorabilia for almost $700,000," Postmedia News story from *Alaska Highway News*, June 21, 2013.

5. Stephen Chase, "Move over, Laurier: Ottawa plans 1812 war monument," *Globe and Mail*, September 12, 2012; "Monument to Mark War of 1812 as military struggles to get Afghan war recognized," Postmedia, version printed in the *Kamloops Daily News*, September 12, 2012.

6. Murray Brewster, "Recalling and recognizing War of 1812 tough for Canadians: DND survey," Canadian Press, August 28, 2012.

7. David Pugliese, "MacKay takes liberties with 1812 history in Bastille Day speech," *Regina Leader-Post*, July 18, 2012.

8. Alex Boutilier, "Ottawa spent $69 million on advertising in 2012," *Toronto Star*, February 7, 2014.

9. Stephanie Levitz, "Bureaucrats proposed birthday party for charter, but Tories refuse to RSVP," Canadian Press, June 7, 2012.

10. George Naismith, *Canada's Sons and Great Britain in the World War* (Toronto: The John C. Winston Co., 1919). From the introduction by Gen. Sir Arthur Currie.

11. For the best Canadian study of the remaking of war memory, see Jonathan Vance, *Death So Noble: Memory, Meaning and the First World War* (Vancouver: UBC Press, 1997 edition).

12. Noah Richler, *What We Talk About When We Talk About War* (Fredericton: Goose Lane Editions, 2012), 70–71.

13. Ibid., 86.

14. Lee-Anne Goodman, "Is government trying to reshape Cdn history?," Canadian Press, October 16, 2013.

15. Richler, *What We Talk About*, 204–205.

16. The author has served as a contract consultant to the Canadian War Museum on research connected to media and war.

17. Richler, *What We Talk About*, 67.

18. James Loney, "War Never Again," *Blacklock's Reporter*, March 23, 2014.

19. Tom Spears, "New e-passport's historic scenes a study in 'triumphalism,' historians say," *Ottawa Citizen*, October 26, 2012.

20. Quoted in Stephen Maher, "Canadians seem to be getting tired of the often nasty man at 24 Sussex," Postmedia News, May 9, 2014.

21. Richard Madan, "Families of fallen soldiers invited to Ottawa service must pay own way," CTV.ca, April 2, 2014.

22. Mike Blanchfield, "DND cited concerns of 'militarization' and cancelled planned ceremony on Parliament Hill," Canadian Press, March 17, 2014.

23. Nimijean, "Domestic Brand Politics and the Modern Publicity State," 176.

24. Jane Taber, "Placement of 'Mother Canada' statue has Cape Bretoners on war footing," *Globe and Mail*, March 7, 2014.

25. David Pugliese, "Pearson Centre for peacekeeping could shut its doors," *Ottawa Citizen*, September 26, 2013.

26. Maria Cook, "NCC adds military content to sound and light show on Parliament Hill," *Ottawa Citizen*, July 9, 2013.

27. Murray Brewster, "Canadian soldiers go back to the future with British-style ranks," Canadian Press, July 8, 2013.

28. Rabinovitch had a special place on the Tories' list of villains because he was one of the architects of Pierre Trudeau's National Energy Program.

29. Mike De Souza, "Stephen Harper's Conservatives plan review of Canadian history," Canada.com, May 2, 2013.

30. Kathryn Blaze Carlson, "'Muscular' guide to be released; Conservatives re-write citizenship handbook to focus on responsibilities," *National Post*, November 12, 2009; "Rewrite of citizenship guide ordered," Canadian Press, April 29, 2009.

31. Jim Bronskill, "Federal snooping agency gets big budget increase, watchdogs face cuts," Canadian Press, February 27, 2014.

32. Lee Berthiaume, "Veterans urge Stephen Harper government to avoid 'Cadillac' version of war commemorations," Postmedia News, February 10, 2014.

33. Interview with Gordon Moore, April 4, 2014.

34. Darcy Knoll and Scott Taylor, "Ombudsman Stogran: Lookin' to fight for the veteran," *Esprit de Corps* (December 2007): 22.

35. Interview with Pat Stogran, April 2, 2014.

36. Jack Granatstein, "The disgrace at Veterans Affairs Canada," *Globe and Mail*, October 15, 2010.

37. Interview with Sean Bruyea, April 4, 2014.

38. Yves Frenette, "Conscripting Canada's past: The Harper government and the politics of memory," *Canadian Journal of History* 49 (Spring 2014): 49–65.

CHAPTER 7. THE WAR ON BRAINS

1. Max Paris, "Experimental Lakes closure risks federally funded research," CBC.ca, March 19, 2013; the explanatory material on nanosilver is from www.beyondpesticides.org/antibacterial/nano.php.

2. C. Scott Findlay, "Ottawa's dangerous unscientific revolution," *Toronto Star*, October 11, 2012.

3. Bob Weber, "2,900 from around the globe sign petition against Tory science cuts," Canadian Press, July 19, 2012.

4. Mia Rabson, "Scientist takes on Ottawa to try to save ELA," *Winnipeg Free Press*, October 27, 2012.

5. Mike De Souza, "NRC managers frustrate staff: 3 out of 5 science-agency employees surveyed question decisions made," Postmedia News, February 13, 2014.

6. Douglas Quan, "Scientists and journalists call on Harper to end gag order," Postmedia News, February 18, 2012.

7. Editorial, "Frozen Out," *Nature* 483.6 (March 1, 2012).

8. Quan, "Scientists and journalists call on Harper to end gag order."

9. Ibid.

10. Janet Davidson, "Are Canada's federal scientists being 'muzzled'?," CBC.ca, March 27, 2012.

11. Margaret Munro, "Environment minister's office kept scientist from speaking, documents reveal," Postmedia News, November 30, 2012.

12. Lawrence Martin, "Should Peter Kent still be in the broadcasters' hall of fame?," *iPolitics*, December 5, 2012.

13. Quirin Schiermeier, "River reveals chilling tracks of ancient flood," *Nature*, March 31, 2010.

14. Gary Corbett, "Harper government's disdain for science," *Ottawa Life*, September 2012.

15. Mike De Souza, "Federal scientists muzzled on oilsands," Postmedia News, November 5, 2012.

16. Richard Jolley, "Cuts and red tape are gagging US and Canadian science," *New Scientist* (April 14, 2012).

17. Laura Payton and Max Paris, "Health Canada library changes leave scientists scrambling. Main Health Canada research library closed, access outsourced to retrieval company," CBC.ca, January 20, 2014.

18. Interview with Katie Gibbs, February 10, 2014

19. Joseph Hall, "Historical letters not wanted at Library and Archives Canada, critics say," *Toronto Star*, March 10, 2013.

20. Much of the file is still hidden. It will stay that way because the Supreme Court of Canada refused to hear Bronskill's appeal of a lower court's decision that the file—which holds reports written from the 1930s until Douglas's death almost three decades ago—holds material that could jeopardize ongoing investigations and burn secret sources.

21. Ex Libris Association Backgrounder on Library and Archives Canada, "Timeline on Library and Archives Canada Service Decline after 2004," http://exlibris.pbworks.com.

22. Margaret Munro, "Federal librarians fear being 'muzzled' under new code of conduct," Postmedia News, March 15, 2013.

23. Editorial, "Ottawa's muzzling of librarians' free speech is intolerable," *Calgary Herald*, March 25, 2013.

24. Daniel J. Caron, letter, "Re: New code a 'muzzle,' March 16," *Ottawa Citizen*, March 21, 2013.

25. "Head of Library and Archives resigns over Spanish lessons. Billed taxpayers nearly $4,500," Canadian Press, May 15, 2013.

26. Teresa Smith and Chris Cobb, "Big-spending head of library resigns; 'Titanic expenses' totaled about $170,000 in two years," *Ottawa Citizen*, May 15, 2013.

27. Randy Boswell, "Library and Archives Canada buys War of 1812 memorabilia for almost $700,000," Postmedia News, June 21, 2013.

CHAPTER 8. FRAT BOYS AND CHEERLEADERS

1. Michael Harris, "Harper and the 'Merchant of Venom,'" *iPolitics*, March 16, 2014.

2. Nicholls, *Loyal to the Core*, 128.

3. For an interesting discussion of Harper's connection to the American right, see Brooke Jeffrey, "The Harper Minority and Majority Myth: Implementing the Conservative Agenda," presentation to the Canadian Political Science Association 2011 Annual Conference, Waterloo, Ontario, May 18, 2011. I used a draft version available through Google Scholar. The material on Rove and Luntz is from p. 8 of the draft version that was online in June 2014, while the connection between Luntz's language manipulation and Harper's framing of the 2008 coalition attempt is from p. 11.

4. Andrew Heard, "The Governor General's Decision to Prorogue Parliament," *Constitutional Forum* 18.1 (2009), quoted in Jeffrey, "The Harper Minority and Majority Myth."

5. See "'Four Sad Faces and a Smiley': A Political Topology of Civic and Olympic Spaces at the 2010 Winter Games," in *Rethinking Matters Olympic: Investigations into the Socio-Cultural Study of the Modern Olympic Movement Tenth International Symposium* (London, ON: International Centre for Olympic Studies, The University of Western Ontario 2010), 233.

6. Allan Woods, "Harper shows Stairs the door: Emerson affair costs communications chief his job, source says," *Ottawa Citizen*, February 21, 2006; Don Martin, "Harper the real captain at helm of lousy communications strategy," *Edmonton Journal*, February 23, 2006.

7. Keith Beardsley, "Tory backbenchers rise up against the boys in short pants," *National Post*, October 15, 2012.

8. Glen McGregor, "PMO denies claim that depression paralyzes Harper," *Ottawa Citizen*, April 16, 2014; Martin, *Harperland*.

9. McGregor, "PMO denies claim that depression paralyzes Harper."

10. Abbas Rana, "Conservatives could lose next election if Harper keeps picking fights, says Flanagan," *Hill Times*, May 12, 2014.

11. Samara, "By Invitation Only: Canadians' Perceptions of Political Parties," report, February 16, 2014.

12. Marchand is a cousin of the author.

13. Andrew McIntosh, "Ex-MP must pay $16,362 to Bloc for underspending," *National Post*, December 4, 2003.

14. Campbell Clark, "Speaker rebukes Bev Oda over document in Kairos case," *Globe and Mail*, February 10, 2011.

15. Martin, *Harperland*, 117.

16. James Adams, "Canadian Conference of the Arts vows to live on, despite funding loss," *Globe and Mail*, June 20, 2012.

17. Index on Censorship: The voice of free expression (indexoncensorship.org), August 16, 2013.

18. Garth Turner, *Sheeple: Caucus Confidential in Stephen Harper's Ottawa* (Toronto: Key Porter, 2009), 128.

19. *Blacklock's Reporter*, December 13, 2013.

20. Tom Korski, "Energy Board Spies on Pipe Critics; Calls RCMP & CSIS," *Blacklock's Reporter*, November 4, 2013.

21. Interview with Elizabeth May, May 5, 2014.

22. Mark Hume, "RCMP, intelligence agency accused of spying on pipeline opponents," *Globe and Mail*, February 6, 2014.

23. Tom Korski, "RCMP to Watch 'Anti-Oilsands' Crowd: Memo," *Blacklock's Reporter*, Tuesday, November 5, 2013.

24. Tom Korski, "Oil Lobby Made the Law?," *Blacklock's Reporter*, December 13, 2013.

25. "Climate change scientist calls conservatives 'Neanderthal,'" CBC.ca, April 27, 2013.

26. Evan Solomon and Kristen Everson, "7 environmental charities face Canada Revenue Agency audits," CBC.ca, February 6, 2014.

27. Jason Fekete, "Budget will crack down on charities with links to charity, organized crime: Flaherty," Postmedia News, February 7, 2014.

28. Matthew Millar, "Flaherty cites terrorism when asked why CRA is auditing environmental charities," *Vancouver Observer*, February 13, 2014.

29. Mike De Sousa and James Woods, "Feds list First Nations, green groups as oilsands 'adversaries,'" Postmedia News, April 3 2012.
30. Tom Korski, "MPs vote 258 to 1 on seal bill," *Blacklock's Reporter*, May 29, 2014.
31. Michael Harris, "Tory MP insists he did not want reporter fired," *iPolitics*, November 5, 2012.

CHAPTER 9. HOUSE OF CLOWNS

1. George MacDonald Fraser, *Flash for Freedom*, quoted in Tony Smith, "Parliamentary ethics and political failure: a state of confusion," *AQ* 83.4 (June 2012): 4.
2. The author worked as Turner's assistant business editor at the *Toronto Sun* in 1979–80.
3. Turner tells his story in *Sheeple*.
4. Garth Turner, *National Post* excerpt of *Sheeple*, April 29, 2009.
5. Turner, *Sheeple*, 126.
6. Ibid., 15.
7. Donald J. Savoie, *Breaking the Bargain* (Toronto: University of Toronto Press, 2003), 223.
8. David E. Smith, *The People's House of Commons* (Toronto: University of Toronto Press, 2007), 23.
9. For an excellent examination of the role of MPs and the coercive power of prime ministers over those on the government side of the House of Commons, see Savoie, *Whatever Happened to the Music Teacher?*, ch. 2.
10. Steven Erlinger and Stephen Castle, "British parliament votes down air strike," *New York Times*, August 28, 2013.
11. Interview with Elizabeth May, May 5, 2014.
12. Jason Fekete and Lee Berthiaume, "Truant Trudeau says he's in touch with Canadians outside Ottawa," *Ottawa Citizen*, May 2, 2014.
13. Library of Parliament Research Office.
14. Tom Korski, "Accidental sugar tax is averted," *Blacklock's Reporter*, October 9, 2013.
15. Hansard, March 25, 1994.
16. "MP Rathgeber refuses to be 'cheerleader' and quits Tory caucus," CBC.ca, June 6, 2013.
17. Josh Wingrove, "Former Tory whip slams party's decision to strip private member's bill," *Globe and Mail*, February 28, 2014.
18. Joan Bryden, "Conservative MPs challenge their own government," Canadian Press, January 24, 2014.
19. David Oldroyd, "The Role of Accounting in Public Expenditure and Monetary Policy in the First Century AD Roman Empire," *Accounting Historians Journal* 22.2 (December 1995): 124.

20. Report of the Auditor General of Canada, 1976, 9.

21. Ibid., 14.

22. Interview with Kevin Page, May 22, 2014.

23. Savoie, *Breaking the Bargain*, 222–223.

24. Julian Beltrame, "Watchdog warns of Tory secrecy; MPs losing ability to do their job, Kevin page tells Commons committee," Postmedia News, from *Kamloops Daily News*, February 16, 2011.

25. Interview with Kevin Page, May 22, 2014.

26. Laura Ryckewaert, "Hill journalists say there's too much government information control and Parliament has lost its power," *Hill Times*, March 1, 2014.

27. Bill Curry, "Internal memo reveals Ottawa cut labour market data spending," *Globe and Mail*, June 11, 2014.

28. Jordan Press, "Nominee for privacy commissioner questioned," *Ottawa Citizen*, May 29, 2014.

29. Ibid.

30. Daniel Leblanc, "Critics decry new Privacy Commissioner's appointment," *Globe and Mail*, June 2, 2015.

31. Paul McLeod, "Watchdogs' efforts to pry lid off government secrecy often doomed to fail," Halifax *Chronicle Herald*, March 3, 2014.

32. "Ex-McGill hospital boss Arthur Porter arrested in Panama," CBC.ca, May 28, 2013.

33. Minutes of the House of Commons Committee on Procedural and House Affairs, May 1, 2014.

34. Tonda MacCharles, "Canada's lawyers demand Stephen Harper withdraw criticism of chief justice," *Toronto Star*, May 13, 2014; Tonda MacCharles, "Joe Clark, Paul Martin criticize PM's attack on chief justice," *Toronto Star*, May 20, 2015.

35. Savoie, *Whatever Happened to the Music Teacher?*, 146.

36. Among the people who vetted the appointment was respected economist Don Drummond, whose sweeping recommendations for efficiency in the Ontario government would later be ignored by premiers Dalton McGuinty and Kathleen Wynne.

37. Interview with Kevin Page, May 22, 2014.

38. Jessica Bruno, "Page's high profile, high transparency, scaring some backbenchers off: Tory MP," *Hill Times*, April 2, 2013.

39. Interview with Kevin Page, May 22, 2014.

40. Meagan Fitzpatrick, "Parliamentary Budget Officer says she's not getting requested information," CBC News, July 22, 2013.

41. Joan Bryden and Bruce Cheadle, "Tory cabinet minister launches astonishing personal attack on elections watchdog Marc Mayrand," Canadian Press, April 8, 2014.

42. Joan Bryden, "Elections bill illustrates Harper's vindictiveness, pragmatism, Flanagan says," Canadian Press, April 28, 2014.

43. Tonda MacCharles, "Tories drop RCMP complaints commissioner," *Toronto Star*, November 27, 2009.

44. For the best recent analysis of the prime minister's role and power, see Savoie, *Whatever Happened to the Music Teacher?*, ch. 4.

Chapter 10. The Secret Government

1. Martin, *Harperland*, 130.
2. Ken Rubin and Kirsten Kozolanka, "Managing Information," in Kozolanka, *Publicity and the Canadian State*, 196.
3. Ibid., 197.
4. Ken Rubin and Kirsten Kozolanka, "Managing Information," in Kozolanka, *Publicity and the Canadian State*, 214.
5. Robert Marleau, Report of the Information Commissioner of Canada, 2006. See pages 1, 8–9, 22.
6. Canadian Newspaper Association, "Government Unfairly Slows Access to Information, Information Commissioner Concludes," press release, Canadian Newswire, September 8, 2008.
7. Jennifer Ditchburn, "Tory staff interfered in access to info: Watchdog," Canadian Press, April 10, 2014.
8. Canadian Journalists for Free Expression, "Our right to information is disappearing," www.cjfe.org, November 30, 2012.
9. Robert Marleau, Report of the Information Commissioner of Canada, 2009–2010.
10. Suzanne Legault, Report of the Information Commissioner of Canada, 2010–2011.
11. Suzanne Legault, Report of the Information Commissioner of Canada, 2012–2013.
12. Jim Bronskill, "Feds losing ground on timely access-to-information responses: Commissioner," Canadian Press, January 14, 2012.
13. Elizabeth Thompson, "PM's former chief of staff criticizes government secrecy, calls for greater access to documents," *iPolitics*, September 30, 2013.
14. Jennifer Ditchburn, "Bureaucrat muzzled in midst of Senate scandal," Canadian Press, March 4, 2014.
15. James Cudmore, "Army commander promises discipline against media leaks," CBC.ca, January 13, 2014.
16. David Pugliese, "Harper muzzle will hurt DND: Retired general," *Ottawa Citizen*, December 12, 2007.
17. James Cudmore, "How one defence staffer stood up for Access to Information," CBC.ca, March 2, 2014.
18. The Bloc Québécois and Green Party had MPs elected in the 2011, but only the Conservatives, New Democrats and Liberals had the minimum of twelve that are needed to qualify for official party status.
19. Kady O'Malley, "MPs drop bid to impose lifetime gag orders on Hill staff," CBC.ca, March 26, 2014.

20. Elizabeth Thompson, "Political parties collecting 'creepy' amount of information on voters: privacy expert," *iPolitics*, September 27, 2013.

21. Tom Korski, "Feds go Facebook creeping," *Blacklock's Reporter*, December 1, 2013.

22. Tom Korski, "Facebook creeping makes better gov't: Treasury Board," *Blacklock's Reporter*, December 3, 2013.

23. Hansard, December 2, 2013.

24. Susana Mas, "Cyberbullying bill surveillance powers alarm Ontario privacy watchdog," CBC.ca, May 23, 2014.

25. Michael Geist, "From Toews to Todd: The Unraveling of the government's lawful access sales strategy," Michael Geist blog (Michaelgeist.ca), May 23, 2014.

26. Tom Korski, "Federal agency had secret file on 'Occupy' protesters," *Blacklock's Reporter*, August 27, 2013.

27. Hansard, December 2, 2013.

28. Alex Boutilier, "Taxpayers shelling out for Ottawa's Snooping," *Toronto Star*, May 1, 2014.

29. Susan Delacourt, "No gifts please, we're politicians. Just send postal codes," *Toronto Star*, March 5, 2013.

30. David Pugliese, "Government orders federal departments to keep tabs on all demonstrations across the country," *Ottawa Citizen*, June 4, 2014.

31. Katie Collins, "Espionage in a post-privacy society," Wired.com, May 20, 2014.

32. Justin Ling, "The Canadian government's 'secure' phones come straight from the NSA," motherboard.vice.com, April 25, 2014.

33. The trade goes back thousands of years. Mary, Queen of Scots, was done in by signals intelligence. Tudor spies collected her secret messages and broke the code. So were German pilots who flew into clouds of Spitfire and Hurricanes in the Battle of Britain because geniuses in Poland and England had unravelled the secret of the German Enigma code machine. And four Japanese aircraft carriers are on the bottom of the Pacific Ocean because the Americans cracked Japan's Purple code before the Battle of Midway.

34. Jim Bronskill, "Federal snooping agency gets big budget increase, watchdogs face cuts," Canadian Press, February 27, 2014.

35. Dale Smith, "Critics show teeth on spy agencies: 'We need action,'" *Blacklock's Reporter*, January 29, 2014.

36. Jim Bronskill, "Spy agency uncovers 'serious breaches,'" Canadian Press, March 16, 2014.

37. Paul McLeod, "Telecom data regularly tapped," *Chronicle Herald*, March 25, 2014.

38. Paul McLeod, "Government makes over a million requests a year for data," *Chronicle Herald*, April 29, 2014.

39. Carl Meyer, "Little-known federal monitoring centre tracked bee protest," *Embassy*, February 12, 2014.

40. Alex Boutilier, "Ottawa imposes life-long gag order on bureaucrats, lawyers," *Toronto Star*, March 13, 2014.

41. Elizabeth Thompson, "Canadian government increasingly asking for content to be pulled offline," *iPolitics*, November 23, 2012.
42. Bill Curry, "Judge raps Justice officials for treatment of whistle-blower," *Globe and Mail*, January 16, 2013.

CHAPTER 11. BAFFLE THEM WITH BULLSHIT

1. Dave Feschuk and Michael Grange, *Leafs AbomiNation: The Dismayed Fan's Handbook to Why the Leafs Stink and How They Can Rise Again* (Toronto: Random House, 2009), 13.
2. J. Grant Glassco, *Royal Commission on Government Organization* (Ottawa: Queen's Printer, 1962), 69–70, quoted in Randal Marlin, *Propaganda and the Ethics of Persuasion* (Peterborough: Broadview Press, 2013), 283–284.
3. Nimijean, "Domestic Brand Politics," 175.
4. Steve Bandera, "Ottawa communications firm linked to federal departments and F-35 manufacturer," CTVnews.ca, September 22, 2012.
5. "B.C. scientist reinstated by Ottawa after phrase flap," CBC.ca, September 19, 2006.
6. David Taras and Christopher Waddell, "The 2011 Federal Election and the Transformation of Canadian Media and Politics," in *How Canadians Communicate IV*, 373.
7. Chris Purdy, "Man who killed police dog sentenced to 26 months in prison," *Globe and Mail*, February 28, 2014.
8. Eric Reguly, "Canada's $207,000 oil sands ad: Putting a price on deception," *Globe and Mail*, May 9, 2014.
9. Bill Curry, "Government spends millions on ads for 'Economic Action Plan' that ended two years ago," *Globe and Mail*, January 25, 2014.
10. Ibid.
11. Alex Boutelier, "Ottawa spent $69 million on advertising in 2012," *Toronto Star*, February 7, 2014.
12. Curry, "Government spends millions on ads for 'Economic Action Plan.'"
13. Dean Beeby, "Canadians getting tired of Economic Action Plan ads, surveys suggest," Canadian Press, February 17, 2012; Dean Beeby, "Harper 'Action Plan' ads 'creating apathy' for many Canadians: Survey," Canadian Press, July 23, 2013.
14. Dean Beeby, "Canadians getting tired of Economic Action Plan ads."
15. Editorial, "Action-plan ads are ineffective," *Globe and Mail*, July 23, 2013.
16. Tim Naumetz, "Conservatives painting Government of Canada website blue, organizing by themes not departments, NDP says new look obscuring sensitive facts," *Hill Times*, March 19, 2014.
17. Peter O'Malley, "Harperites' secret plan to 'streamline' websites likely to cut public access to vital information," Straightgoods.ca, April 4, 2013.

18. Karolyn Koorsh, "'We're nothing to you': Spouse of veteran with PTSD confronts Fantino over funding," CTV.ca, May 28, 2014.

19. Laura Stone, "Veterans Affairs Canada spent $100,000 on promoted tweets: Documents," Globalnews.ca, May 13, 2014.

20. Flanagan, *Harper's Team*, 232.

21. Martin, *Harperland*, 131.

22. Alex Marland, "Political photography, journalism, and framing in the Digital Age: The management of visual media by the Prime Minister of Canada," *International Journal of Press/Politics* 17.214 (February 2012): 220.

23. Ibid., 224.

24. Details of Marland's study are from Marland, "Political photography, journalism and framing in the Digital Age."

25. Stephen Maher, "Conservatives' email blast targets Aga Khan followers," Postmedia News, March 5, 2014.

Chapter 12. Attack, Attack, Attack!

1. Many writers erroneously claim the prize was given to the *Edmonton Journal* when, in fact, the coverage of the time shows it was meant to honour all of the papers that fought the press law. As the main daily in the provincial capital, the *Edmonton Journal* accepted the prize on behalf of the newspapers. Aberhart's colourful descriptions and the details of his Press Bill are from W.H. Kesterton, *A History of Journalism in Canada* (Toronto: McClelland and Stewart, 1967), 226–233. *Toronto Star* reporter/photographer Paul Watson was awarded a Pulitzer Prize in 1994 for an iconic photograph of Somalis abusing the body of an American.

2. Kathryn Blaze Carlson, "New book describes Harper as controlling, 'Nixonian' leader," *Globe and Mail*, April 10, 2014.

3. Adam Daifallahand Tasha Kheiriddin, *Rescuing Canada's Right* (Toronto: Wiley, 2005), 92–93.

4. Edge, *Asper Nation*, 108.

5. "Ex-Harper aide Bruce Carson charged with influence peddling," CBC.ca, July 27, 2012.

6. Laura Payton, "Bruce Carson, former PMO staffer, faces new charges," CBC.ca, May 12, 2014.

7. Linda Diebel, "Meanness is a way of life in Ottawa," *Toronto Star*, November 20, 2013.

8. Tim Harper, "Tribunal will rule whether Ottawa retaliated against native rights advocate Cindy Blackstock," *Toronto Star*, October 22, 2012.

9. Ian Macleod, "The implications of the federal government's monitoring of social media," *Ottawa Citizen*, November 29, 2013.

10. http://ezralevant.com/2008/02/ive-been-threatened-with-anoth.html

11. The author's wife is currently a corporate counsel to the Canadian Human Rights Commission. The author has no idea what she does in the course of her work. She started working for the commission in 2010, after the Steyn and Levant cases were resolved.

12. Amy Minsky and Tom Clark, "Ministerial staff asked to develop blacklists in lead-up to shuffle: source," Global News, July 7, 2013; Amy Minsky, 'Request for 'enemy' list speaks to PMO need for control: Opposition," Global News, July 16, 2013.

13. Mark Kennedy, "Rae accuses PMO of disrespecting Parliament," Postmedia, February 25, 2011.

14. In previous incarnations, this type of overeager, hyper-loyal, amoral and often annoying young people were called "ratfuckers," a term that emerged during the Watergate scandal. Nixon White House operative Donald Segretti self-identified as a ratfucker and admitted to running a dirty tricks squad engaged in forgery, smears, and petty dirty tricks. Segretti did a short stretch in jail after Watergate. In 2008, he was head of Republican presidential candidate John McCain's election campaign committee in Orange County, California.

15. Althia Raj, "Trudeau protest was manned by Tory interns and organized by PMO," Huffington Post, June 25, 2013.

16. James Munson, "Mackay's office won't comment on link to 'bozo eruption' tape," iPolitics, June 5, 2014.

17. Rick Westhead, "Canada muzzles foreign diplomats," Toronto Star, June 21, 2013.

18. Roland Paris, The Digital Diplomacy Revolution: Why Is Canada Lagging Behind? (Canadian Defence and Foreign Affairs Institute, June 2013).

19. Pierre Karl Péladeau, "All's not fair in war," Torontosun.ca, April 27, 2011.

20. Laurie Watt, "PM's office sends details of Trudeau's talk at Georgian," Barrie Advance, July 17, 2013.

21. Glen McGregor, "Cotler calls spark complaint against polling firm," Ottawa Citizen, December 16, 2011.

22. Joan Bryden, "Tory pollster rebuked for misleading campaign against MP Irwin Cotler," Canadian Press, November 28, 2012.

23. Althia Raj, "Irwin Cotler: Speaker says Tory phone calls in Liberal's riding 'reprehensible,' but finds no breach of privilege," Huffington Post, February 27, 2012; Althia Raj, "Irwin Cotler: Liberal MP expresses outrage over Tory calls claiming a byelection looms in his riding," Huffington Post, February 27, 2012.

24. "Ex-Tory adviser Saulie Zajdel arrested in corruption probe," CBC.ca, June 12, 2013.

25. Kathryn May, "Budget bill contains surprise reforms aimed at weakening public service unions," Ottawa Citizen, October 22, 2013.

26. People for the American Way Foundation, "The new face of Jim Crow: Voter suppression in America," pfaw.org, undated.

27. Rachel E. Berry, "Democratic National Committee v. Edward J. Rollins: Politics as usual or unusual politics," *Race and Ethnic Ancestry Law Digest*, footnote 27, quoted in Chandler Davidson, Tanya Dunlap, Gale Kenny, and Benjamin Wise, "Republican Ballot Security Programs: Vote Protection or Minority Vote Suppression—or Both? A Report to the Center for Voting Rights and Protection" (September 2004), 96.

28. Details of the North Dakota and North Carolina robocalls campaigns are from Jason C. Miller, "Regulating robocalls: Are automated calls the sound of a threat to democracy?," *Michigan Telecommunications and Technology Law Review*, 2009.

29. Mackenzie Weigner, "Reports: Robo-calls lying to Wisconsin voters," Politico.com, May 6, 2012.

30. Steve Benen, "Conviction in GOP voter-suppression scheme," *Washington Monthly*, December 7, 2011.

31. Kim Zetter, "Malicious robocalls aim at suppressing election day turnout," Wired.com, February 2, 2010.

32. Tom Korski, "Elections Canada allowed ballot boxes in a gated community clubhouse, a suburban supermarket, a law bowling club," *Hill Times*, March 26, 2012.

33. This type of vote suppression is described in Chandler Davidson, Tanya Dunlap, Gale Kenney and Benjamin Wise, "Vote caging as a Republican ballot security technique," *William Mitchell Law Review* 34.2 (2008): 536–538.

34. People for the American Way Foundation, "The new face of Jim Crow."

35. Laura Beaulne-Stuebing, "Elections Commissioner: I was not consulted on Fair Elections Act," *iPolitics*, April 1, 2014.

36. Peter Mazereew, "Elections Act changes drop Canada from lofty status: Electoral scholars," *Hill Times*, April 16, 2014.

37. Jeffrey Simpson, "The Fair Elections Act is ever so telling," *Globe and Mail*, April 16, 2014.

38. Joan Bryden, "Fair Elections Act: Sheila Fraser slams Bill C-23 as attack on democracy," Canadian Press, April 4, 2014.

39. McLachlin had other reasons had other reasons to be horrified by the PMO's selection process. One of the four Federal Court judges on the six-person long-list had been warned by the Federal Court of Appeal for cutting and pasting arguments from federal pleadings into his decisions. See Sean Fein, "The secret short list that provoked the rift between Chief Justice and PMO," theglobeandmail.com, May 23, 2014.

40. Leslie MacKinnon, "Beverley McLachlin, PMO give dueling statements on Nadon appointment fight," CBC.ca, May 2, 2014; Sean Fine, "Harper says Chief Justice tried to discuss court case with him," *Globe and Mail*, May 2, 2014; Statement to the Media by Owen M. Rees, distributed to the Canadian Parliamentary Press Gallery, May 2, 2014.

41. Glenn Kauth, "Bar alarmed at 'extraordinary' situation between Harper, McLachlin," *Canadian Lawyer* blog (canadianlawyermag.com), May 5, 2014.

42. Tonda MacCharles, "Stephen Harper changes version of events around phone call by Beverley McLachlin," *Toronto Star*, May 14, 2014.
43. Interview with Thomas Mulcair, foyer of the House of Commons, May 5, 2014.
44. Tonda MacCharles, "Canada's lawyers demand Stephen Harper withdraw criticism of Chief Justice," *Toronto Star*, May 13, 2014.
45. Tim Naumetz, "Prime Minister's Office one of least trusted of federal institutions: poll," *Hill Times*, May 28, 2014.

CHAPTER 13. A RADICAL SOLUTION

1. Allan Gregg, "In defence of reason," *Toronto Star*, October 8, 2012.

Index

371